W9-BBJ-381

For Karl Kroeber
    in appreciation of the
    unflagging vigor with
    which you propelled
    this study from its
    studently beginnings to
    its present end.
                Regina Hewitt
                Sept. 12, 1990

American University Studies

Series IV
English Language and Literature
Vol. 120

PETER LANG
New York • Bern • Frankfurt am Main • Paris

Regina Hewitt

Wordsworth and the Empirical Dilemma

PETER LANG
New York • Bern • Frankfurt am Main • Paris

Library of Congress Cataloging-in-Publication Data

Hewitt, Regina
    Wordsworth and the empirical dilemma / Regina
Hewitt.
       p. cm. — (American university studies. Series IV,
English language and literature ; vol. 120)
      Includes bibliographical references.
      1. Wordsworth, William, 1770-1850—Philosophy.
2. Wordsworth, William, 1770-1850—Criticism and
interpretation.   3. Empiricism in literature.
I. Title. II. Series.
PR5892.P5H49   1990   821'.7—dc20   90-5912
ISBN 0-8204-1358-5   CIP
ISSN 0740-0700

CIP-Titelaufnahme der Deutschen Bibliothek

Hewitt, Regina:
Wordsworth and the empirical dilemma / Regina
Hewitt. — New York; Bern; Frankfurt am Main;
Paris: Lang, 1990.
    (American University Studies: Ser. 4, English
    Language and Literature; Vol. 120)
    ISBN 0-8204-1358-5

NE: American University Studies / 04

© Peter Lang Publishing, Inc., New York 1990

All rights reserved.
Reprint or reproduction, even partially, in all forms such as microfilm,
xerography, microfiche, microcard, offset strictly prohibited.

Printed by Weihert-Druck GmbH, Darmstadt, West Germany

Contents

Contents

Preface

As all readers of Romantic literature know, Wordsworth's canon—ranging from lyrical ballads to sonnet sequences, from *An Evening Walk to The Excursion*—forms one of the largest and most varied bodies in English poetic literature. Yet Wordsworth's own prose and the documents of others recording his convictions indicate that he thought of his poems as parts of a network, that he considered them bound up in a deliberate enterprise. My study springs from a fascination with this apparent disparity between Wordsworth's diffuse production and his conjunctive aim.

Though I do not wish to reduce Wordsworth's poetry solely to his statements about it, I do suggest that Wordsworth's declarations can carry more weight than they are customarily allowed to bear. Granting that Wordsworth's canon represents a specifiable enterprise lays a foundation for investigating what factors explain Wordsworth's commitment to such an endeavor, what characteristics shape its divers forms, and what values account for its dubious success. In short, a sense of Wordsworth's purposive undertaking opens the way for a reassessment of Wordsworth's interaction with his contemporaries at a fundamental intellectual level, a reassessment made timely as reader-response criticism and reception theories heighten our awareness—and suspicion—of reading as a dynamic and culturally-informed activity.

My investigation begins by identifying one of the most significant problems dominating the late eighteenth-century intellectual world in which Wordsworth emerged—the problem of whether people have any real ties to each other and to the environment. Chapter One establishes solipsistic fear as an "empirical dilemma" that had been growing since Locke sired it. Developments not only in philosophy but in religion, literary theory, and periodical writing mark the passage of concern about individual isolation from a specialized question worrying Locke and his fellow philosophers to a turgid issue pressing on almost all thinkers. Arguments about an "intellectual milieu" inevitably suffer from a degree of speculation, but an overwhelming amount of evidence (which I try to marshall) defines late eighteenth-century thought as devoted to finding some way to secure the individual and give ontological reality to the otherwise chimerical idea of community.

Chapter Two places Wordsworth within the atmosphere in which individuality was a highly charged concept. The context defines Wordsworth's poetic enterprise as a response to this pervasive cultural preoccupation. Wordsworth's poetics posits literary discourse both as a representation of functional relationships among perspectives and as a means to bring readers into relationships that would dispel their fears of isolation without denying the independence of every view. The second chapter confines itself to addressing the declarations with which Wordsworth proposed such a solution to the empirical dilemma and argues that the relational features with which Wordsworth distinguishes poetry form likewise the distinguishing features of his canon. Subsequent chapters analyze these features in poems ranging widely among Wordsworth's works.

These chapters also try to capture the tensions that complicated Wordsworth's endeavor. Wordsworth's approach to the empirical dilemma diverged from those of his contemporaries by offering a solution contingent upon accepting individual perception rather than recovering a consensual ideal. Simultaneously at the heart of contemporary concerns and at odds with dominant values, Wordsworth challenged his readers to a self-reliance most

Preface

were afraid to embrace. Contemporary reviews of Wordsworth's poetry evidence a resistance to and cooptation of his work that not only supports a sense of his involvement in a far-reaching controversy but also suggests a rationale for his stylistic variety: reader resistance may have encouraged him to search for a way to make his solution less threatening to an audience he genuinely wished to engage. I refer throughout to contemporary reviews when they seem most useful in documenting the cultural and intellectual centrality of Wordsworth's undertaking.

Considering Wordsworth in the context of contemporary concerns and reactions provides a way to assess not only what Wordsworth attempted and achieved but also what significance remains to his enterprise. A longer study than the present one would be necessary to address Wordsworth's influence, but my final chapter includes some remarks on how attention to Wordsworth's enterprise can assist modern self-consciousness. From an historical distance, readers can trace in the struggle between Wordsworth and his reviewers a lesson in the complexity of literary relations. I leave educement of this and other possibilities to more adept theorists.

Current interest in Wordsworth's relationship with his readers is growing rapidly, as evidenced in particular by the recent publication of Susan Edwards Meisenhelder's *Wordsworth's Informed Reader: Structures of Experience in His Poetry* (Nashville, Tennessee: Vanderbilt University Press, 1988). I wish to express my admiration for Meisenhelder's book, which appeared after I completed my manuscript, and to suggest that our divergences make our studies complementary. Meisenhelder concentrates on ways in which Wordsworth's texts offer his own experiences as a moral paradigm for a general

ix

readership. She identifies Wordsworth's experiences during the French Revolution as the catalyst for his interest in educating others, posits his knowledge of eighteenth-century aesthetic theories to account for his choosing poetry as his means, and discovers his first efforts to help others mature as he did in *The Prelude*. In contrast, I concentrate on the ways in which Wordsworth's texts aim at enabling his contemporary readers to cope with their fundamental differences from him and from each other. I see Wordsworth's experience of individuation as subsuming his involvement in the French Revolution and his use of poetry to examine its implication for community as beginning in work as early as *An Evening Walk*. Meisenhelder's and my separate contexts, analyses, and conclusions testify to the complexity of Wordsworth's thought and of the milieu in which he worked.

I owe my commitment to understanding Wordsworth in the context of his time to Carl Woodring. Recollection of the sentence with which he begins *Politics in English Romantic Poetry*—"Poems contain ideas"—often reminded me of how important extra-literary events are in the production and reception of texts, but Professor Woodring has lent this study more than its orientation toward intellectual relations. It exists because of his kind encouragement, patient endurance of early drafts, and careful criticism of misapprehensions and omissions. Its shortcomings stem from my intractability, not his oversight.

The advice, assistance, and support of Karl Kroeber have also substantially improved this study. Professor Kroeber's willingness to share his insights into Wordsworthian community rescued it from many isolating blind alleys; his attention to differences between historical and contemporary interpretations fostered its conceptualization of the problems of reading. Without his lengthy

Preface

discussions and provocative questions, its sense of Wordsworth's commitment to others would have remained inchoate.

I am also grateful to Robert M. Ryan for guiding my research into the religious dimension of the empirical dilemma and for energizing me to persevere in the work; to Mark Reed for clarifying the dates of Wordsworth's acquaintance with Holcroft; to Theresa Kelley for suggesting the inclusion of "Gipsies"; and to Linda Palumbo for giving me access to her work on *Ecclesiastical Sonnets* while still in manuscript. Their help has broadened and deepened the study as has the graciousness of the Coleridge Estate and the Harry Ransom Humanities Research Center, The University of Texas at Austin, in allowing me to use a manuscript by Henry Nelson Coleridge, which has now become available to all readers in the note "Table-Talk by William Wordsworth," in Samuel Taylor Coleridge, *Table Talk*, ed. Carl Woodring (2 vols., Princeton University Press, 1990), 1: 549-50. I wish to thank Research Librarian Cathy Henderson in particular for assistance with the manuscript. I also acknowledge the kind permission of Oxford University Press to cite Wordsworth's poetry from *The Poetical Works of William Wordsworth, Edited from the Manuscripts, with Textual Notes and Critical Notes,* ed. Ernest de Selincourt and Helen Darbishire (5 vols., rev. ed., Clarendon-Oxford University Press, 1952-59).

I have previously published portions of this book in the following articles, which I incorporate respectively in Chapters 2, 4, and 6 by permission of the publishers: "Towards a Wordsworthian Phenomenology of Reading: 'The Childless Father' and 'Poor Susan' as Paradigms," *Essays in Literature* 16 (1989): 188-202; "Faery Lands Fit and Forlorn: Keats and the 'Problem' of

Wordsworth's 'Ego'," *Essays in Literature* 14 (1987): 65-79; "'Wild Outcasts of Society': Stigmatization in Wordsworth's 'Gipsies'," *Nineteenth-Century Contexts* 12 (Fall 1988): 19-28. All rights reserved. I thank editors Thomas P. Joswick and Stuart Peterfreund for generously facilitating the reprinting of the pertinent parts of these materials.

My efforts to turn my manuscript into a legible book would have met with little success without the help of Pat Schuster, who accomplished the transition through her talent for text design and expertise at word processing. My thanks to her should surely be echoed by any reader who moves smoothly through these chapters.

A further contribution to legibility comes from the new MLA style, which obviates much cumbersome bibliographic apparatus. The list of Works Cited elucidates all references in the text and notes, except for abbreviations of volumes of *The Letters of William and Dorothy Wordsworth*, which are as follows: *The Early Years* (*EY*), *The Middle Years* (*MY*), *The Later Years* (*LY*).

Chapter 1

The Empirical Dilemma

With the publication of *An Essay Concerning Human Understanding*, Locke gave individuals unprecedented power and responsibility by positing that their knowledge comes from their own sensory perceptions:

> Let us then suppose the Mind to be, as we say, white Paper, void of all characters, without any *Ideas*; How comes it to be furnished? . . . To this I answer, in one word, From *Experience*: In that, all our Knowledge is founded; and from that it ultimately derives itself. (II.i.2)

Having privileged individual experience in this hypothesis, Locke stressed its primacy throughout his argument. He paused, for example, in his discussion of language to emphasize "how much the Foundation of all *our Knowledge of corporeal Things, lies in our Senses.* . . . The whole extent of our Knowledge, or Imagination, reaches not beyond our own *Ideas*, limited to our ways of Perception" (III.xi.23) . Historically, Locke's insistence on forming ideas from experience provided an alternative to Scholasticism and its method of deriving knowledge from axioms.[1] Locke's concerns, however, exceeded the confines of parochial controversy. As Yolton's study of Locke's contemporary reception shows, Locke countered a widespread belief that only recourse to innate ideas of some kind could account for human knowledge and behavior (26-30). Almost everyone in Locke's day made knowledge depend upon and support some preconceived view of reality—whether that view came from systems of religion and morality generally or from the Aristotelian tradition of metaphysics as "first philosophy" (Yolton 26-49, 109; Gibson 9-10, 30-32). According to Locke, proceeding from reality "began at the wrong end" (I.1.7).

Locke began by "enquir[ing] into the Original, Certainty, and extent of human knowledge" (I.1.2). His revolutionary approach liberated people from received ideas and made them epistemologically self-reliant.[2]

Many studies document the ascendancy of Locke's philosophy during the eighteenth-century and attest to its eagerly-embraced advantages. It enabled people to think of their minds as "instruments" for use instead of as "adjunctive" faculties placing them within a pre-ordained reality (Quintana 39, 51). It put knowledge within the reach of all by making knowledge the product of democratic sensation rather than the possession of intellects sufficient to develop their implicit knowledge explicitly (Tuveson 21-24). Empiricism provided not only affirmations of the human capacity to know but also consolations for human failure to do so. After Locke, people did not have to rely on their minds alone for understanding but could turn to the environment to build up knowledge:

> By adopting an attitude of humility as to what man can accomplish
> without external aid, and by earnestly seeking aid from outside
> oneself—in morality from God; in science, from God's
> Creation—one can learn both to love and to know. (Greene 52)

To many, Locke advanced human dignity and prevented human despair.

Despite these advantages, epistemological self-reliance proved a problematic endowment. Locke's theory provided no direct link to join individuals to the environments on which they rely. As Gibson explains, Locke approached philosophy from a new angle, but he did not begin with new premises:

> [Locke] had . . . *taken it for granted* that the contents of our ideas
> of the primary qualities of matter are qualifications of a reality
> which exists beyond and independently of the mind . . . . No

serious attempt is made to get beyond these presuppositions or to
offer a formal justification for them. (172, emphasis added)[3]

Because of his ontological assumptions, Locke deprived perceivers of shared views and verifiable data. He left them to face the threat of isolation within their own perceptions, cut off, ironically, from the environment in which their knowledge originated.

The isolation implicit in Locke's theory stems from his treatment of knowledge of objects as indirect. Perceivers do not know the objects of their own perception. Instead, they know their ideas:

> Since *the Mind*, in all its Thoughts and Reasonings, hath no other
> immediate object but its own *Ideas*, which it alone does or can
> contemplate, it is evident, that our Knowledge is only conversant
> about them. (IV.i.1)

Between perceiver and perceived Locke wedged "Substance," an unknowable "*substratum*, or support, of those *Ideas* we do know" (I.iv.18). "We have no Idea of what [substance] is, but only a confused and obscure one of what it does" (II.xiii.19). Modern commentators reject a simplistic reading of Locke's statement as an endorsement of a mysterious primal matter. For example, Alexander argues that Locke uses substance to counter the notion that matter or thought can exist as independent bodies. He finds that Locke equated material substance with solidity—a feature of all objects but not a separate feature because all solids have qualities (103-04; 9-10); furthermore, he theorizes that Locke posited by analogy an equivalent immaterial substance but that he did not find a feature to epitomize it (11-19). Whatever justification for Locke's reliance on substance a sophisticated interpretation may provide, the refinement does not bring perceivers closer to objects themselves.[4]

Lockian perceivers can gain no comfort or compensation for their isolation from the environment by recourse to shared views, for they know other people as indirectly as objects. No individual has access to another's ideas. Everyone's ideas "are all within his own Breast, invisible and hidden from others, nor can [they] of themselves be made to appear" (III.ii.1). One must learn of another's ideas through words, but words are approximations, removed from ideas themselves. Words function "by voluntary imposition, whereby such a Word is made arbitrarily the Mark of such an Idea" (III.ii.1). Words help to overcome the particularity of everything because they can stand for general ideas. Words and ideas

> become general, by separating from them the circumstance of
> Time, and Place, and any other Ideas, that may determine them to
> this or that particular Existance; [thus] . . . they are made capable
> of representing more Individuals than one; each of which, having
> in it a conformity to that abstract Idea, is (as we call it) of that
> sort. (III.iii.6)

Although Locke celebrates language as the means by which human community may be established (III.i.1), his emphasis does not change the fact that this community is artificially designed and tenuously bound. Nothing securely joins people together; moreover, pursuit of independent aims can thrust the community apart.

Human action stems from "uneasiness" at not having what one desires (II.xxi.34). Locke identifies happiness as the object of all desires (II.xxi.41), defines it as "the utmost Pleasure we are capable of," and further specifies that whatever "has an aptness to produce Pleasure in us, is that we call Good" (II.xxi.42). People, then, inevitably pursue their own satisfaction, irrespective of what means they choose to that end (II.xxi.54-55). They can "suspend" pursuit of immediate desires to evaluate how their gratification conduces to a future greater good (II.xxi.47), but they might choose evil by imperfectly conceiving a future good (II.xxi.58, 63). Despite his view of action as individual gratification, Locke does not reduce society to a Hobbsian "war of each against all." He locates good and evil as pleasure and pain (II.xx.2) with respect to moral good and evil as compliance with or departure from divine or civil law or social custom, through which pleasure or pain is effected (II.xxviii. 5-7). Though he maintains that moral law is not arbitrary and can be understood by reason as certainly as can mathematics (IV.iv.7), his connection of it to individual gratification reinforces the artificiality and tenuousness of community. Assertions such as "there is no body so brutish as to deny" God's right to impose divine law (II.xxviii.8) do little to draw people together.

Equally isolated from objects and from others, Lockian perceivers can be certain of only their individual mental processes. They have a "more perfect and distinct" idea of relations (II.xxv.8), which Locke defines as "the referring, or comparing two things, one to another; from which comparison, one or both comes to be denominated" (II.xxv.5). Relations, which include time, space, and causality (II.xxvi.1-3), are ways of thinking about the world, ways that "lead the Mind" to ideas (II.xxv.10). To be consistent, Locke must confine certainty to the realm of ideas, which he has made the only objects of thought. Hence, he defines knowledge as "nothing but *the perception of the connexion and agreement, or disagreement and repugnance of any of our Ideas*" (IV.i.2) Since Locke believes that ideas refer to a reality beyond themselves, he accepts the ideational agreement as a reflection of an ontological one, but the reality of the agreement obtains only by what Yolton (99-101) and Gibson (193-95) describe as an act of projection. Certainty, knowledge, and truth become, at best, relational. Locke's philosophy opened a Pandora's box of "extreme subjectivism" (Gibson 126) and "radical individualism" (Quintana 54): "Man is alone with his experience, his intellectual life being the ceaseless pursuit of such understanding as the terms of human existence allow, his moral life the application of knowledge to his personal and social needs" (Quintana 54).

The isolation Locke's theory implies might have been less threatening if Locke had confronted it, but he avoided doing so. He argued that people know of their own existence by intuition (IV.ix.3), of God's existence by reason (IV.x.1-3), and of others' existence by assumption:

> The notice we have by our Senses, of the existing of Things
> without us, though it be not altogether so certain, as our intuitive
> Knowledge, or the Deductions of our Reason, employ'd about the
> clear, abstract Ideas of our own Minds; yet it is an assurance that
> *deserves the name of Knowledge*. If we persuade ourselves, that our
> Faculties act and inform us right, concerning the existence of those
> Objects that affect them, it cannot pass for an ill-grounded
> confidence: For I think no body can, in earnest, be so sceptical, as
> to be uncertain of the Existence of those Things which he sees and
> feels. (IV.xi.3)

Locke's effort to show that reason supports this assumption cannot endow the premise with certainty (IV.xi.4-8). His insistence works against reassurance, for he dismisses the issue disdainfully:

> He that can doubt [the existence of things] . . . will never have any
> controversie with me; since he can never be sure I say any thing

contrary to his Opinion. As to my self, I think GOD has given me
assurance enough of the Existence of Things without me. (IV.xi.3)

He counsels doubters to be humble, reminding them that human knowledge is not meant to encompass "the full extent of Being, . . . free from all doubt and scruple" but to convey information sufficient for the preservation of the human condition (IV.xi.8). With this, Locke expects doubters "cannot but be satisfied" (IV.xi.9).

Many were not satisfied. For every admirer who appreciated Locke's demonstration of what people can and cannot properly know, there arose a critic who resisted his separation of perceivers from reality.[5] Following Locke's "way of Ideas," perceivers faced a dilemma. They had either to assume the ontological reality of people and objects besides themselves or to accept confinement within their own mental processes. The development of empiricism can be seen in part as an attempt to resolve this dilemma and join perceivers more securely with the community and environment. Berkeley contributed to this effort by subordinating objects to minds; Hume by absorbing minds into objects. Though these and other philosophers have their own characteristics and aims, all empiricists inherit the problem of isolation and can be examined according to how they deal with it. An example of how Berkeley countered Locke on two grounds—with respect to words and with respect to substance—can illustrate this dimension.

Berkeley believed that Locke was mistaken in construing words as representative of abstract general ideas and that Locke's misapprehension of words had led to a misapprehension of abstract and universal ideas themselves (Introduction 11, 18).[6] To Berkeley, Locke's theory implied that abstract words and ideas exist independently of the particulars from which they have been derived. They become barriers between the perceiver and his perceptions of particular things.   In countering Locke's position, Berkeley carefully explained that his own view does "not deny absolutely there are general ideas" (Introduction 12).   Berkeley argued that "an idea which, considered in itself, is particular, becomes general by being made to represent or stand for all other particular ideas of the same sort" (Introduction 12).   He gives the following example:

> Suppose a geometrician is demonstrating the method of cutting a line in two equal parts. He draws, for instance, a black line of an inch in length: this, which in itself is a particular line, is nevertheless with regard to its signification general, since, as it is there used, it represents all particular lines whatsoever; for that which is demonstrated of it is demonstrated of all lines. . . . And, as that *particular* line becomes general by being made a sign, so the *name* "line," which taken absolutely is particular, by being a sign is made general. And as the former owes its generality not to its being the sign of an abstract or general line, but of all particular right lines that may possibly exist, so the latter must be thought to derive its generality from the same cause, namely, the various particular lines which it indifferently denotes. (Introduction 12)

By bringing general words and ideas closer to their particular origins, Berkeley took a step toward reintegrating the perceiver with his environment. According to one commentator, Berkeley's objection is not to universals but to something like Platonic forms (Van Iten 53).[7]

Berkeley saw universality itself as "not consisting in the absolute, positive nature or conception of anything but in the relation it bears to the particulars signified or represented by it" (Introduction 15). He believed that knowledge would be advanced by the admission that abstract generalities do not exist because such an admission redirects mental energy away from trying to probe the fantastic and reorients it toward trying to discover what can be known (Introduction 24). The new orientation can be seen even in the relationship Berkeley establishes with his reader. Berkeley's reader does not confront Berkeley's general words in the text; rather, the words that represent Berkeley's particular ideas elicit the reader's particular ideas of the same sort, and it is these the reader contemplates. With this exhortation to the reader, Berkeley moves from his Introduction to his main text:

> Whoever, therefore, designs to read the following sheets, I entreat him to make my words the occasion of his own thinking and endeavor to attain the same train of thoughts in reading that I had in writing them. By this means it will be easy for him to discover the truth or falsity of what I say. He will be out of all danger of being deceived by my words, and I do not see how he can be led into an error by considering his own naked, undisguised ideas. (Introduction 25)

Berkeley's denial of abstract words and ideas prepares his denial of abstract objects, i.e. objects independent of perceivers. Berkeley states:

> For as to what is said of the absolute existence of unthinking things without any relation to their being perceived, that seems perfectly unintelligible. Their *esse* is *percipi*, nor is it possible they should have any existence out of the minds of thinking beings that perceive them. (3)

By developing this position, Berkeley eliminates any "unthinking substance or *substratum*" between the perceiver and what he perceives (7, 9). Minds, not inert substances, "support" objects. Objects exist as ideas through their relationship to perceivers, and they are "real" because their relationship to individual perceivers is ratified by their relationship to God as omniscient perceiver (7, 87-94).

In a parallel to his argument that denying abstract words and ideas leads to discovery of genuine knowledge, Berkeley proceeds from denial of material substance to apprehension of reality:

> Color, figure, motion, extension, and the like, considered only as
> so many *sensations* in the mind, are perfectly known, there being
> nothing in them which is not perceived. But if they are looked on
> as notes or images, referred to *things* or *archetypes* existing without
> the mind, then are we involved all in skepticism. We see only the
> appearances, and not the real qualities of things. . . . So that, for
> aught we know, all we see, hear, and feel may be only phantom
> and vain chimera, and not at all agree with the real things existing
> in *rerum natura*. All this skepticism follows from our supposing a
> difference between *things* and *ideas*, and that the former have a
> subsistence without the mind or unperceived. (87)

Understanding objects as ideas in the mind affords surer understanding not only of the physical environment but of the human community. Knowledge of others comes from attributing effects to other perceivers (145) who themselves appear as objects of perception (148). Even belief in God follows from attributing to Him the effects of nature (146-47).

Berkeley's position can be—and has been—attacked from many quarters. Whether it succeeds or fails as a philosophical system, it does try to define the relationship between the individual perceiver and his perceptions, and it should be acknowledged as an attempt to locate the individual within his milieu. Berkeley does not, however, provide an easy solution to the empirical dilemma. In revising Locke, Berkeley gives a great deal of responsibility to every individual perceiver. Each must look to his own mind and the objects predicated upon it for knowledge. Each is denied the comfort of assenting to an absolute and externally verifiable system. Even if Berkeley's approach is as reliable as he claims, it requires an extraordinary amount of individual effort and independence. In short, it destroys hope that the relationship between individual and environment, individual and community, can be understood in fixedly imposed terms.

Some early criticism of Berkeley's philosophy indicates that people felt increasingly threatened and frustrated by the unavailability of certain knowledge from an outside source. Many associated the individual initiative in Berkeley's epistemology with selfishness, i.e. with an impulse inimical to community. In fact, commentators on Berkeley brought the term "egoism" into common English use and opened the way for its frequent conflation with "egotism." The practice of trivializing Berkeley in these terms represents an attempt to lighten the burden of individual responsibility he would place on the shoulders of every perceiver. The details of the controversy, though involved, reward close attention.

Neither the last edition of Bailey's *Dictionary* nor the fourth edition of Johnson's *Dictionary* contains an entry for "egoism." The *Oxford English*

Dictionary cites its first discovered use in English in a 1785 work of philosopher Thomas Reid. It identifies the word as a specialized term in metaphysics and defines it as "the belief, on the part of an individual, that there is no proof that anything exists but his own mind." It adds that the term is "chiefly applied to philosophical systems supposed by their adversaries logically to imply this conclusion." The *Oxford English Dictionary* cites a slightly later (1800) usage of "egoism" as an ethical term: "The theory which regards self-interest as the foundation of morality." It continues: "Also, in practical sense: Regard of one's own interest, as the supreme guiding principle of action; systematic selfishness."

Both Johnson and the *Oxford English Dictionary* define the confusingly similar word "egotism" first as a rhetorical term. In Johnson's words, "egotism" is "the fault committed by the too frequent repetition of the word ego or I; too frequent mention of a man's self in writing or conversation." The *Oxford English Dictionary* shows the condemnatory sense expanding by 1800 when "egotism" could be considered "the vice of thinking too much of oneself: self-conceit, boastfulness; also selfishness." The increasing broadness of the definitions of "egoism" and "egotism" would suggest how easily the terms could be interchanged even if the *O.E.D.* did not document the use of one for the other as early as 1807 and in the work of no less than Thomas Jefferson ("Egoism" 4). Dictionary evidence seems to support Steiner's conclusion following his survey of the use of the terms: "The words are charged with a negative implication; they are intended quite clearly as terms of derogation, except when used in the technical sense of Idealism" (450).

Bracken's research, however, shows Steiner's conclusion to be misleading. Bracken traces "egoism" to early reviews of Berkeley's work, in which context it was used derisively. Bracken explains that the Jesuits and the Malebranchists had an ongoing debate about "the existence of bodies" (15-17). The Malebranchian position, which holds that matter cannot be known to exist by means of the senses but only through belief in the Scriptural attestation of it, threatened the Jesuits' cosmological and teleological methods (17). To protect the Jesuits from an idea that they could not countenance, the editor of the Jesuit journal *Memoires de Trevoux* made Berkeley "the *reductio ad absurdam*" of Malebranche, claiming that he dared an outright denial of matter (16-17). The review tries to instill fear of extreme Malebranchianism by endowing the misrepresented Berkeley with followers:

> Berkley [sic] . . . has pushed without discretion *the principles of his*
>
> *sect* greatly beyond common sense, and has concluded that there
>
> are neither bodies nor matter, and that spirit alone exists. (17)[8]

Moreover, the review tries to give Berkeley a reputation for solipsism by associating him in readers' minds with an unspecified French Malebranchist "who goes farther than Mr. Berkley . . . [and believes] that he may be the only created being who exists" (18).

The review was effective. Bracken shows that association of Berkeley with the notorious—and probably fictitious—"egomist [sic] or egoist of Paris" was echoed by other critics and started the still current debate over whether Berkeley is a solipsist (18-19). For example, Pfaff's *Oratio de Egoismo* indicts Berkeley for his "'new philosophical heresy,' *Egoism*," by citing four reviews—including the Jesuit one—but never referring to Berkeley's own words. When Reid brings "egoism" into regular English usage, he does so in the context of these associations. In fact, his editors' research confirms Bracken's conclusion about the influence of the Jesuit article.

Analyzing Berkeley's philosophy, Reid decides that it provides adequate assurance of God's existence but objects that it fails to provide similar assurance of the existence of other beings. If I am a Berkeleyan, Reid opines, "I am left alone, as the only creature of God in the universe, in that forlorn state of *egoism* into which it is said some of the disciples of Des Cartes were brought by his philosophy" (1: 285). Hamilton, one of Reid's editors, notes that he is "doubtful about the existence of this supposed sect of Egoists" and tries unsuccessfully to trace Reid's derivation of it from the Cartesians (1: 285n). His note indicates knowledge of the Jesuit article but admits to not having seen it. Following up on Hamilton's intention, an anonymous editor of Hamilton's *Reid* searched Hamilton's manuscripts for his derivation. He found reference to Pfaff and to the Jesuit article to be "the only further historical evidence advanced to shew the existence of persons professing Egoism" (Reid 2: 988). "Egoism," then, entered common parlance marked by controversy that qualified its "objective" technical status. Given this background, all uses of "egoism" have negative connotations, and, even apart from the background, Reid's use is hardly non-judgmental.

The arrival of a pejorative term for epistemological self-reliance suggests the gravity and pervasiveness of the empirical dilemma. With increasing vehemence, Locke's heirs resisted the independence he had bequeathed and sought a means to secure the individual within the environment and community. Attempts to answer the questions and remove the doubts that Locke had raised were not confined to the academic regions of philosophy and theology. The Lockian legacy of individual liberation and isolation had culturally pervasive ramifications that shot up in the spiritual lives of many Protestants, entwined around the social and moral concerns of most educated thinkers, and even reached into the activities of all who could write and read. Many aspects of eighteenth-century intellectual life that exceed the confines of the narrowly philosophical nevertheless bear noticeably the mark of the new way of ideas.

For example, a new self-reliance affected religious leaders and their followers in fundamental ways. As Brantley shows by tying Wesley's "experiential emphasis [in] theology" to Locke's "experiential emphasis" in epistemology (*Locke* 2), the development of Methodism is significantly bound up with the empirical dilemma. According to Brantley, Wesley shifted the dominant concern of believers from general knowledge of God to personal and individual knowledge of their own salvation (4-5). Individual believers, like individual perceivers, were thus denied confirmation of their place in the universe by reference to an absolute system external to themselves. Believers could no longer trust adherence to practice and precept as a likely means of attaining salvation. Instead, they became obliged to establish their own relationships with God to effect their separate salvations.

Wesley's *Journal* offers his own experience as an epitome of this redirection. The *Journal* pinpoints Wesley's new orientation as beginning on May 24, 1738 at Aldersgate. Prior to that time, Wesley had been unsuccessful at leading what he considered to be a religious life. At school, he writes, "I still said my prayers both in public and in private, and read with the Scriptures, several other books of religion, especially comments on the New Testament. Yet I had not all this while so much as a notion of inward holiness" (1: 466). He devoted himself to numerous charitable causes, though he "was convinced . . . that outward works are nothing, being alone" (1: 469).

Despite his scrupulous observances, Wesley believed himself cut off from religious life until he experienced what he interpreted as an individual relationship with God:

> In the evening I went very unwillingly to a society in Aldersgate Street, where one was reading Luther's preface to the *Epistle to the Romans*. About a quarter before nine, while he was describing the change which God works in the heart through faith in Christ, I felt my heart strangely warmed. I felt I did trust in Christ, Christ alone for salvation; and an assurance was given me that He had taken way *my* sins, even *mine*, and saved *me* from the law of sin and death. (1: 475-76)

Wesley "testified openly to all" at Aldersgate about this occurrence (1: 476) and made it his task to acquaint more people with the possibility of such individual assurance. The relationship between the believer and God became for him the cornerstone of religion: "'Is a man a believer in Jesus Christ, and is his life suitable to his profession?' are not only the main, but the sole inquires I make in order to [accept] his admission into our society" (5: 116).[9]

In the *Appeals* he wrote to explain Methodism to the uninitiated, Wesley emphasizes the personal dimension of faith for every believer: "Justifying faith implies . . . a sure trust that Christ died for *my* sins, that he 'loved *me* and gave himself for *me*'" (*Works* 11: 107).[10] Although Wesley encouraged believers to persist in the practices of their churches, he separated justification from attendance at worship or participation in the sacraments and preserved it as an individual act of belief (11: 121-22). Though he showed exhaustively that his doctrine is consistent with Anglican orthodoxy, he imposed no creed or rubrics upon believers and upheld "the right every man has to judge for himself . . . [as] sacred and inviolable" (11: 279).[11] Wesley's respect for the integrity of the individual believer led him to resist prescription and, sometimes, even direction.

An incident recorded in his *Journal* illustrates the free rein he gave to his followers. In conversation with Wesley, a Calvinist stated his belief in predestination and informed Wesley that many Methodists likewise accepted that tenet. Unconcerned, Wesley said: "I never ask whether they hold it or no. Only let them not trouble others by disputing about it" (2: 353). Wesley recounted this conversation to his followers, but he was vague in advising them about how to deal with the issue:

> I mentioned this to our society, and, without entering into the
> controversy, besought all of them who were weak in the faith not
> to "receive one another to doubtful disputations," but simply to
> follow after holiness, and the things that make for peace. (2:353)

Wesley left his followers essentially on their own. His doctrine may be well defined in his *Appeals*, but his consistency did not unite his community.

As Brantley's exposition demonstrates, Wesley's individual believers seem left to accumulate their own spiritual knowledge as Locke's individual perceivers are left to accumulate their own sensory knowledge. They also seem to face a similar threat of isolation. Nothing external to believers can verify their justification. Assurance comes from "an inner sense" that Wesley never precisely defined, though he maintained that it is not unreasonable and that it is not merely emotional.[12] Believers could give accounts of their experiences—such as Wesley's *Journal* gives of his—but these could attest only to their authors' conditions. Some believers manifested their assurance with nearly hysterical behavior, perhaps in an effort to have some tangible sense of it.

Though Wesley did not endorse such displays, he was reluctant to condemn them, for he thought that they did not "hinder the work of [God's] Spirit in the soul, which may be carried on either with or without them" (*Works* 11:121). No regular practices, then, identified believers as a group.

Despite Wesley's insistence that good works must follow from true faith, his theology makes works and faith distinctly separate activities (*Works* 11: 106; *Journal* 2: 354-60). Thus, believers could not refer to a pattern of behavior for assurance. Nor could they accept it on authority, for Wesley's use of lay preachers (*Works* 11: 297-98) suggests the knowledge of the minister to be of no different kind from that of his congregation. In short, believers had no uniform means to represent and confirm their central belief.

As the development of empiricism can in some sense be seen as an effort to compensate for the implied isolation of the individual perceiver, so certain developments within Methodism seem attempts to compensate for the parallel predicament of the individual believer. Movements developed among Methodists to constitute themselves apart from the Church of England. The gradual tendency toward group definition suggests a plea for ties among individual believers.[13] Wesley's insistence in the *Appeals* on unity with the Church of England may even show a complementary tendency, for it indicates a need to locate the highly individuated Methodists within a controlling group. Less obviously, Methodists' writing of journals and autobiographies grew sufficiently to make those forms popular in secular literature.[14] Beneath the impulse toward individually confessional writing may lie the hope that common traits might be extracted from the mass of separate documents. Even the hysterical behavior of those Methodists who testified with manic fervor cries out for a definition of norms that Wesley would not provide.

If the individuality of Methodism presented difficulties to believers, it proved even more troublesome to people of other convictions. Self-reliance was often construed as a threat to community and Methodism attacked less for what it was than for the extreme to which it might lead. For example, George Horne denounced Methodists as Antinomians because he believed that separation of works from faith in the matter of justification would lead to anarchy: if the individual could be justified by faith alone, he would have no reason to conform to any law.[15] The fact that Wesley's *Appeals* insist that works necessarily follow from justifying faith and thus distinguish Methodism from Antinomianism would be beside the point for Horne even if he knew the documents (and Wesley suspected that he did not [*Works* 11: 443]). As the Jesuits found it useful to make Berkeley a solipsist, so Horne finds it useful to make Wesley an Antinomian. He is not evaluating Wesley or Methodism. He is associating and exaggerating to protect the Church of England from the threat of individualism, in which campaign Wesley and Methodism can serve as examples.

More widespread reactions to Methodism appear unified in their concentration on its potentially divisive individuality. Lyles' analysis of eighteenth-century satires of Methodism reveals a persistent association of independent judgment with pride, arrogance, and anti-social tendencies. Condemnations of Methodism, like condemnations of Berkeleyanism, begin with a distortion of the individual responsibility at issue. For example, many satires attack the Methodists' idea of assurance, i.e., that justification can give an individual a conviction of his sins having been forgiven at a particular time. Critics turned this idea into one that justification provided an unconditional and irreversible promise of final salvation. After making the idea suggest that the individual finds himself perfect enough for heaven, satirists could easily dismiss it as "impudence" (Lyles 55).

Similarly, lay preachers were attacked for arrogance in assuming that they could fill a specialized office for which others had prepared for years. Part of one poem Lyles quotes illustrates this point:

> Brimful of *Righteousness*, unaw'd by *Sense*,
>
> By *Inspiration* urg'd and *Impudence*,
>
> The *Bricklayer's-Labourer*, with horny *Fists*
>
> On *Faith* in Preference to Works insists. (64)

Moreover, satirists construed the presumption of lay preachers as a direct threat to the order of society and the division of labor. They predicted that it would lead to a world "in which the trades and the shops were empty because all were preaching God's word" (Lyles 62).

Whether they focus on doctrine or practice, satirists seem intent on exposing Methodist attachment to individual faith as a rationalization for following one's own inclinations (Lyles 47-54). Perhaps their apprehension of individualism is responsible for what Lyles reveals as the most common kind of satire on Methodists, the personal attack (60). Instead of systematically addressing ideas, critics often contented themselves with mocking people. For example, they would turn a characteristic squint into a sign of impaired intellectual insight or narrow-mindedness (Lyles 112-13). The significance of the personal attack may go beyond Lyles' assessment of it as an attempt to show "the absurdity and danger of the movement" by showing a leader of or participant in it "as ridiculous and dangerous" (112). Through personal attack, the critic suggests that the movement stems from the unsupported and unshared whims of one character. The danger of the movement is diffused by trivializing it. The technique makes it possible to dismiss the movement without dealing with ideas that may be difficult to confront. Moreover, it confirms the importance and coherence of the group, which can identify and control deviant elements.

The associations with selfishness and arrogance that crowded around empiricism and Methodism suggest the volatility of all aspects of individualism for this era. By projecting fears of isolation onto particular systems that centered on self-reliance, the larger society could rid itself of an uncertainty that threatened its cohesion. Conflict between the larger society and its targeted groups might issue in a clearer definition of the individual's ties to the world. The process reveals a general resistance to the Lockian inheritance and a general demand for some way to repudiate it.

One influential and ecumenical attempt to solve the dilemma of the individual's isolation from others appears in Shaftesbury's work. Shaftesbury challenged the practice of grounding human behavior in individual gratification, a practice that places community at risk (*Characteristics* 1:74-85).[16] He grounded human behavior in "affections" and asserted that people possess social affections that lead them to value the good of others (1:285-86). From the observation that such social affections are characteristically human, it followed for Shaftesbury that their fulfillment is likewise so. He thus theorized that people possess a "moral sense" by which they apprehend the moral qualities of actions. The moral sense develops the apprehension of virtue into an attraction toward it and inclines people to act altruistically. In Shaftesbury's words:

> In a creature capable of forming general notions of things, not only the outward beings which offer themselves to the sense are

the objects of the affection, but the very actions themselves, and
the affections of pity, kindness, gratitude, and their contraries,
being brought into the mind by reflection, become objects. So
that, by means of this reflected sense, there arises another kind of
affection towards those very affections themselves, which have
been already felt, and are now become the subject of a new liking
or dislike. (1:251)

For Shaftesbury, the moral sense ensures the reality of community, making
people as connected as organs in a body. The good of the individual is
identical with the good of others because only the good of all maintains the
whole organism without which individuals are incomplete and unfulfilled
(1:280-82).

Though the coincidence of virtue and interest batters the barrier of
individual isolation, it does not topple it. The coincidence could result from
the priority of interest as convincingly as from the priority of virtue. Shaftesbury's approach seems to enlist an empirical method to support assumed moral
certainties. As Grean points out, Shaftesbury returns to an innate idea of
virtue in his claim that there are good qualities all can recognize as such (204,
182). Tuveson supposes that the "moral sense" arose by analogy with the
physical senses. If people have faculties that detect the qualities of objects,
they ought likewise to have a faculty that detects the values of actions (45-49).
Blending the old ontology with the new epistemology, Shaftesbury produced
"a faith that sustains aspirations" (Grean 213). The unstable compound of
"moral sense" philosophy attests to the desire of Locke's heirs to salvage the
comforting assurance that individual minds gain knowledge from experience
while jettisoning the disturbing concomitant that experience imposes limits on

what minds can know. Shaftesbury's endeavor seems best summarized in Engell's account: Shaftesbury tried "to extrapolate from the senses an order and relation behind experience that is deeper than the senses alone can supply" (24-25).

Shaftesbury inaugurated numerous attempts to forge a link between the individual and others, though most succeeding writers replaced his system of the affections and the moral sense with the concept of the sympathetic imagination. Shaftesbury himself had an idea of sympathy, which Grean extracts from his notebooks, but for Shaftesbury the bond of fellow feeling was simply one of many social ties predicated upon the operation of the affections (160-63). Though Shaftesbury passed over the concept of sympathy, others seized it as the key to overcoming isolation. Adam Smith, for example, made the imaginative bond of sympathy the cornerstone of this ethics.[17] In Smith's system, the imagination compensates for the individual's isolation by making available to each individual an "analogous" experience of another's perception (I.i.1.4). From this analogous experience arises the sympathy or "fellow feeling" that joins people together. One perceiver imaginatively "chang[es] places" with another and "come[s] either to conceive or be affected by what [the other] feels" (I.i.1.3). Smith makes this shared experience in varying degree the basis of love, friendship, and society (VI.ii.1.1-VI.ii.3.3). He even makes it the source of conscience and altruism, for perceivers check their self-interest by imagining how their behavior may affect others (III.1.5, III.3.4-7). In short, the capacity for sympathy indicates that people, "who can subsist only in society, [are] fitted by nature to that situation for which [they were] made" (II.ii.3.1).

Like Shaftesbury's, Smith's philosophy blends an assumption about the reality of society with experiential confirmation. Rooted in experience, Smith's imagination does not simply give one person the experience of another; rather, it allows observers to think of themselves as participants in a given situation and to share the emotion of the truly affected person by experiencing how they would feel if they were likewise affected. Smith's vivid writing seems aimed at reinforcing his idea in his language:

> Though our brother is upon the rack, as long as we ourselves are at our ease, our senses will never inform us of what he suffers. They never did, and never can, carry us beyond our own person, and it is by the imagination only that we can form any conception of what are his sensations. Neither can that faculty help us to this any other way, than by representing to us what would be our own, if we were in his case. It is the impressions of our own senses only, not those of his, which our imaginations copy. By the imagination we place ourselves in his situation, we conceive ourselves enduring all the same torments, we enter as it were into his body, and become in some measure the same person with him, and thence form some idea of his sensations, and even feel something which, though weaker in degree, is not altogether unlike them. His agonies, when they are thus brought home to ourselves, when we have thus adopted and made them our own, begin at last to affect us, and we then tremble and shudder at the thought of what he feels (I.i.1.2).

Though Smith's system depends upon the bond of sympathy, he advances no argument for the ontological reality of that bond. Sympathy may be a product of the imagination in the Humian sense—a fleeting and possibly illusory combination of impressions that does not necessarily reflect a reality beyond itself.[18]

Dwelling on the ways in which sympathy enhances the human condition, Smith's account testifies to the ongoing preoccupation with shared experience. "Nothing pleases us more than to observe in other men a fellow feeling with all the emotions in our own breast," he writes; "nor are we ever so much shocked as by the appearance of the contrary" (I.i.2.1). The desire for sympathy can even lead those passionately affected by grief to moderate their emotion to a degree comprehensible to observers so as to elicit the sympathy the excess of passion would prevent (I.i.4.7). Smith's work describes a functional set of human relations. His philosophy is problematic because he insists that the relations reflect a "real" sympathy, that people in fact share experience by imaginative transfer. Rooted in each individual's own experience, sympathy might reflect the projection of one individual's feeling onto another as easily as the apprehension of another's feeling by a given individual. As Engell points out, sympathy *assumes* an accurate reproduction of another's circumstances (158). The spectre of isolation remains unexorcised.

So important was the link with others that most writers preferred to whittle away at the role of individual interest in human action rather than confront the speculative nature of their enterprise. Anxiety over isolation seems to have produced an antagonism toward the independence of every perceiver. As late as 1805, Hazlitt tried to circumvent the element of self-interest in human behavior while retaining a modicum of individual experience. Hazlitt worried that action as interest implies

> an attachment to self [that] could signify nothing more than a
> foolish complacency in our own idea, an idle dotage, and idolatry

of our abstract being, . . . [and that] must leave the mind indif-

ferent to everything else. (1: 18)

Consequently opposing any philosophy that finds human action motivated by
the desire to attain one's own good, Hazlitt countered that action follows from
an idea of good built up from knowledge of a variety of goods (1: 12-13).[19]
The idea stems from one's own experience but is unrelated to one's own
satisfaction because it is impossible to conceive of a future self or another self
(1: 6-11). Imagination makes sympathy possible by allowing perceivers to think
of another's situation in terms they themselves have previously experienced (1:
25). Imagination thus transfers knowledge of past experience to anticipation
of future experience—whether it be one's own or another's (1: 25-27).

Hazlitt even tried to exploit the projecting capacity of the imagination to
circumvent another aspect of the empirical dilemma—the isolation of perceivers
from the physical environment. The assumption that sympathy involves the
accurate reproduction of another's feeling leaves people separated from the
physical environment, which has no emotional characteristics for people to
reproduce. Hazlitt allowed the imagination to initiate a relationship with an
object and then to become so overwhelmed by the object's nature that the
barrier between perceiver and object falls.[20]   Such a theory compounds the
existing dilemma. At the very least, the possibility of sympathy with objects
pushes the possibility of sympathy with people farther back into the realm of
projection rather than of apprehension.[21] Sympathy with objects and with
people may be equivalent—and equivalently illusory—occurrences. Furthermore,
Hazlitt reserves the fullest sympathetic capacity for artists and poets, a
circumstance that may diminish the extent to which average perceivers can

overcome their isolation or that may increase the extent to which average perceivers must depend on artists as intermediaries.

The empirical dilemma had provoked aesthetic controversy long before Hazlitt entered the lists. One specifically literary aspect surfaced in the eighteenth-century preoccupation with original genius, which traditionally dates from 1759 with the publication of Edward Young's *Conjectures on Original Composition* (the same year in which Adam Smith published his *Theory of Moral Sentiments*). In his *Conjectures*, Young called on modern authors to rely on their own views of nature to inform their art instead of imitating their predecessors. He posited originality as a value in itself, extrapolating:

> But suppose an *Imitator* to be most excellent, (and such there are),
> yet still he but nobly builds on another's foundation; his debt is, at
> least, equal to his glory; which therefore, on the balance, cannot
> be very great. On the contrary, an *Original*, though but indifferent
> (its *Originality* being set aside), yet has something to boast. (7)

Young exhorted his contemporaries not to be intimidated by the achievements of former authors, however magnificent: "treat even *Homer* himself as his royal admirer was treated by the cynic,—bid him stand aside, nor shade our Composition from the beams of our genius" (10-11). Thus excerpted, Young seems to argue for the merit of any independent effort in an extreme that justifies Howard Mumford Jones's estimation of him as "virtually solipsistic" (270). Potentially, Young's theory isolates the genius from his predecessors, contemporaries, and successors, for if the genius's work is entirely unique, it is inaccessible to readers and unrelated to literary history.

Young prevented his theory from leaving every author ignorant of and uninterested in any but himself by restating originality as right imitation. In other words, he argued that every original genius, insofar as his work stems from personal interaction with his environment, replicates the process by which the great writers of the past produced their masterpieces:

> Imitate [ancient writers] by all means;—but imitate aright. He that imitates the divine *Iliad*, does not imitate *Homer*; but he who takes the same method, which *Homer* took, for arriving at a capacity of accomplishing a work so great. Tread in his steps, . . . drink where he drank, . . . that is, at the breast of nature. Imitate; but imitate not the *Composition*, but the *Man*. . . . Let us build our Compositions with the spirit, and in the taste, of the antients [sic]; but not with their materials. (11)

Thus, Young saved the original writer from isolation by positing a link of "noble contagion" (12) among geniuses. They have a common goal, a common procedure, and a common source.

Young's qualifications give his original writers enough of a shared enterprise for Samuel Johnson to express his bewilderment at "Young['s] receiv[ing] as novelties, what he thought very common maxims" (Boswell, *Life* 5: 269). As Bate explains, Johnson would find an author who imitates the ancients in particulars to be negligent of his obligation to seek "general nature" (70). Johnson was apparently able to see in Young a kindred spirit construing the writer's task as the apprehension of some unchanging principle and the expression of it in a timely manner.[22] When Young's ideas are aligned with Johnson's, they do not describe the genius as isolated and self-fulfilling; instead, they make him a partaker of what Fussell calls "the sacrament of authorship" (91). For Young as for Johnson, the best composition "is the realization of a paradigm, . . . a virtual translation into local terms of a pre-existing model" (Fussell 113). Like Smith's ethics, Young's aesthetics attempts to overcome the problem of isolation by supporting a given ontology with individual experience.

Most late eighteenth-century theories of original genius make a similar effort to connect the author with others in some way, an effort that Cox traces in the works of Young, Duff, and Gerard. Cox sets up a parallel between the problem of the isolated consciousness that knows only its own perceptions (13-34) and the problem of the isolated writer who must achieve some original insight (35-58). He also proposes parallel solutions: if sympathy can break through the isolation of each consciousness (27-28), so sensibility can break through the isolation of the writer who, in expressing his original insights, makes others "feel the same concern, and share in the same distress" (40); if social interaction allows the individual to define his moral position (29-32), so critical interaction allows the writer to define his literary position, a position that is intelligible only when compared with the positions of others (54-55). Unfortunately, the potential for bonding is as assumptive in theories of genius as in theories of morals. Moreover, bonding threatens theories of genius with reductionism. If the product of genius is to be recognized by the sympathy it evokes, the genius may be forced to resort to "a few stock situations" in order to elicit "an automatic response" (Cox 53-54). The author who fails to do so might be seen as less than a genius or as an irresponsible genius who has not given his fellow human beings the benefit of his insight.

The result of clutching tightly to those safeguards that prevent the dislocation of genius may be seen in applied literary criticism of the late eighteenth and early nineteenth centuries. As Hayden's study of then current reviewing practices reveals, reviewers saw their duties as ones of defining, upholding, and furthering certain standards (3-4, 243-60). They shared a sense of purpose despite a multiplicity of biases because their differences about specific standards dissolved before their agreement that standards can and should be ascertained, communicated and adopted. In particular, they agreed that "literature . . . had a moral purpose, variously described but always present either explicitly or implicitly" (Hayden 246). In effect, reviewers enlisted literature in the culturally pervasive endeavor to overcome individual isolation, an endeavor in which they were highly involved.

As Klancher's study shows, the turn of the nineteenth century found British periodicals engaged in a struggle to define and control their readership. Since the French Revolution had disturbed the expectations with which groups of people—including writers and readers—approached each other, authors could not easily assume that they addressed a mirror-image of themselves (19-23). They addressed instead a wide range of middle classes more readily character-ized by their responses—advocacy, antagonism, or bafflement—to recent political events than by socio-economic status (38-44). Consequently, periodical writers defined their readership by its "potential" (50) and turned periodicals into a "space for imagining social formations still inchoate and a means to give them shape" (24). Klancher details the ways in which numerous journals designed the new middle class identity (51-75), and he raises a parallel between efforts at molding that constituency and efforts in other journals to shape professional and radical constituencies (81-111).

What is remarkable about the *agon* in the periodical arena is the despera-tion with which the participants sought consensus. In some sense, the political upheaval of the 1790's attests to the impossibility of fusing individuals into a uniform and sufficient structure: the Revolution manifested in the Body Politic the factitiousness of shared experience. British periodicals might have responded to the failure of the old order by becoming a forum in which to consider the validity of consensus as an concept, a forum in which to revalue the idealization of shared knowledge. That they responded instead by seeking a means to turn their individuated readers into a homogeneous audience betrays a deep-seated fear of confronting individuality. Moreover, periodical writers' recourse to perception itself as the means to effect the desired bonding locates their enterprise within the broadly philosophical context.

Preoccupation with perception underlies the various techniques Klancher identifies. Periodical writers directed their readers' attention to their mental processes to ensure—or to attempt to ensure—that "innumerable acts of reading . . . produce a centralized intellect" (Klancher 60). Articles in the *New Monthly Magazine* might anatomize how events from trials to games were distinct "signs of the times," but their catalogues aimed at joining their readers in the belief that they were a classless unity who could comprehend those distinctions (61-68); articles in the *Quarterly* and *Edinburgh Review*s might formulate key concepts to explain all aspects of contemporary life, but their technique meant to bring readers together as interpreters of "master-signs" (68-73). In general, periodical writing posited an audience that would believe itself united in consequence of its mastery of the discourse (74-75). The plan to unite the middle class as readers has a parallel in plans to unite the less educated "mass" audience and the less extensive radical audience. Writing for the masses typically celebrated how common humanity subsumed social diversity (91-96); writing in the service of radical interests usually forced its readers collectively into the role of the excluded underclass (99-103).

The separate audiences depended upon each other. The knowledge each audience allegedly shared included assumptions about the "others" functional for its comprehensive illusions.[23] In essence, periodicals formed an audience around the act of reading as a promise of consensus, as a solution to the empirical dilemma. Individual perceptions inevitably obtruded upon this ideal, challenging the proponents of consensus either to reveal the foundation for their claims or to investigate potential alternatives.[24] One such challenge came from William Wordsworth. While most of Wordsworth's contemporaries were trying to circumvent the limits of perception, Wordsworth seems to have tried to turn them to advantage. The variety and complexity of Wordsworth's poetics may stem from a deliberate attempt to determine whether literature could open the issue of individual perception to approaches beyond denial. The following study locates Wordsworth's work within the context of the empirical dilemma. It begins with Wordsworth's own declarations, which, in effect, return the empirical dilemma to the Lockian drawing-board. Responding to a pressing contemporary concern by shifting the lines of inquiry, Wordsworth pushed contemporary thought toward redefinition of the consensual ideal.

Chapter 2
Wordsworth's Response

Understanding Wordsworth's situation as part of the empirical dilemma requires, paradoxically, a more general approach than that taken in most philosophically-oriented studies of his work. Many scholars have located Wordsworth within the history of ideas. Beatty shows Wordsworth's debt to Hartley, to which Stallknecht adds that to Boehme; Hirsch aligns him with Schelling, and Chandler with Burke. Havens and Grob pursue more broadly conceptual inquiries, an approach perhaps best exploited by Rader, who argues for Wordsworth's eclecticism and traces the source of Wordsworth's ideas in whatever he read—whether in Newton or Paley. However valuable these and other philosophically-oriented studies of Wordsworth may be, their very specificity and attention to nuance of controversy deflects their focus from the generalized and pervasive preoccupation with self and environment, self and society, that is the hallmark of the empirical dilemma.[1] Responding to the intellectual milieu, Wordsworth's poetic commentaries take up the question of individual and communal prerogatives. His statements provide more than a gloss on his poetic practices. They locate those practices within a sophisticated and consistent poetics and indicate that he started and continued to write poetry in an effort to join the struggle to secure the individual. Wordsworth begins by accepting the individuality of all perception that his contemporaries wished to circumvent. He then explores how writers and readers can take advantage of this condition if they abandon their pursuit of a chimerical consensus and channel their efforts into the creation of functional relationships.

Wordsworth's earliest theoretical statement, the *Preface* to *Lyrical Ballads*, posits a counter-poetics to that taking shape in the consensus-seeking periodicals, for Wordsworth's work calls attention to those features of literature that make it uniquely suited to reconciling people with the individuality of their perceptions. Readers cannot share an author's insight. The integrity of each individual's perception prevents a replication of perspective. If readers accept that limit and overcome the temptation to surrender their minds to an author's, they can use literature to compensate for their isolation and even to grow as a result of it. Wordsworth's *Preface* emphasizes independent reader response, for readers can exploit the limits of perception only if they accustom themselves to wresting meaning from literature instead of receiving—or hoping to receive—an author's insight through it.

Wordsworth's emphasis on reader response in the *Preface* takes two forms: indictment of what hinders independent response and exhortation to it. Principally, he indicts sensational literature, poetic diction, and critical authority. He complains about the popularity of "frantic novels, sickly and stupid German tragedies, and deluges of idle and extravagant stories" (*Prose* 1: 128) because they act "to blunt the discriminating powers of the mind, and, unfitting it for all voluntary exertion, to reduce it to a state of almost savage torpor" (1: 128). He rejects poetic diction not because its terms are themselves objectionable but because they have become formulaic:

I have . . . abstained from the use of many expressions, in themselves proper and beautiful, but which have been foolishly repeated
by bad Poets till such feelings of disgust are connected with them

as it is scarcely possible by any art of association to overpower. (1:
132)

He dismisses criticism that operates by scanning works to see if they conform
to a fixed set of rules:

There is a numerous class of critics who when they stumble upon
these prosaisms as they call them [i.e., the language of prose in a
poetic line] imagine that they have made a notable discovery, and
exult over the Poet as over a man ignorant of his own profession.
(1: 132)

In short, Wordsworth targets an attitude of unthinking acceptance of established ideas and identifies it in three manifestations.

Specifically "endeavor[ing] to counteract" the trend represented by the
novels, tragedies, and stories (1: 130), Wordsworth offers his poems drawn
from "low and rustic life" (1: 124) and using "the very language of men" (1:
130). He substitutes his concept of the poet as "a man speaking to men" (1:
138) for the notion of the poet as a guardian of a certain discourse. He
subordinates the authority of the collective critical establishment to each
reader's independent judgment:

I have one request to make of my Reader, which is, that in judging
these Poems he would decide by his own feelings genuinely, and
not by reflection upon what will probably be the judgment of
others. How common is it to hear a person say, "I myself do not
object to this style of composition or this or that expression, but to
such and such classes of people it will appear mean or ludicrous."
This mode of criticism so destructive of all sound unadulterated

> *judgment* is almost universal: I have therefore to *request that the*
> *Reader would abide independently* by his own feelings, and that if he
> finds himself affected he would not suffer such conjectures to
> interfere with his pleasure. (1: 154 emphasis added)

As this passage especially bears out, Wordsworth defends his alternatives not
because of their greater intrinsic merit but because of their usefulness in
eliciting responses. Wordsworth's efforts should awaken readers to the uses of
their mental powers and should encourage them to try their own and analyze
the evidence of the efforts of others.

Wordsworth further invites his readers to scrutinize their epistemological
processes by making perception itself the cynosure of his poetry. Again and
again, Wordsworth calls attention to how perception figures in his lyrical
ballads. The Poems exist to explore it:

> The principal object then which I proposed to myself in these
> Poems was to make the incidents of common life interesting by
> tracing in them . . . the primary laws of our nature: chiefly as far
> as regards the manner in which we associate ideas in a state of
> excitement. (1: 122-24)

They take shape from its operation:

> But speaking in less general language, [the purpose of the poems]
> is to follow the fluxes and refluxes of the mind when agitated by
> the great and simple affections of our nature.   (1: 126)

And they invest all other elements with its power:

> But it is proper that I should mention one other circumstance
> which distinguishes these Poems from the popular Poetry of the
> day; it is this, that the feeling therein developed gives importance

>   to the action and situation and not the action and situation to the
>   feeling. (1: 128)

Wordsworth's combined emphasis on the topic of perception and the goal of
response yield, in effect, a new function for literature, a function not of
disseminating a view but of stimulating thought. Literature becomes a means
by which readers can revalue the merit of any given mode or notion. It not
only prevents intellectual stagnation but fosters intellectual growth. Literature
possesses such potential, however, because of the limits of perception. If
readers collectively received an idea from literature, all evaluation and
stimulation would be precluded by the domination of one thought. Only
through individual interaction with texts can readers realize an infinite number
of ideas. Though readers develop their own understandings, they are joined
to all other readers by the common text.

The link to the text and to other readers does not bring the individual into
contact with some absolute meaning or reality; rather, it enables the individual
to work within a functional relationship to a posited object—the written text
and other readers or, by extension, natural objects and other perceivers in a
"real" environment. The approach serves as a coping mechanism in an
isolating situation. Once people stop denying the limits of their individuality,
they can begin to create meaning from self-conscious effort and to relate to
others as individuals. Such courses of action are not available to those
engaged in a search for perfect meaning and agreement. Wordsworth's literary
theory, then, discovers the liberating potential within the empirical dilemma.
Faced with an issue of individual isolation as a problem to be solved or
deplored, Wordsworth turned it into a condition to be cultivated and exploited.

One might characterize Wordsworth's work as an adaptation of a traditional view of literature to contemporary demands. As Tompkins points out, literature had been directly involved in stimulating readers' extra-literary activity since ancient times. The connection between reading the pages of a text and acting in the social sphere did not break down noticeably until the eighteenth-century (202-14). Insofar as Wordsworth affirms a link between reading and responding and brings the activity of reading to bear on the analysis of a contemporary issue, he works from a time-honored view of literature as socially functional. His application, however, is unprecedented. Previous notions of response entail collective results. Readers of classical rhetoric, Renaissance poetry, or Augustan satire expected to enact some specific moral or practical improvement, eliminate some moral or practical problem, or otherwise transform the author's words into action. Doubts about the reliability of such shared results reached a crisis by Wordsworth's time and prompted his plan to accommodate an infinite range of integrally individual responses.

The novelty and magnitude of Wordsworth's proposal might be more readily apparent by reference to Wolfgang Iser's *Wirkungstheorie*, a view with which Wordsworth's is remarkably consonant. Such an approach in no way argues that Wordsworth "anticipated" Iser or that a one-to-one correspondence obtains between them. It posits only that both share a basic orientation and that the work of one can highlight the work of the other.[2] Like Wordsworth, Iser holds that a text can help "the reader to break out of his accustomed framework of conventions."[3] But, he stresses, it does *not* accomplish this by offering the reader a given perspective to adopt (8, 11, 24, 27, 49, 140). The text confronts the reader with a number of perspectives drawn from recognizable areas of life and thought (96). The amalgamation constitutes what Iser calls the "repertoire":

> The repertoire consists of all the familiar territory in the text. This
> may be in the form of references to earlier works, or to the social
> and historical norms, or to the whole culture from which the text
> has emerged. (69)

The text, however, dislocates the familiar elements from the "context" or "frame of reference" in which the reader normally encounters them (71). It uses certain "strategies," such as allocating the elements among perspectives, to induce the reader to reassemble the repertoire in a new way (69, 86-103). Exploiting the condition that no one perspective is entirely adequate or entirely accessible to any other (96-97, 126, 166), the text sets up a relationship of "tension" or "conflict" between the reader and itself (37, 46, 89).

The text presents the perspectives in "continually interweaving and interacting" portions and not as separate or successive wholes. Iser calls each portion as the reader's attention focuses on it a "theme" and the accumulation of themes, the "horizon." Every new theme that the reader encounters qualifies his view of past themes and directs his attitude toward each new one (97). Thus, reading proceeds by "a dialectic of protension and retention" (112). As the reader thinks the "alien thoughts" (154, 126-27) of each perspective and watches the perspectives qualify each other, he gains distance from the reality in which he is usually trapped (140). The distance gives the reader insight into a different dimension of the object or idea (140, 134). Such insight is possible because the theme-and-horizon structure requires the reader to make use of portions of the text that have passed into his memory in order to interpret new portions he encounters. When the reader recalls the necessary themes, he recalls them in the "context" of his mind. Thus the reader brings to consciousness the text and his apprehension of it, and this puts him in a position to evaluate both (116-17).

By engaging with the text, the reader "bring[s] into the world something that did not exist before," i.e., his "actualization" or "realization" of the text (22, 37, 203) and catches himself in the process of doing so (134). Engagement with a text educates the reader out of an excessive reliance on a given perspective—his own or that of others—and inculcates the habit of evaluating "reality" and the perception of it (8). Of the power of such engagement Iser writes:

> Suddenly we find ourselves detached from our world, to which we are inextricably tied, and able to perceive it as an object. And even if this detachment is only momentary, it may enable us to apply the knowledge we have gained by figuring out the multiple references of the linguistic signs, so that we can view our own world as a thing "freshly understood." (140)

In addition, through such engagement, a reader "can bring into light a layer of his personality that he had previously been unable to formulate in his conscious mind" (50).

Although the interaction between a text and its reader is unique to each reader, it is *not*, Iser insists, "private" or "arbitrary" (24). Personal applications *follow* the act of reading, as the reader carries his comprehension of the text into his own world (22-23). These two parts of the reading process reflect a distinction between "meaning" and "significance" that Iser incorporates from Ricoeur: "meaning" refers to a reader's deriving an organization of the text's elements; "significance" involves the reader's "absorption of the

meaning into existence" (151). The composition of meaning has "intersubjec-
tively verifiable characteristics" (22) because it is governed by certain
"response-inviting structures" in the text (34). These structures consist chiefly
of the text's deployment of repertoire and strategies, which "anticipate[s] the
presence of a recipient without necessarily defining him; . . . prestructures the
role to be assumed by each recipient; [and] . . . impels the reader to grasp the
text" (34). Iser calls the totality of these structures the text's "implied reader"
(34). The implied reader does not manipulate—or try to manipulate—the reader
into agreeing with the author or with any perspective presented, for that would
make the reader passive and preclude the interaction on which reading is
based (28-29). Its function is to unify the otherwise isolated responses of
readers: "each actualization . . . [of a text] represents a selective realization
of the implied reader" (37). Because these discrete structures underpin
readers' infinite interactions with the text, the implied reader "provides a link
between all the historical and individual actualizations of the text and makes
them accessible to analysis" (38). It joins not only readers contemporary to the
text but later readers, giving the former new insight into their milieu and the
latter access to an otherwise remote and alien environment (74).

Among the similarities between Iser's and Wordsworth's theories, the
responsibility of the individual reader for wresting meaning from the text and
locating it with respect to other points of view stands out most clearly. If Iser
has been criticized by some of his contemporaries for not giving the individual
a large enough role in the reading process,[4] Wordsworth was criticized in his
day for giving the individual too great a role. The vehement and systematic
criticism that marks many contemporary reviews of Wordsworth's work
confirms the hypothesis that he held a controversial position on the issue of

individuality which brought him into conflict with consensus-seeking readers. Like Berkeley's and Wesley's systems, which fully reward only those who can rise to independent judgment, Wordsworth's poetry could completely satisfy only those readers who could meet it with their own thought. Strategically lacking absolutes for readers to seize, Wordsworth's poetry is literally egoistic insofar as it depends upon an individual perspective. That perspective, however, is not Wordsworth's. It is each reader's. Readers unable or unwilling to rely on their individual perspectives thrust their roles back onto Wordsworth, faulting him for failing to communicate a universal view. Most significantly, the notion of Wordsworth's "egotism" may have its provenance in reviewers' turning the philosophically egoistic dimension of Wordsworth's work into a fatuously egotistical one. The development of Wordsworth's reputation for "egotism" resembles nothing so much as the development of Berkeley's reputation for "egoism": both judgments emerge from the pages of periodicals engaged in prior controversies, and both remain independently of the struggles that made them functional.[5]

Reviewers allude dozens of times to Wordsworth's "egotism," "vanity," "arrogance," "singularity," "peculiarity," "eccentricity," and "affectation" in one hundred twenty-five articles reprinted by Reiman.[6] Cumulatively, the reviews convey an impression of Wordsworth's poetry as an exercise in self-indulgence too dominant and pervasive to be dismissed with reference to personality alone. Reviewers consistently derive their sense of Wordsworth's self-absorption from those features of his poetry that emphasize the individuality of perception. A glance at the pattern of criticism shows its implicit reliance on shared ideas.

Reviewers often decry Wordsworth's subjects as "mean," "unworthy," or not "properly poetical."[7] As the critic of *Peter Bell* and *The Waggoner* for the *Literary and Statistical Magazine* pronounces:

> There are limits below which poetry can never descend with success. . . . [Wordsworth] will never bring men to think that poetry may profitably scatter its beauties on washing-tubs, baby-clothes, bull-dogs, and donkies.

Ranking poems according to the propriety or impropriety of their subjects attempts to make poetry embody and encourage consensus. It directs readers to fit individual points of view into pre-determined and discrete categories that promise to solve the problem of isolation if only they can subsume all perspectives. Conventional subjects, then, constitute what Klancher might call a "master sign," recognition of which signals the readership's community (71-72). Given the factitiousness of that community, enumeration of "properly poetical" subjects cannot easily be achieved, and reviewers seldom attempt it. Instead, they dismiss Wordsworth's unconventional practices on the ground of their unconventionality, drawing their readership together in recognition of Wordsworth's deviance. Francis Jeffrey makes the most absolute rejection of Wordsworth in his famous analogy:

> Poetry has this much, at least, in common with religion, that its standards were fixed long ago, by certain inspired writers, whose authority it is no longer lawful to question.
>
> (*Edinburgh Review, Thalaba*)

Other reviewers echo him, calling Wordsworth a "heretic" (*Monthly Review, Duddon; British Critic, Excursion*), a "schismatic" (*Eclectic Review, White Doe*), and a "danger . . . to public taste" (*Annual Review*, 1807 poems) insofar as he is an "apostle" (*Literary Gazette, Collected Edition* of 1820) who might induce others to join the sect he wants to found on the "ruin of all existing authority" (*Edinburgh Review, Thalaba*).

The persistence of such criticism into Wordsworth's "later" period when his poetry became more apparently conventional reinforces a sense of consistency in Wordsworth's undertaking that emerges from his own theoretical declarations. The *Preface* to *Lyrical Ballads* seems to be only the first direct statement about a "campaign" in which Wordsworth consistently engaged. Though Wordsworth claimed that he added the *Preface* in 1800 only at Coleridge's urging and that he wished he had not done so, his statements do not necessarily mean that he repudiated the ideas the *Preface* expresses.[8] They are more likely to indicate that he regretted the irreparable compromise of his poetical experiment by theory. All of Wordsworth's efforts aim at marshalling the advantages of individual perception. Literature, and especially literature as Wordsworth was writing it, has characteristics to facilitate this: it can condense and qualify a number of views; it can refer to familiar things in unfamiliar ways; it can make readers observe themselves in the process of thinking. Other kinds of writing, such as criticism, philosophy, or history, have fewer of these devices available to them. In general, these kinds of works must present a complete position to readers who in turn must accept or reject it. This is not to say that theoretical writing is simplistic. It points out, rather, that the dominant traits and goals of theoretical writing are different from those of literary writing.[9] Adding a theoretical preface to a poetical collection without stating a position that readers should adopt—or that readers will think they are meant to adopt—is an almost impossible task.

Writing the *Preface*, then, involved Wordsworth in something like an act of tightrope walking. He had always to balance between directing readers to the features of the poems that would educe response and telling them to adopt a restricted interpretation of anything. The demands of one kind of writing threaten always to vitiate the other, and Wordsworth voices in the *Preface* itself his concern for the preservation of his literary enterprise: he fears that the *Preface* will seem to be motivated "by the selfish and foolish hope of reasoning [the reader] into an approbation of these particular poems" (*Prose* 1: 120).

Having once engaged in theoretical writing, Wordsworth was almost bound to continue that enterprise. Further evidencing a lifelong campaign, Wordsworth's later prose is largely consistent with his earlier. For example, his early concentration on reader activity prepares his illustration in the 1815 *Essay* of false reader engagement. Wordsworth dismisses reader espousal of a specific view as somehow beside the point of poetry. Irrespective of whether readers agree or disagree with, share or cannot share, an expressed view, they have attended to something other than poetry—perhaps valuable but nevertheless distinct—if they focus on the view alone. Wordsworth gives the following example:

> Men who read from religious or moral inclinations, even when the subject is of that kind which they approve, are beset with misconceptions peculiar to themselves. Attaching so much importance to the truths which interest them, they are prone to over-rate the Authors by whom those truths are expressed and enforced. (*Prose* 3: 64-65)

Wordsworth does not discourage his readers from an interest in or commitment to religious doctrines or moral codes; rather, he wants his readers to acknowledge that doctrines and morals are not identical with poetry or representative of the poetic enterprise. Readers of poetry must be concerned with the fact that a perspective on or an insight into an object or concept has been achieved and captured. Apprehension of the mental activity of the poet and engagement in their own mental activity as a result matters more than agreement on the nature of the object or concept.

The consistency of Wordsworth's theory and the variety in his poetry suggest his sensitivity to readers. Seeing how threatening readers found the exaggerated and aggressive treatment of individual perception that distinguishes his early poetry, Wordsworth may have deliberately modified his strategy to greet readers with gentle encouragement instead of forceful surprise.[10] Concern for readers pervades Wordsworth's poetics, leading him to redefine "genius" as a leader of people. In the *Essay, Supplementary to the Preface* of 1815, Wordsworth replaces Young's figure of the genius as Diogenes with that of the genius as Hannibal:

> The predecessors of an original Genius of a high order will have
> smoothed the way for all that he has in common with them,—and
> much he will have in common; but, for what is peculiarly his own,
> he will be called upon to clear and often to shape his own road:
> he will be in the condition of Hannibal among the Alps. (*Prose*
> 3:80)

While Diogenes stands alone, Hannibal appears among a crowd. In the company of others, he opens a path for still others to follow should they exert themselves to do so. Just as importantly, his functional relationship to others in no way compromises him or them.

Wordsworth's figure revives an aspect of genius previously suppressed or neglected.   As Cox points out, most eighteenth-century theories were concerned with relations among extraordinary individuals, although Young does celebrate all "mental Individuality" (37-38).   The more numerous ordinary individuals who read the works of the extraordinary were of interest only insofar as their sensibility was said to have been enlarged by their contact with works of genius, as it could not have been otherwise. The genius, then, imparted his experience to his readers, who received it passively and lived it vicariously. Wordsworth's genius, in contrast, does not transfer experience to readers.   Noting the incalculable number and kind of things, situations, emotions, and words in the "intellectual universe," Wordsworth explains that "the genius of the poet melts these down for his purpose; but they retain their shape and quality to him who is not capable of exerting, within his own mind a corresponding energy" (*Prose* 3: 82).   The poet may have achieved a new perspective and represented it in his work, but readers will not find the insight meaningful unless they make an effort at mental activity too. The readers' expanded sensibility—and Wordsworth agrees with his predecessors that the poetry of genius evidences itself with a "widening of the sphere of human sensibility" (3: 82)—is not imparted to readers by the poem but effected by readers in interaction with it. It is the "co-operating *power* in the mind of the Reader" (3: 81) that makes reading poetry a meaningful experience.

One need not imagine Wordsworth deliberately revising Young's *Conjectures* to construe the replacement of Diogenes with Hannibal as indicative of contrasting developments in the theory of genius.[11]   Wordsworth's "revisions" tend to be of dominant ideas. He clears away what he suggests to be erroneous interpretations of sound premises, interpretations that usually involve consensus-seeking circumventions of individual conditions. Like Young, Wordsworth sees the genius as one who engages directly with his environment and who achieves a unique insight qualified by context and tradition:

> Genius is the introduction of a new element into the intellectual universe: or, if that be not allowed, it is the application of powers to objects on which they had not before been exercised, or the employment of them in such a manner as to produce effects hitherto unknown. (*Prose* 3:82)

What Wordsworth denies is the dichotomy predicated on the theory, which separates the genius from others or reduces him to "rightly imitating" the activity of other geniuses whose perspective he thus presumably replicates.

If Wordsworth's poet as Hannibal differs from Young's as Diogenes, it seems to epitomize Johnson's description of literary courage:

> It is the proper ambition of the heroes of literature to enlarge the boundaries of knowledge by discovering and conquering new regions of the intellectual world.[12]

Ironically, Wordsworth's antagonism toward Johnson is nowhere more directly expressed than in the 1815 *Essay*. Its interplay of accepting and rejecting Johnson may clarify Wordsworth's method and position. Owen and Smyser's notes to the *Essay* document enough references to *Ramblers* 106 and 137 and to the *Lives of the Poets* to suggest Wordsworth's taking a Johnsonian subtext. Such a procedure would not be unthinkable of Wordsworth. In a separate article, Owen posits that Wordsworth constructed the *Essay* on Francis Jeffrey's rhetoric, "drawing on it (while criticizing it incidentally)" ("Wordsworth and Jeffrey" 163). Wordsworth may be making a more central use of Johnson to define the position from which he and eighteenth-century theorists start and from which they diverge. Johnson's and Wordsworth's geniuses are both leaders, but they open up different courses to their followers. Johnson's poet must bring his readers to a particular perception. His goal, as Bate stresses, is "the inculcation of the truth" (61), an aim inimical to Wordsworth's campaign of reader engagement. Wordsworth's poet shows his readers the act of perceiving. His campaign centers on stimulating their intellects to activity beyond accepting or rejecting "truths" that may or may not be concomitant to the enterprise.

Wordsworth may conjure Johnson's figure to exorcise "the false notions about the dignity of writing" (Robinson, *Books* 1: 103) he thought Johnson had and with which he invests his literary leader. Wordsworth returns to the idea of the poet as leader but gives him a different goal. Such an approach enables Wordsworth to do more than put his theory before the reader. It gives the reader access to the critical context of Wordsworth's views, a context that may be helpful for the reader to ponder. Moreover, it lets Wordsworth's text exemplify the idea, for it affords Johnson the position of a previous, original writer with whom Wordsworth has something in common but from whom he now departs to make his own contribution.

The oblique acknowledgement of Johnson's importance balances the *Essay*'s direct criticisms of him, most of which, significantly, involve Johnson's commitment to "truth." For example, Wordsworth resists what he perceives to be Johnson's prescriptiveness: "Doctor Johnson, 'mid the little senate to which he gave laws, was not sparing in his exertion to make [Percy's *Reliques*] an object of contempt" (*Prose* 3: 75). Wordsworth perhaps exaggerates Johnson's attitude toward Percy, playing it off against his own praise.

Wordsworth says that Percy "redeemed" English poetry, influencing many writers including Wordsworth himself. Thus Wordsworth judges Percy's merit by his ability to stimulate correspondent activity, activity that would be stifled by passive acceptance of absolute value as decided by a critical establishment. Wordsworth directs his hostility toward Johnson as an important and respected critic whose views threaten reader engagement.

As Wordsworth evaluated Percy on the basis of influence, so he wanted his readers to evaluate his own works. He wrote to Alford on February 21, 1840 that he best liked reactions to his poems that reported their effects (*LY* 2: 1007). Such reactions involve the reader's grappling with the text and differ markedly from static approval or disapproval. That Wordsworth was most concerned about sparking this activity is evidenced by the fact that he resisted unsubstantiated accolades as much as unjust scorn. He took little interest in an American review of his works because, he explained to Reed in a letter dated September 18, 1844, "I am indifferent to praise merely as such" (Christopher Wordsworth 2: 419). This letter echoes one Wordsworth wrote on July 29, 1803 in which he expressed his displeasure at the "unreasonable value" De Quincey set on his poems (*EY* 400).

Wordsworth's desire for a thoughtful response from readers can shed light on the notorious distinction between the Public and the People he makes in the 1815 *Essay*. Cruttwell asserts the widely held view that the Public represents real readers who scorned Wordsworth's poetry, while the People comprises a "dream-public . . . whose taste was, miraculously, both unlettered and correct" (75). The notion that Wordsworth made this distinction to fulfill a fantasy of truly appreciative readers is hard to reconcile with his avowed distaste for passivity, acceptance, and absolutes. It is easier to imagine

Wordsworth's distinction as separating passive from active readers. The Public is an undifferentiated group waiting to receive a poet's insight or a reviewer's direction. They require the communication of a specific perception in limited ways that they can recognize. Wordsworth's characterization of the Public in the letter in which he worked out the distinction reinforces the view because it describes the Public in terms of conformity and custom. His catalogue of the concerns of the public includes:

> routs, dinners, morning calls, hurry from door to door, from street to street; . . . the Westminster Election or the Borough of Honiton; . . . endless talking about things nobody cares anything for except as far as their own vanity is concerned, and this with persons they care nothing for but as their vanity or *selfishness* is concerned. (*MY* 1: 145-46)

The Public devotes its collective mental powers to the maintenance of an order and does not exercise them beyond its bounds. They give up their individual judgment to a system in all matters, including the matter of poetry. The People, in contrast, are those who have kept their independent psyches. They respond individually to all things, including poetry, and their engagement has fostered the art. Hence, Wordsworth pays tribute to them with an active metaphor in the *Essay*:

> To the People, philosophically characterized, and to the embodied spirit of their knowledge, so far as it exists and *moves*, at the present, faithfully *supported by its two wings*, the past and the future, [the Poet's] devout respect, his reverence, is due. (*Prose* 3: 84 emphasis added)

Wordsworth's statement that his poetry cannot be "popular" with the Public follows logically from his concentration on the process of perception. Poetry requiring a response cannot please an audience waiting to receive an insight.

Perhaps Wordsworth detected a hint of concession to the Public in Johnson's acceptance of subjects for the *Lives of the Poets*, and anger at such accommodation informs his allegations that these volumes were largely a profit-making project (*Prose* 3: 79). Wordsworth seems to fault Johnson for failing to exercise more judgment, for missing the opportunity to write about the most influential poets in literary history and writing instead about many who figure passingly in the public taste. But the undertaking itself may have represented a marshalling of strengths and weaknesses in absolute terms that repelled Wordsworth. That is not to say that Wordsworth did not accept the idea of any absolutes, but except in cases of "fundamental principles of right and wrong" (2: 19) he found the idea of received standards detrimental to the development of judgment and taste.

Wordsworth's *Reply to Mathetes*, which declines Wilson's request that he assume the role of teacher of the upcoming generation and explains how they should instead learn, provides a parallel to Wordsworth's view of how readers should read:

> Everything great and good is obtained . . . [by] steady dependence
> upon voluntary and self-originating effort, and upon the practice
> of self-examination sincerely aimed at and rigourously enforced.
> (*Prose* 2: 13)

The student must be free to attain knowledge at "perfect liberty" (2: 24), for he can have a surer conviction later for having experienced and rejected error (2: 20-22). A teacher—especially one who is loved and respected—can impede this process, for attachment to the teacher's views can lead the student's mind to a "mistrust of its own evidence" (2: 23). If that happens, the student learns only to mouth

> words muttered by rote with the impertinence of a Parrot or a
> Mockingbird, yet which may not be listened to with the same
> indifference, as they cannot be heard without some feeling of
> moral disapprobation. (2: 23)

Wordsworth's writing itself invites the analogy between the teacher and the student, the poet and the reader. "Every great poet is a Teacher," he wrote to Beaumont in the winter of 1808. "I wish to be considered as a Teacher or as Nothing." Wordsworth's characterization of himself cannot consistently mean, as Colville would have it, that Wordsworth has a "philosophy, . . . a religion, . . . a way of codifying the meaning of human experience" (35) to impart. But it can mean that he is willing to initiate intellectual exploration.[13]

Wordsworth's desire to lead readers in a revaluation of individual perception appears not only in his published declarations but surfaces in a private conversation preserved in manuscript by Henry Nelson Coleridge.[14] In the recorded discussion, Wordsworth speaks about writing poetry as incompatible with ascertaining and disseminating an absolute world view:

> There were to be two other parts in the "Recluse," not so long as
> the "Excursion"; one of them severer and entering into the
> metaphysics of the mind, the other easier and more diffuse on the
> influences of nature. But it is impossible to reconcile the exact
> truth with poetry. . . . If we abandon the old mythical conception
> of Gods and Nymphs &c. what can we substitute? We may call
> the phaenomena of the visible world Powers if we please, but in

fact they are not so. . . . To call them Laws is not better, and yet
how can we deal with the face of Nature and Nature's goings on
. . . under this notion of their being only Rules or Laws? W. said
he could not do it, and he regretted he had ever attempted such
a subject. So long as he was called upon to operate with the
imagination on the visible world, and to evoke the spirit that seems
to lie hidden in its varied forms in sympathy with man, he felt he
was able to do it; but to deal with . . . nature as it really in a
religious view is, was what he could not manage.[15]

Wordsworth's emphasis on the multiple relations effectively informing reality
supports his published commitment to dynamic and independent thought. The
conversation clearly indicates that Wordsworth did not wish to subsume his
readers' judgments under a unified or unifying perspective.

Even in conversation, Wordsworth concentrated on the interaction that
should obtain between a reader and a text. Echoing the objections to
sensational literature he voiced in the *Preface* to *Lyrical Ballads*, Wordsworth
complained to Henry Nelson Coleridge about the fact that "newspapers and
magazines are read to a most pernicious extent; they cannot improve the mind
in any way; they injure it, weaken it and debase it grievously." Wordsworth's
abhorrence of passive reading seems to stem from an exalted idea of individual
potential and a desire to see such potential realized as fully as possible.
According to Henry Nelson Coleridge, Wordsworth held that

nothing great or ennobling could be learnt from without or a
posteriori; the seeds of grandeur of thought and feeling are in the
man himself, tho' called forth and developed by occasions and
circes [sic].

Wordsworth expected literature to provide such occasions, a function it cannot fulfill if it merely offers a perspective for readers to adopt. In fact, Wordsworth concluded his conversation with a statement that emphasizes the primacy of independent intellectual growth over the discernment of a given "truth": "The ancient philosophers, tho' so often wrong in particulars, were far superior to many moderns in proposing the improvement of the mind as the grand object of their labors."

In other remarks to Henry Nelson Coleridge, Wordsworth suggests his technique to involve experiment with multiple perspectives and reveals his dismay at having belief in any one of these views imputed to himself:

> He [Wordsworth] thought himself entitled to avail himself as a
> verseman of many notions wch [sic] he was not prepared to defend
> literally as a proseman, and he complained of the way in wch he
> had been made answerable for mere plays of the imagination.

Wordsworth's uneasiness might consistently include displeasure at the consensus behind such an assessment as well as unhappiness at the resultant misrepresentation of his own intentions. Only the reign of consensus can account for such an assessment: it prevents readers from conceiving of a perspective that is not contending with all others to represent the "right" vein.

If Wordsworth felt frustrated by hostile readers, he might have felt equally frustrated by admiring ones. Many who embraced his work closed their minds to the possible advantages of independent perception as soundly as did those who rejected Wordsworth's poetry. Praise often proceeded by cooptation, a process of assimilating a threatening idea into a prevailing structure and making it seem to support the very system it challenges. Iser's terms would explain such a response as an extraction of the repertoire from the strategy of the text: readers seize the familiar elements from the text and disregard the unfamiliar combinations that would induce a revaluation of the familiar. Reviewers could coopt Wordsworth into the service of consensus as surely as their colleagues could enlist class distinctions in support of some marvelous scheme of human community (Klancher 60-61, 88-92). The *Monthly Censor*'s combined review of *Ecclesiastical Sketches* and *Memorials of a Tour on the Continent* exemplifies the process.

After a long retrospective that dwells on the "egotism" of Wordsworth's earlier works, the reviewer announces that these volumes depart significantly, though not entirely, from Wordsworth's customary style:

> Mr. Wordsworth with a very perverse obstinacy indeed, adhered
> for a short time to his original theories. . . . He has subsequently
> corrected some of the obliquities of his taste, and abated some of
> the offensive peculiarities of his compositions.

Comparing the poems dealing with an Italian itinerant and a Swiss goatherd from the *Memorials* to the collective *Lyrical Ballads*, the reviewer writes:

> The subject is quite as ignoble as any in the *Lyrical Ballads*, . . .
> but [Wordsworth's] taste is unfettered by system, and he has
> created a beautiful and touching picture out of materials which in
> the hands of almost any other poet would have been very
> unmanageable.

The reviewer seems to credit Wordsworth with fitting anomalous figures into familiar categories that align them with a preconceived and shared point of view. Seizing one perspective from these poems leaves the reviewer with something recognizable and acceptable to him. If he analyzed them more thoroughly, he might find qualifications that would interfere with what he takes to be their view, but this he does not do. He emphasizes the perspective that can represent for him a comforting and communal view, and he tries to rid it of as much individuality as possible. Though he praises Wordsworth for a unique talent in handling the subject, he implies that the talent is for bringing troublesomely individuated figures into the range of known types. Moreover, he sees Wordsworth as having been passively open to a given condition rather than as having actively created meaning from it: "it is delightful to observe how with the universality of genius his spirit has expanded itself over all that he saw and drank in large draughts of inspiration." Looking in Wordsworth for a view to adopt, the reviewer finds in poems of subtle strategy a familiar repertoire that he can fit back into his milieu, so he enlists the poems in the service of the shared perspective he seeks and praises Wordsworth for having revealed it to him.

Since cooptation can occur most readily when poems have only subtle and slight strategies controlling their repertoires, readers began to employ it primarily with respect to Wordsworth's later, more apparently conventional works. Ironically, Wordsworth's sensitivity to his readers may have undermined his campaign. As De Quincey reports, Wordsworth's reputation was "triumphant" by 1830 (117),[16] but this circumstance does not necessarily indicate that people had freed themselves from their attachment to consensus as a result of Wordsworth's work. It seems instead to suggest that they reclaimed Wordsworth for the dominant tradition.[17] Wordsworth's reputation was secure when a sufficient quantity of his canon was available for cooptation.

Considered together with Wordsworth's declared consistency and poetic variety, contemporary reader resistance conveys a sense of the gravity of the empirical dilemma in Wordsworth's time, a gravity easily underestimated by twentieth-century minds. Finally reconciled to the fact of individuation, readers can now appreciate the magnitude of the campaign Wordsworth undertook. The recent privileging of Wordsworth's early, more forcefully individualistic work suggests that readers have arrived at what Jauss terms the "horizon of expectations" appropriate to the work and now have "access to . . . the form" (35).[18] The possibility of accepting Wordsworth's challenge to individuality in no way involves substituting new, "right" interpretations for old, "wrong" ones. On the contrary, it involves valuing the function of previous interpretations and striving for self-consciousness about that of current ones.[19] Recognizing the current preoccupation with Wordsworth's individuality as part of the poet's legacy greatly enhances that self-consciousness.

Without the context of the empirical dilemma, emphasis on individual perception and reader activity in Wordsworth seems merely a modernization of his work. Though hardly an "invalid" enterprise, modernization alone is especially limiting in Wordsworth's case, for it ignores the progressive and purposeful way in which he approached his writing. Wordsworth's pioneering efforts to lead readers to the independence they now embrace deserve to be acknowledged. The readings of Wordsworth's poems in the following chapters call attention to the strategies by which they liberate texts and readers from the confines of a shared view. Having examined some of Wordsworth's declarations to establish a notion of his poetic campaign, one must turn to his poetry to see his enactment of it.

Chapter 3

The Dilemma and Wordsworth's Poetry:
An Evening Walk

Wordsworth's first publications, *An Evening Walk* and *Descriptive Sketches*, are usually considered together, or rather, they are usually dismissed together, as juvenilia.[1] But even these works evidence Wordsworth's preoccupation with perception and with his reader. Although they antedate his declarations, they manifest the spirit of his subsequent work. They thus provide a context of long-term meditation for Wordsworth's avowed concern with how literature can assist readers' understanding of themselves as percipient beings. That Wordsworth challenged his readers to such self-consciousness even in his early work should be clearer upon examination of what Iser would call the "response-inviting structures" with which the poems perform the task. Although a case could be made for either poem, I confine myself to one from the earliest "period" for purposes of economy.[2]

An Evening Walk draws its "repertoire" from the geography of the Lake District and from the genre of loco-descriptive poetry. The opening fifty-two lines serve as something of an introductory section that orients the reader toward a reorganization of these elements. The first-person speaker begins by enumerating features of the country by reference to their place names and to poetically conventional attributes. Only their names distinguish Derwent, Lodore, Rydale's mere, and Winander from innumerable other scenes that purportedly depict a river's course through "forest glooms" to "tremulous" cliffs or capture lakes frowned upon by yews or shyly peeping around foliage. The highly specific place names, which single out particular rivers, cliffs, and lakes against all other phenomena of similar kind, appear among a collection of poetic generalizations, which blur the features of natural phenomena and subordinate them to a role as evocators of preconceived emotion.

Arguing for Wordsworth's deliberate exploitation of the "graveyard" orientation may seem at first an unjustified interpretive leap, but a number of factors support its likelihood. Hartman finds Wordsworth working "to combat the melancholy use of nature" as early as in "Lines left upon a Seat in a Yew-Tree" (*Unremarkable* 39).   Perhaps nothing is so quintessentially Wordsworthian as antagonism toward preconceived responses, and Wordsworth could not have failed to recognize the limitations of a half-century old convention.   In *An Evening Walk*, he calls attention to the approach as a convention. He does not "combat" it with a substitute view; rather, he allows it to appear in conjunction with another view that qualifies its scope.

Taking the place names as indicative of that qualifying view may also seem an act of over-interpretation, but Wordsworth's interest in place names makes it unlikely that he would use them lightly. By 1800, he had written at least four poems in which the private and public significance of names figures and which eventually became part of his "Poems on the Naming of Places." Clearly names and naming were not trivial to him, a circumstance that would in itself make his use of six place names in the first sixteen lines of *An Evening Walk* remarkable. That use is made even more remarkable by the fact that the practice is unusual in this genre.

A glance at some eighteenth-century poems that purport to describe a scene reveals an avoidance of place names. Dyer's "Grongar Hill" uses only two—"Grongar Hill" and "Towy," the latter only twice and both times as "Towy's flood," subordinating the name to the generic phenomenon (11. 23 and 69); Gray's "On a Distant Prospect of Eton College" mentions "Eton" only in the title and includes only "Windsor" and the Thames in the body. Like Dyer's "Towy," Gray's "Windsor" appears in the genitive ("Windsor's heights," 1. 6). His "Thames" (1. 9) becomes "Father Thames" at line 21, moving away from a place name toward a personified abstraction. Goldsmith might have turned to place naming as a device to recreate "The Deserted Village," but he does not. He names the Village—Auburn—and refers to its sites in general terms:

> The shelter'd cot, the cultivated farm,
>
> The never failing brook, the busy mill,
>
> The decent church that topp'd the neighbouring hill,
>
> The hawthorne bush, with seats beneath the shade
>
> For talking age and whispering lovers made.
>
> (11. 10-14)

Goldsmith generalizes from his observations and does not use particulars that would interfere with Auburn's emblematic function. Cowper begins Book IV of *The Task* with "Hark! 'tis the twanging horn! O'er yonder bridge." Later editorial conventions call attention to the lack of specificity about the bridge. Editing selections from Cowper in 1968, Brian Spiller noted that Cowper refers to "The 'Long Bridge' over the Ouse at Olney, rebuilt 1832" (465). Spiller's editorial approach contrasts with Robert Southey's, who, in preparing the 1836 edition of Cowper's works copiously annotated literary allusions and analogues but ignored possible references to actual localities. Since Southey's edition appeared only four years after the rebuilding of the bridge, his readers might have found it a curiosity, but the specificity is apparently regarded as unimportant.

Although these four almost random observations hardly constitute an authoritative search, they do support the premise that Wordsworth's multiplication of place names is unusual, and perhaps they allow for a generalization: place names divert attention from a preconceived idea of a scene. When the poet's aim is to use the hill, the college, the village, or the bridge to direct a certain kind of meditation, he avoids labelling it in a way that ties it to the ordinary or that might hold other associations for some readers. The locality serves as a springboard for the preconceived view. As Woodring explains in addressing the evolution of aesthetic categories, almost any scene could be "picturesque" if an "asymmetrical arrangement of natural forms" could be found in it ("New Sublimity" 88).[3] To be properly affective, the scene would need to be stripped of attributes other than those desired. If one poet would avoid place names in an effort to conjure a given attitude, another poet might make a point of naming places to throw the other approach into relief.[4]

Wordsworth's place names in *An Evening Walk* can have just such a highlighting function. The first fourteen lines of the poem put before the reader two opposite approaches to nature—one represented by common nomenclature and confinement to the particular object as given; the other, by stylized but still familiar language and the imposition of qualities upon a given thing. The reader's knowledge that the two approaches are usually mutually exclusive in their "real" contexts and characteristic of two social strata accents the antagonism for him. To borrow Iser's terms, lines 1-14 juxtapose the two parts of the repertoire as a strategy and involve the reader in the first theme. The new context of the poem establishes a peaceful coexistence between two things that are usually opposite in their "real" contexts.

As the reader considers the first theme, he discovers two perspectives that will interact in the poem, and he forms certain expectations from them.[5] He expects, for example, that the poem will either separate the views it has brought together, confirming his experience of them, or explain the basis for their coexistence, expanding his knowledge of them. Lines 15 and 16—"Where twilight glens endear my Esthwaite's shore,/ And memory of departed pleasures, more"—fulfill the latter expectation. By establishing a parallel between the effect of imposing poetic conventions upon an object and the effect of imposing personal associations upon it, the lines suggest a rationale for joining two approaches to a scene. They unite disparate views as products of individual minds. Both views represent perceivers' attempts to give meaning to their surroundings. They differ according to the needs and characters of the perceivers, but they spring from the same impulse. Some orientations, such as recollection of personal experiences, are unique to one perceiver; others, such as poetic language and place naming, are common to many. All have the effect of making an otherwise remote and alien environment special to the perceiver. Thus, the poem pointedly brings together two generally opposed approaches and establishes their identity. In doing so, it raises a question about what one gains from either approach. As the reader recalls the first fourteen lines from his memory, he might realize that the seemingly specific place names give no access to the objects they designate but indicate, like their stylized counterparts, a collective attempt at a particular kind of access.

Holding this idea in abeyance, the poem impels the reader on to the next theme, in which the narrator addresses multiple views. In lines 17-26, he contrasts his childhood idea of the landscape with his adult perception. By calling attention to the disparity between the narrator's former and current views of the scene, these lines emphasize the uniqueness of every perceiver's view. Indeed, each is so unique as to be limited not only to an individual but to moments of that individual's life. The narrator does not re-experience his former happiness but conjures it from memory by contrast with his current melancholy. The lines show that the narrator cannot gain direct access even to his own former perceptions. He must rely instead on the mediation of memory, which yields an approximate and vicarious experience of the former perceptions. He derives the nature of his former emotion by working backward from his closest current experience: "Then did no ebbing of chearfulness demand/ Sad tides of joy from Melancholy's hand" (11. 21-22). The lines do more than narrate the procedure. They represent the nature of its result in an oxymoron, and they describe and enact the purpose of poetic diction, i.e., recourse to a predetermined trope to produce a predetermined result.

Because line 22 not only epitomizes the method of a particular style of writing but refers openly to its elements, it lets the reader generalize from the narrator's predicament. If the narrator cannot reproduce his former perception, it follows that perceptions are inaccessible to all but the perceiver at the moment of perception; if the narrator turns to conventions under these circumstances, it follows that conventions ought to compensate for the condition; and if the narrator receives an approximation of the perception as a result, it follows that conventions do not substitute for experience but give the illusion of doing so.

The theme qualifies the reader's understanding of place naming and poetic diction from the earlier section. Instead of being the devices to gain access to the environment they had seemed, they now appear as barriers to it. This section might leave readers with the image of all individuals trapped in their own minds were it not for a number of safeguards. For one thing, the narrator addresses the scene for the first time (1. 18). Thus, the uniqueness that separates perceptions also makes them possible. If perceptions were not separate and inaccessible, they would collapse into each other in the perceiver's mind. They would rob him of the experience by leaving him truly trapped in his mind, or they would render him impercipient of any object because of his coincidence with it. When individuation is construed as desirable, conventions rise in stature too. They mediate between the uniqueness of every perception and the situation in which perceivers find themselves. They are not poor substitutes for experience but good devices to capture an element from experience, to hold and communicate it.

These qualifications should make the reader dissatisfied as he enters the third theme with the narrator's obviously futile apostrophe: "Return Delights! with whom my road begun" (1. 27). The shift in addressee, however, can happen only in consequence of the second section. By invoking neither the landscape nor the former self but the condition that had obtained between them, the narrator carries forward the idea of interaction he has introduced. Moreover, he indicates his untroubled acceptance of the limits of perception he has realized, for he sets up reflections on the passing of the former experiences (11. 27-48) and dismisses them as inappropriate: "But why, ungrateful, dwell on idle pain?" (1. 49). He immediately proposes an alternative disposition that will occupy the rest of the poem: "Say, will my friend, with soft affection's ear,/ The history of a poet's ev'ning hear?" (11. 51-52).

A number of things are remarkable about this transition. It suggests turning to new experience as a preferable course to trying to replicate other experiences, whether of one's past summoned from memory or of others' conveyed through conventions. Furthermore, it reminds the reader that the full title of the poem—*An Evening Walk. An Epistle In Verse. Addressed to a Young Lady, from the Lakes of the North of England.*—specified an addressee who has not been—and who still is not—addressed. The somewhat awkward avoidance of the second person here follows from the premise that experience cannot be directly communicated. Thus the narrator keeps the distinction between reporting an experience to another and having an experience. He makes it all the more pointed for having previously addressed the scene that contributed to the perception and the condition resulting from the interaction. In addition, the impersonal quality of the third person imposes a negative limit on the friend's role. It diminishes her status so she cannot seem a recipient of a private communication that, presumably, would not be directed to anyone else.[6]

The narrator's additional shift from first to third person with respect to himself likewise follows from the premise that reported or recollected experience is removed from experience itself. The third person specified—a poet—extends the account from the merely personal and invests the narrator's perspective with authority. No individual's perception is intrinsically better than any other's, but certain individuals have heightened faculties because they have carefully cultivated and reflected upon their experiences. The narrator has done so in the preceding sections and, in fact, demonstrates Wordsworth's later description of a poet as "a man who being possessed of more than usual organic sensibility had also thought long and deeply" (*Prose* 1: 126). Such individuals can assist others in understanding their own perceptions, as implied by the presence of the addressee from the beginning and by the narrator's stated intention: "To shew her yet some joys to me remain" (1. 50). In a sense, she has assisted him as he will assist her because the need to explain to her occasioned the articulation that clarified his thoughts. The poet's perspective derives its authority from the function of poetic diction in the earlier parts of the poem. Poets have given readers one means of grasping their experiences. Hence the aim and communicatory office of previous poets helps to define the nature of the narrator's new endeavor and distinguish it from personal indulgence.

In sum, lines 1-52 set before the reader the four perspectives that will interact in the poem together with an indication of how they interact. The narrator's perspective holds a privileged position in a hierarchy because it is one of demonstration. It will try to manage the difficulties arising from what it has experienced of human perception in its encounters with the other perspectives. The orientations of place naming and poetic diction function as character perspectives, each representing a partial truth about perception. The narrator's task is to attain a more complete understanding of perception, and he has found the perspectives of the characters insufficient to help him attain it. He resolves, therefore, to supplement them with the perspective of the plot, i.e., the proposed evening walk. The venture has been undertaken because of an axiomatic need to communicate with another, whom the outcome will in turn benefit. The addressee represents the other and defines the perspective of the reader as catalyst of invention and recipient of knowledge. It should be noted that the addressee is an in-text reader. The reader *in* the text, one of many perspectives, should be carefully distinguished from the reader *of* the text, who must put together all the perspectives including the in-text reader's.

The *donnée* of communication has launched the narrator's reflections on what can be perceived, understood, and communicated, and how it can be so. These reflections have been traced through a number of encounters between the perspectives of the narrator and "characters," as a result of which the narrator has accepted certain premises about the matter. His assent is signalled by his bringing an adjusted perspective to bear on each successive encounter, a perspective that does not reject what it has considered but which qualifies it and which builds up the qualifications cumulatively. For example, the narrator does not try to communicate experience directly, for to do so would force him to commit an act forbidden by conditions he has previously accepted.

All of these qualifications form the horizon that the external reader brings to bear on the main part of the poem. The reader does not expect the narrator to interact with the plot in a way contradictory to that in which he has interacted with the "characters," yet the reader expects to find a recognizably new element in the engagement. He may be disappointed. The plot seems to lead the narrator only into a recapitulation of the introductory section. The device of the walk, itself highly evocative of poetic conventions, seems to reproduce the juxtaposition between stylized and common language evidenced in the opening lines. The only apparent difference between the two openings seems to be the use in the main part of generic local terms—"intake" (1. 65), "gill" (1. 72)—instead of place names. Marginal notes define the words and reinforce the idea that common terms stand in the same position outside of experience as stylized ones. Place names appear in the main section as marginal explanations of scenes described, thus continuing to allow them the function of communication while emphasizing the limits of the group that can share any code.

For example, the poem gives this description:

> Beyond, along the visto of the brook,
>
> Where antique roots its bustling path o'erlook,
>
> The eye reposes on a secret bridge
>
> Half grey, half shagg'd with ivy to its ridge.
>
> (11. 81-84)

The accompanying note states: "The reader, who has made the tour of the country will recognize in this description the features which characterize the lower waterfall in the gardens of Rydale." Thus, the description is acknowledged accessible in a special way to those who have seen the object. Only occasional references to the narrator's passage mark his interaction with the walk: "eve's mild hour *invites* his steps abroad" (1. 88), and he in turn is "*wooing*" the rill (1. 86, emphasis added). The adjustment seems minor. The narrator is engaged with the scene, but he communicates little of it. In presenting his local terms, he contributes to the supply of formulae available to assist communication but does not alter the nature of it or provide a new insight into it.

This theme continues until line 177, at which point the narrator turns his attention from what he sees to what he does not:

> When up the hills, as now, retreats the light,
>
> Strange apparitions mock the village sight.
>
> A desperate form appears, that spurs his steed,
>
> Along the midway cliffs with violent speed;

> Unhurt pursues his lengthen'd flight, while all
> Attend, at every stretch, his headlong fall.
> Anon, in order mounts a gorgeous show
> Of horsemen shadows winding to and fro.
>
> (11. 177-84)

Because this report distinguishes between what the villagers see (the equine apparitions) and what the narrator sees (interplay of light and shadow), it is consistent with the now familiar idea of unique perceptions. But because it calls attention to the exaggerated result of the villagers' interpretation of the natural phenomenon, it adds a new dimension to the poem. It stresses the mind's role in what emerges from its engagement with its environment. The apparition belongs to the collective village sight because the natives are predisposed to find it in the scene. It is not part of the narrator's view because he is not so disposed. Perception depends not only on the mind's interaction with the scene but on the mind's interaction with all other scenes, which cumulatively qualify what the individual can see before him at any time.

As the narrator would be mistaken if he wished to surrender his own educated skepticism in an attempt to see with the eyes of the credulous, so he would be mistaken if he thought his view better than theirs. The tone of the passage neither exalts nor denigrates the alien perspective it reports; instead, it adopts a tone of amused enjoyment. The amusement stems from the narrator's treating a view he cannot share. It maintains his distance. The enjoyment follows from the equal valuation of this view with his. It celebrates the uniquely productive nature of the mind. The lines themselves carry the tone, but an added note emphasizes the desired attitude toward the matter: "See a description of an appearance of this kind in Clark's 'Survey of the

Lakes,' accompanied with vouchers of its veracity that may amuse the reader."
This suggests that distance is to be maintained with respect to the judgment of
other perceptions but does not discourage appreciation of their variety.

The external reader should enhance his appreciation of this passage by
extracting from his horizon the positive valuation of individual perception
suggested by lines 17-26 and allowing those lines to act upon his reading of
these. As Iser explains, recollection of certain lines involves recollection of
their context, and so provokes an interplay between reader and text.[7] Mindful
that individuality was earlier accepted as a good, the reader can look back on
the main section from line 178 and find more than a reshaping of the
vocabulary available for description. The poem has been purposefully and
gradually individuating the narrator's perspective all along. It starts with the
narrator's experience of a scene presumably available to everyone and communicable, albeit qualifiedly, through specialized terms. But it is the narrator's
store of a unique combination of experiences that enables him to interact with
the scene as he and no one else does. His absorption of Beattie makes him
find "embattl'd" (1. 55) a meaningful epithet for clouds; his immersion in the
district informs his assumption that "intake" and "gill" are usefully specific.
In short, he, as much as the ghost-seeing rustics, has been describing something
that is not there—even when he is being most seemingly precise about the
scene. His perception bears the same relation to the aspects of the walk as
does the villagers' to the rays of light. No view is ever presented as entirely
fanciful because it is always tied, however loosely, to some object, but no view
is presented as more faithful than another to that object. The diversity is cause
for amused enjoyment. It does not impede perception but facilitates it,
continually exercising and expanding the individual's experience. Nor does it

impede communication. A listener or reader stands in the same relation to a speaker or text as does the perceiver to an object. The relationship precludes a one-sided flight of fancy. However different the outcome of each perceiver's engagement might be, an anchor in an object underlies it. As Iser says of reading, what matters is "the sameness of the process and not the differences in realization" (143).

The poem further individuates the narrator's view as the plot takes him from the site of the apparitions to the shore along which the swans glide. The narrator describes the swans in a manner consistent with his previous mode of description (11. 200-18); however, he becomes increasingly engaged with them, and his engagement leads him further from them. Thus, this next theme masterfully demonstrates the progress of the narrator's perception. The narrator addresses the swans, wishing them perpetual enjoyment of what he has described their condition to be (11. 219-26). Continuing in the second person, he elaborates a scheme of their habitual activities (11. 227-38). In sum, the swans stimulated the narrator to exercise his past experience to interpret them, and in doing so, the narrator in turn incorporated them into his present experience. His experience of the swans then became an object to him, and he interacted with it to describe the habitual state of what he had observed once.[8] This kind of interaction requires a broader definition of "object" than that of a verifiably external thing. An object is that which the perceiver casts into the role in a relationship by which perception proceeds. The emphasis is on the function of an object not on its actual status.[9]

At line 239, another element of the narrator's experience—the "human wanderers"—enters by way of contrast his description of the swans: "Ye ne'er, like hapless human wanderers, throw/ Your young on winter's winding sheet of snow" (11. 239-40). The human wanderers are not really a new element here. Latent knowledge of and pity for their condition has likely informed the idyllic quality with which the narrator invests the swans' domestic condition (indeed may have suggested the concentration on domesticity in the first place) and spurred his urgency to see it protected. The contrast does not so much enter as break out at line 239. The human wanderers gradually usurp the swans in the narrator's preoccupation. Lines 239-40 address the swans and make them the primary focus of an incidental contrast with humans. Lines 241-42 address the female swan but transform her back into an object, an object in an incidental contrast imputed to a singled-out female wanderer, who is now the primary object of the narrator's description: "Fair swan! by all a mother's joys caress'd,/Haply some wretch has ey'd, and call'd thee bless'd." The narrator then abandons the swans for the female wanderer (11. 243-300). She, who is not present, becomes more visible to him than the swan, which is. The narrator's somewhat ironic "I see her now" (1. 257) calls attention to this aspect of his perception.

The narrator extends his description of the wanderer to the supposed demise of her children and breaks off. The transition to the next object is as abrupt as the transition between swan and wanderer was elaborate: "Thy breast their death-bed, coffin'd in thine arms./ Sweet are the sounds that mingle from afar" (11. 300-01). If the reader comes to this transition from the horizon of the earlier one, he will see the same process at work. The earlier case displays all the intricate steps of succession and masks what would be an otherwise equally jarring result. Having seen that process, the reader should be prepared to understand its role in yielding the result, which is presented alone in the second instance.

The sequence from the observation of the swans to the abandonment of the wanderer summarizes some of the previous themes while carrying them forward. It relies on the reader's recalling from preceding themes the premise that objects underlie perceptions—no matter how apparently diverse. Having become comfortable with this point, the reader recognizes it instantly in the narrator's engagement with the objects in view and extends it easily to his interaction with those in the narrator's psyche. He is not tempted to think that the latter are independent of objective referent because he has worked through that problem before. Thus, he can concentrate on the new element in this theme, the succession of perceptions. By finding the markers of the plot and of the narrator's experience in his conclusions, the reader can see that perceptions are unique but not random. Subtle connections provide a rationale for the narrator's associations. The poem manifests the links between swan and wanderer and trusts the reader to understand connections between wanderer and sounds. The section details the more difficult of the two since the former passage is intellectual, the latter sensory. It demonstrates a process for the reader, gives him a chance to test it, and prepares him for more daring action.

Before it puts its final challenge to the reader, the poem returns to the apparition theme. The reader, of course, should recall the appearance of the ghostly village horsemen as he reads the lines summarizing the deepening darkness:

> —'Tis restless magic all; at once the bright
> Breaks on the shade, the shade upon the light,
> Fair Spirits are abroad; in sportive chase
> Brushing with lucid wands the water's face,

> While music stealing round the glimmering deeps
> Charms the tall circle of th' enchanted steeps.
>
>   . . . .
>
> No night-duck clamours for his wilder'd mate,
>   Aw'd, while below the Genii hold their state.
>   (11. 345-50; 357-58)

Like the first passage on spirits, this one uses the same topic of apparitions
coming from the same source of mingled light and shadow. The similarities
between the two pointedly induce the reader to pull the first from his horizon
as he reads the second. In addition, they can help him to remember that the
first apparition theme prompted consideration of the infinite variety and equal
value of perceptions. It led to the conclusion that perception is always
underpinned by some object. This premise provided the rationale for the
succeeding demonstration of the narrator's associations, a demonstration that
emphasized the object as function over the object as thing.

The second apparition section leads to what serious commentators on the
poem see as its crisis. After the last tantalizing gleams of light, darkness
overtakes the scene:

> —The pomp is fled, and mute the wondrous strains,
>   No wrack of all the pageant scene remains,
>   So vanish those fair Shadows, human joys,
>   But Death alone their vain regret destroys.
>   (11. 359-62)

The narrator refuses to accept the lacuna the plot attempts to create and
searches for objects to fill it:

> Unheeded Night has overcome the vales,

On the dark earth the baffl'd vision fails,

If peep between the clouds a star on high,

There turns for glad repose the weary eye.

(11. 363-66)

Hartman (*Poetry* 97-98) and Ramsey (383-85) both read the passage as indicating the alienation of the narrator (whom they identify as Wordsworth) from his environment and his turning inward to his imagination to compensate. A search for compensatory objects, prepared by the Young allusion, does indeed seem to begin and to proceed with increasing success (11. 371-98); however, the narrator's previously complex relationship with what he perceives would make his sudden alienation unlikely and a desire to restore a simple harmony contradictory.

At this crux, the poem confronts the implications of the object as function that it has been practicing as a device. The narrator always proceeds as if his unillumined gazes have correspondent objects, however nebulously defined, until the moon rises to redeem the scene (11. 399-406). Indeed, the moon itself might be the narrator's projection, for it is compared to hope (1. 407), a mental resource that compensates for losses. Even if this is the case, the narrator dissociates it from himself, referring to it as the personified abstraction Hope and thus endowing it with external characteristics.[10]

The narrator stays scrupulously within the bounds that the poem has allotted to perception. Deprived by the darkness of the sight of objects with which to interact, he compensates through the productivity of his own mind. But he cannot interact with the compensatory objects unless he believes them to be external. Hence he casts them into objective roles and proceeds as he had before nightfall. This development does not merely sidestep what Nuttall calls "solipsistic fear" (11). Its insistence on the object as function redefines the issue. The poem builds up from certain premises—chiefly, the impossibility of knowing objects apart from one's perception of them and the inconceivability of being without objects when perception thrusts them before one. Instead of trying to deny or circumvent these two conditions that seem to govern human experience, the poem embraces their limits and tries to assess their use. Hence it leaves the issue of verifying an object's existence and actual characteristics as insoluble. It concentrates on how objects appear because that is what generates thought and communication. It posits the idea of a relationship between perceiver and object that depends upon the apparent integrity and separateness of each. The limits, then, are positive guides rather than troublesome barriers. Once one accepts them as such, one can explore how they allow for individuality and community of thought.

The poem pays exaggerated attention to the objects as seen, whether with the physical or in the mind's eye. It bestows such care not because the actuality of the object can somehow be affirmed by it but because the use of the object can be activated by it. The apparent characteristics of objects are presented as "actual," as indeed they are for purposes of the vital relationship. Wordsworth uses this technique, which others have described as his "literalness" or "matter-of-factness," to maintain one limit of perception while allowing perspectives to expand.[11] In *An Evening Walk*, it informs the variety of his descriptions.

With the reestablishment of the narrator in a productive relationship, *An Evening Walk* draws to a close. The narrator goes home contentedly. The ending may seem unsatisfying because the narrator does not sum up and pronounce anything conclusive about his experience. He continues to demonstrate the relational pattern of perception, so he has shown the addressee, whom he has ignored since line 51 and whom he never acknowledges again, that some joys remain to him. The anticlimactic ending stems directly from the limits of perception accepted. The narrator cannot, without denying the impossibility of direct communication, do more for the reader than display the limits and show that he gladly pursues a course consistent with them. If he makes a theoretical statement, he compromises his emphasis on individuality.

The poem sacrifices the narrator's privileged perspective to the limits of perception. Deprived of the narrator's authoritative conclusion, the reader must educe the poem's import for himself. Significantly, the addressee has disappeared. The role of the reader as recipient of a privileged perspective, which she defined, is superfluous if the perspective loses its authority. The poem transfers the authority to the external reader, whom it has prepared for the role through a series of increasing demands. It suggests a new way of approaching the question of perception and plays out its implications. But it does not present a theory to which the reader can give himself up or not. It invites the reader to participate in forming a theory from certain conditions. Inasmuch as the poem must become an object with which its readers interact, insofar as it is the springboard of their individual interpretations and the anchor of their common enterprise, it is itself an emblem of its subject.

Wordsworth's first readers seem to have sensed the challenge even of his early work. Criticism of *An Evening Walk* and *Descriptive Sketches* by Dorothy Wordsworth and by reviewers indicates that she and they apprehended the limits of perception to be at issue in Wordsworth's poetry, though she appears willing to revalue the concept while they appear to resist any such exploration.[12]   Dorothy Wordsworth's and the reviewers' responses reveal them to be reading within the context of the empirical dilemma and confirm the immediacy of the dilemma for Wordsworth and his contemporaries.

Dorothy Wordsworth may have been the first reader to identify perception as Wordsworth's subject. Writing about his early works to Jane Pollard on February 16, 1793, she concentrated on manipulation of the narrator's perspective: "the Scenes which he describes have been viewed with a Poet's eye and are pourtrayed with a Poet's pencil" (*EY* 89). The success of the poems for her depends not upon a scene but upon the delineation of it; therefore, she calls "Faults" those things that divert attention from the narrator's act of perceiving. The poems

> contain many Faults, the chief of which are Obscurity, and a too
> frequent use of some particular expressions and uncommon words
> for instance *moveless*, which [the Poet] applies in a sense if not
> new, at least different from its ordinary one, . . . [and which] is a
> very beautiful epithet but ought to have been cautiously used, he
> ought at any rate only to have hazarded it once, instead of which
> it occurs three or four times. (*EY* 89)

She does not criticize use of innovative language itself, which presumably could call attention to the uniqueness of the perspective; rather, she suggests that an overabundance of it could weaken its effectiveness as an indicator.

Although Dorothy Wordsworth's comments seem consistent with reviewers' criticisms of these poems, they actually stem from a different apprehension of the purpose of the pieces. Significantly, she construes the perspective impersonally—as "a Poet's," not as "William's" or her "brother's." She assumes the intellectual importance of the perspective and faults what takes attention away from it. The reviewers assume the primacy of what is viewed and fault the intrusion of a perspective that they construe as personal. For them, the success of the poems requires the subordination of the perspective. For example, the critic of *Descriptive Sketches* for the *Analytical Review* writes:

> The diversified pictures of nature which are sketched in this poem, could only have been produced by a lively imagination, furnished by actual and attentive observation with an abundant store of materials. . . . At the same time we must own, that this poem is on the whole less interesting than the subject led us to expect; owing in part, we believe, to the want of . . . [something] to vary the impression.

Hence, when the poem makes this reader aware of the activity of perceiving it is at its best according to Dorothy Wordsworth and at its worst according to the reviewer. As their different premises about what the subject in question is lead to their different conclusions about its successful portrayal, so they inform their different criticisms of Wordsworth's language. The reviewer denigrates "a certain laboured and artificial cast of expression, which often involves the poet's meaning in obscurity." According to the reviewer, Wordsworth errs in using unexpected language rather than, as for Dorothy Wordsworth, in deploying it.

The writer for the *Critical Review* likewise judges the poems by how well they subordinate perspective to some other subject:

> Local description is seldom without a degree of obscurity, which is here [in *An Evening Walk*] increased by a harshness both in the construction and the versification; but we are compensated by that

merit which a poetical taste most values, new and picturesque imagery.

The conjunction between "new" and "picturesque" as well as the predication of both upon "poetic taste" indicates that the poems succeed for the reviewer not to the extent that they present a noteworthy perspective but to the extent that they present an accessible variation of the preconceived notion of the "picturesque." He accepts unfamiliar language provided that it fits in easily with already familiar terms for the poetic convention he transforms into Wordsworth's subject. In addressing Wordsworth's language, he continues: "The beauty of *the moveless form of snow*, need not be pointed out to a lover of poetry." Hence, he praises Wordsworth's language for its communication of the ostensible subject and unwittingly confirms Dorothy Wordsworth's fear that the profusion of such language could divert the reader's attention from perspective as subject.

An additional comparison between Dorothy Wordsworth's comments and Thomas Holcroft's in his articles on *An Evening Walk* and *Descriptive Sketches* for the *Monthly Review* yields similar results. Like his colleagues, Holcroft assumes the primacy of what is viewed and indicates his position by pointing out lines in *Descriptive Sketches* that seem to depart from the portrayal of the actual scene in favor of portrayal of a perspective on it. For example, Holcroft writes:

> The purple morning falling in flakes of light is a bold figure: but
> we are told, it falls far and wide—where?—On the mountain's *side*.
> We are sorry to see the purple morning confined so like a maniac
> in a straight waistcoat.

Holcroft concludes that Wordsworth's preoccupation with perspective—and specifically with his own perspective—has led him to neglect and distort the real subject of his poem. Holcroft ends his review with a summarizing lamentation:

> How often shall we in vain advise those, who are so delighted with
> their own thoughts that they cannot forbear from putting them
> into rhyme, to examine those thoughts till they themselves
> understand them? No man will ever be a poet, till his mind be
> sufficiently powerful to sustain this labour.

According to Holcroft, the success of the poem requires presentation of a scene apparently unmediated by a perspective, and *Descriptive Sketches* fails for him because of its point of view. Holcroft's comments on *An Evening Walk* show his attitude even more clearly: "If [Wordsworth's lines] can possibly give pleasure, it must be to readers whose habits of thinking are totally different from ours." He calls upon Wordsworth to "divest himself of all partiality," and revise his work, presumably subordinating the perspective in the poems to a supposedly "perspectiveless" replication of the scene.

Dorothy Wordsworth's and the reviewers' criticisms of *An Evening Walk* and *Descriptive Sketches* differ in their basic conception of what these poems address. That important disparity between her evaluation and theirs overrides the superficial fact of their common dissatisfaction with the works while it highlights the reviewers agreement among themselves. It indicates that the reviewers reacted to the poems more fundamentally than political prejudices, bureaucratic accidents, or personal preferences can explain. Such criteria account only for individual cases. For example, Sharp argues that the outbreak of war between France and England shortly after the publication of Wordsworth's first works led reviewers to "misrepresent" *Descriptive Sketches* as merely descriptive to avoid dealing with their potentially inflammatory treatment "of the need for freedom and the necessity for political revolution and regeneration" ("Unmerited" 26). In a later article, Sharp takes up the question of why the radical Holcroft failed to exploit the political dimension. He suggests that the pressures of turning out many reviews quickly forced Holcroft to resort to the admitted practice of reviewing what he had not read:

> It seems that Holcroft read little more than the early passages of
> the poem and wrote his review out of his own prejudices against
> descriptive poetry . . . [and did not know] that the remainder of
> the poem was in any way different. ("Principle" 73)

Although political motives are undeniably prominent in reviewing practice, they can here account only for individual cases and account for them randomly. They cannot account for the solidarity of the reviewers among themselves and against Dorothy Wordsworth, and they cannot account for the similar criticisms of *An Evening Walk* and *Descriptive Sketches*—unless the former is construed as likewise inflammatory. Poor working conditions cannot account for Holcroft's reaction to whatever he did read that made him sensitive to the perspective. Oddly, Holcroft's generic prejudice seems to have yielded the most directly personal review. Hence, it would be as generally illuminating to charge him with writing out of his personal opinion of Wordsworth as a man as to charge him with writing without reading, for it is not known whether his personal acquaintance with Wordsworth dates from before or after this review.[13]

In Iser's terms, the early reviewers refuse to acknowledge the poem's new context for the familiar elements in the repertoire. To admit this context in the case of *An Evening Walk*, the reader must see poetic diction and other systems of naming objects as similar and non-authoritative, as conventions that serve an individual perspective and communicate something of it but that do not give direct access to it. The familiar idea that such conventions can or should transcend the individuality of perception, the idea that some external authority can or should subsume individual views, must become part of a "theme-and-horizon structure" and be examined without prejudice. Attachment to the intrinsic value of conventions or to external authority can make such examination impossible. In short, a need for some principle of communication to bind all individuals together, a need for the authority of the text, makes it impossible to accept the limits of perception that the poem suggests as a good.

In the cases of the *Analytical* and *Critical Review*s, the writers show an attachment to universally authoritative poetic systems and find the intrusion of individuality into them to be inappropriate. They will not even add their own perspectives as external readers because that cannot be done without first entertaining the value of individuality. Their refusal to participate leaves them with incomplete poems, for which they compensate by taking the repertoire for the subject. By a process of "cooptation," they fit the poems back into their familiar world instead of revaluing that world through the poems. Holcroft's somewhat more insistent carping on the self-indulgence of these poems is consistent with the others' reactions, though it might stem from political rather than poetic preoccupation. All commitment to practical social change proceeds from a premise that individuals can and should lose themselves in a cause. Some principle of direct communication, some idea with more than individual validity is vital to the orientation. To accept the individual perspective in the poems, Holcroft would have to entertain an idea that could threaten his commitment to shared reform. If he disliked descriptive poetry (for whatever reason), he was left with a repertoire to which he could be less sympathetic than his fellow reviewers.

In each case, the reviewers never seriously consider the alternative benefits of accepting perception as individual. Wordsworth clearly does not see it as leading to solipsism or enslavement to the material world. They never see this because it can be seen only after one is willing to examine individual perception as a possible good, and this they cannot do. Thus, they do not evaluate the consequences of the new idea as wrong or inconsistent. Their commitment to consensus makes them assume a similar intention of coercion on Wordsworth's part, which they resist, pointing to the patent absurdity of everyone seeing a given object in just the way he has described.

When a poem's strategy is subtle, as in the case in *An Evening Walk*, the repertoire can be easily reclaimed from the poem. Thus, readers who found it difficult to face the limits of perception could calmly turn a deaf ear to Wordsworth's earliest call to investigate the advantages of epistemological self-reliance. Wordsworth, however, did not continue to use gentle strategies. After trying the potential of the loco-descriptive genre, he turned to more "experimental" forms. Whether Wordsworth's shifts in style stem from a resolve to range fully through literature's potential or from a desire to shock readers into greater activity (or both), his poetry shows a continued and deepening attention to the involvement of literature with epistemological self-reliance.

Chapter 4

Lyrical Ballads: Genre, Paradigm, Variations

The descriptive genre Wordsworth used in his first poetic ventures had certain advantages for what I have called his campaign. The "want of method" that Samuel Johnson saw as its "defect" could be turned into a virtue if made to represent the apparent randomness of perception. Its potential openness to any natural scene could provide a wealth of opportunities to show interaction between perceiver and objects. Perhaps its chief disadvantage lay in its usual confinement to one perceiver's reflections on a scene. This feature set up expectations of a poem enshrining a privileged view and lulling readers into admiration of it. After his first trials, Wordsworth may have found the descriptive genre and passive reading too inextricably involved with each other to make the loco-descriptive mode the best strategy with which to suggest the individuality of perception. Numerous short poems, however, could allow for the invention of multiple personae and situations, for pointed exaggerations and shifting emphases. They might more easily show readers how perspectives qualify each other and might make readers more willing to put the perspectives together themselves. Finding the descriptive mode wanting, Wordsworth seems next to have tested the advantages of shorter forms in capturing moments of perception.[1] The results remain in his contributions to *Lyrical Ballads*.[2] Although no generalization does justice to the collection, it is at least not unjust to observe that Wordsworth's poems withhold satisfactory conclusions.[3] Avoidance of summary or conclusion, or the presentation of patently inadequate ones, encourages readers to come to their own, as can be seen from a more detailed examination of this characteristic of *Lyrical Ballads*.

The inconclusiveness begins with the genre itself. "No one knows precisely what a 'lyrical ballad' was supposed to be," observes Stephen Parrish, who remains flexible about definition but suggests it involves Wordsworth's extracting desired characteristics from two forms: the ballad provides a "tragic tale" to excite the reader; the lyric, or more specifically the ballad as a "lyrical form," lends its meter to check and control the emotion involved (*Art* 83-86; 113). Langbaum says that by "lyrical," Wordsworth "could not have meant that the poems were to be sung but must have meant that they were lyrical in the sense of subjective, stressing feeling over action" (56). Thus, a "lyrical ballad" in some ways exploits the opposition between the subjective lyric and the objective ballad. A similar idea of opposition seems to underlie Jacobus's assessment of the "achievement" of the lyrical ballads, which, she writes, consists in their "adapt[ing] the ballad to portraying precisely those states and feelings least susceptible to narrative presentation" (233). Woodring challenges the opposition with his definition of the lyrical ballad as "a modest narrative that assumes a rustic tone" (*Wordsworth* 26). The term then implies the poet's transformation of the ballad form; the setting up and breaking through of a literary barrier becomes emblematic of the setting up and breaking through of a social barrier, which Woodring describes as the aim of the project (22). Ryskamp sidesteps the issue by acknowledging that a "lyrical ballad" may pit subjective and objective dimensions against each other but countering that it may also be simply redundant: both terms imply a song (358).

What is remarkable about the range of definitions is not its extent but its existence. Wordsworth surrounded *Lyrical Ballads* with an advertisement, two versions of a preface, and an appendix, yet in all his commentary, he never defined the term. He states his purpose in writing such poems as comprise the collection, and he singles out characteristics that make them different from any other poems. If a definition were to be formed from his own words, it would read something like:

> A lyrical ballad is a poem that "make[s] the incidents of common
> life interesting by tracing in them . . . the manner in which we
> associate ideas in a state of excitement . . . [and that does so]
> by fitting to metrical arrangement a selection of the real language
> of men," commonly called prose. (*Prose* 1: 122, 124; 118; 134)

While this does much to illuminate the features of the poems and their general place in literary history, it does nothing to explain why they stand in a privileged relationship to lyrics and ballads and what exactly that relationship is.

Instead of clarifying the generic issue, the *Preface* considers the difficulties of reading such poems as these exemplify. In order to enjoy *Lyrical Ballads*, readers "must utterly reject" the critical tenet that holds poetry to consist in the metrical arrangement of a language other than prose (*Prose* 1: 132). Indeed, they must open themselves up to the possible identity of poetry and prose:

> Poetry sheds not tears "such as angels weep," but natural and
> human tears; she can boast of no celestial Ichor that distinguishes
> her vital juices from those of prose; the same human blood
> circulates through the veins of both. (1: 134)

Furthermore, readers may not simply shift their allegiance from one critical school to another. They must decide upon the success of the poems by exerting their independent judgment (1: 154). If they do so, they may discover "that the powers of language are not so limited as" they customarily had assumed.

To consider *Lyrical Ballads* as poetry, readers must shatter their trust in specific critical premises that allow poetry to be constituted from only certain elements. This act leads to a shattering of an even more fundamental trust in the implied basis of such premises, i.e., that the "right" combination of elements allows poetry to make a revelatory utterance, to impart to humans a wisdom that transcends their capacity otherwise to derive it. This iconoclasm seems to limit the powers of poetry and deprive readers of its comfort in supplying their deficiencies, but, actually, it exalts both poetry and reader. In leaving his readers to their own resources, Wordsworth invites them to discover how great those resources really are. In limiting poetry only by human capacity, Wordsworth lets it range beyond belief systems that human faculties create. (And he provokes that thought with his pointed references to angels and ichor.) Poetry does broaden its readers' perspectives, but it does so because it relies on the powers of perception not because it transcends them.

The genre of the "lyrical ballad" awaits the reader's definition. Its openness suggests Wordsworth to be using genre as strategy. He takes two familiar forms, the lyric and the ballad, as a repertoire. He removes them from their separate contexts in which their long-standing characteristics prevail and thrusts them together into a new context in which preconceptions are void. He withholds a statement of exactly what the new context is, but he guides the reader in thinking about it. Readers who incorporate the new genre into their idea of poetry have independently reworked their understanding of poetry in order to do so. An anachronistic analogy may illuminate the proposition Wordsworth puts before his readers. The readers of *Lyrical Ballads* find themselves in the position of Jude Fawley when his Latin and Greek grammars first arrive from Christminster. Expecting them to give him a magic cypher with which to understand all classics, he is appalled to discover that understanding can come only through his painstaking efforts at conjugating verbs and declining nouns. He casts the betraying books away. Recovering from his initial dejection, he applies himself to them and finds that his individually won reward exceeds what he had supposed the cypher would impart. Wordsworth's readers must overcome their initial disorientation, retrieve the *Lyrical Ballads*, and examine the expectations they challenge.

Consideration of how the poems carry on the enterprise heralded in the title should begin with a poem Wordsworth singles out as an epitome. In the *Preface*, he sends the readers especially to the last stanza of "The Childless Father" for illustration of his statements (*Prose* 1: 128). Since neither this poem nor "The Reverie of Poor Susan" (the other poem Wordsworth tags as representative) appeared in the first edition, Wordsworth might have added them to the second expressly as examples.[4] The last stanza of "The Childless Father" speculates about the thoughts of a recently bereaved character as he is called upon to join his happy fellow villagers in a hunt:

> Perhaps to himself at that moment he said;
> "The key I must take, for my Ellen is dead."
> But of this in my ears not a word did he speak
> And he went to the chase with a tear on his cheek.

The stanza clearly involves an interplay of associations. It puts seemingly unrelated ideas—carrying a key and Ellen's death—into a causal sequence. The sentence furnishes the illusion of an explanation. Nothing beyond its syntax shows why the character should join these two thoughts. The connection becomes more puzzling when the stanza reveals that one character has ascribed the sequence to another. The statement fills the speaker's need to rationalize what he observes of the silent character's behavior. It inserts a link between the latter's activity and his apparently inappropriate emotion. While its form satisfies the speaker, its emptiness titillates the reader. Serving as an explanation, it creates a new question. Now the issue concerns not only why one character might act as he does but why the other requires an explanation and why he thinks he has found one. Only the context of the entire poem—invoked by this stanza's demonstrative adjective—can do justice to its final challenge.

The poem begins with the direct exhortation to the silent character to join the hunt:

> "Up, Timothy, up with your staff and away!
> Not a soul in the village this morning will stay;
> The hare has just started from Hamilton's grounds,
> And Skiddaw is glad with the cry of the hounds."

The speaker's boisterously excited tone establishes the emotion expected in the situation. He invites Timothy not only to participate in the local sport but also to share the communal gaiety. By beginning with an invitation, the poem suggests that the group activity has a definable and communicable emotion, a point that it develops through assertion and demonstration. The speaker's "Skiddaw is glad" imputes the emotion even to the scene and asserts his belief that the emotion is being communicated directly. His dissociation of the hunt from daily routine—"Not a soul in the village this morning will stay"—suggests his idea of that communicability. He thinks of it as immediate contagion. The villagers leave the situations in which they are individuated and form the group in which they are indistinguishable. The invitation expects Timothy to follow this pattern, and gives him an example of the appropriate response in its reference to Skiddaw. Because the stanza leaves the speaker's identity unclear, it turns the speaker himself into a demonstration of his own point of view. He might be any one of the individuals lost in the group. Thus the poem first presents the reader with a character's perspective and his assumption that it can be directly communicated and fully shared.

Coming clearly from a narrator's point of view, the second stanza reins in the apparently universal validity of the character's perspective. Moved to describe the color of the villagers' garments against the hills over which they chase, the narrator calls it "a holiday show." The development still admits the idea of communicability as the narrator embraces the festive idiom for his interpretation of the scene. His term "holiday" reflects the villagers' happiness and their dissociation of the hunt from everyday activities. The emergence of the narrative perspective, however, adds an element of independent judgment. The narrator is not a participant. He derives his understanding of the scene from observation but remains outside the experience, which he sees as a "show." The stanza calls for a redefinition of communication: it cannot be merely contagion if the narrator arrives at his assessment in a different way.

The very emergence of a narrative perspective weakens the notion of direct communication. It reduces the character's perspective to dependence upon his utterance. The narrator's use of the past tense qualifies the immediacy of the direct quotation, suggesting that he may be using it as a device to emphasize his interpretation of the villagers' view. The indeterminacy of the speaker, which at first enforced the quotation's seemingly universal validity, now contributes to its limits. The narrator may be quoting the words of a villager to Timothy, or he may be recalling his own words to Timothy. By correcting what the poem first presented, the narrator asserts his authority and usurps the poem for his purposes. As he makes the character's perspective revolve around his, so he creates an equally subordinate in-text reader's perspective. His act of narrating requires a passive reader to attend to his clarifications. The narrator's perspective wants to arrogate the privilege of communication to itself. Since it derives its strength from the break-down of direct communication, it rests on a shaky foundation.

The rest of the poem consists of the narrator's presentation of his perspective on the situation, i.e., Timothy's potential participation in the hunt. The narrator remains sure of his own authority. As he unfolds his view, however, he displays its individuality. The inconsistency between the nature of the narrator's knowledge and his authoritative stance should prevent the external reader from identifying himself with the in-text reader whom the narrator's account assumes. The external reader is not to receive the narrator's account as privileged information but to assess it as a point of view. By the end of the poem, the reader should be able to draw some conclusions as to what is known, what is communicated, and what is significant about those conditions.

Exercising his assumed authority, the narrator delays revealing Timothy's response to the invitation in order to give the reader information about a previous event. The transition from the colors on the hill to the "fresh sprigs of green box-wood" (1. 9) is so smooth as to make jarring the realization that the latter are connected to a funeral custom and not to the hunt festivities. The narrator uses the disjunction to elicit the reader's trust and reinforce his dependence. The narrator will explain how the funeral bears on the hunt and give the reader a new understanding of the situation. The transition has already shown the external reader something important about the narrator's perception. The color stimulates him to associate the hunt and the funeral. In that green image coalesce the similarities and dissimilarities between the two events.[5] The separate components are never made explicit, but their latency leads the reader to think what they might include as he ponders the image. For example, he might see that the hunt and the funeral entail departures from ordinary routine. Both also involve shared emotion, albeit different emotions in the different cases.

The transitional association, moreover, makes clear what Wordsworth uses as a repertoire for this poem and provides a strategy with which to organize it into a new context. The poem covers the familiar ground of community activities and the familiar assumption that they unite people in a shared experience. By forging an unexpected and individual link between two different community activities, the poem wrenches them from their separate contexts. The dislocation opens the way for a reconsideration of what community activity is.

When the narrator connects the hunt and the funeral for the in-text reader, he does so by extending his own analogy to Timothy's mind. Timothy does not speak to the narrator, so the narrator works backwards from Timothy's observable behavior to find a rationale for it. Seeing that Timothy participates in the activity of the chase but not in the villagers' exuberance, he decides that a personal association has interfered with Timothy's involvement with the group just as his own association with the box-wood diverted his attention from the hunt. The narrator uses words from the invitation to show Timothy being initially caught up in the group proposal: "Old Timothy took up his staff" (1. 15). He describes Timothy's preparation for departure as "leisurely" (1. 16), indicating that Timothy is untroubled. He assumes that locking the door as he leaves brings two events together for Timothy as the color did for him. Simultaneously present in the act are Timothy's past life in which his child would welcome him home and his life in which he must procure his own entrance to his empty house. This accounts for Timothy's seemingly inappropriate sadness during the hunt.

Having done for the in-text reader what he entered the poem to do, the narrator concludes with satisfied finality. The external reader must carry the narrator's explanation beyond the situation in the poem. The poem has established the primacy of individual association over direct communication by setting up a situation that could be explained only by the former; however, it compromised the explanation by showing it to be the narrator's admitted speculation. Although the narrator replaces one concept with the other, the poem does not. It rejects direct communication as contrary to experience, then redefines the opposition between association and communication. Timothy's grief does not exclude him from the group. The narrator's commitment to his own association does not prevent him from evaluating the behavior of the hunt party; moreover, the narrator never notices a tension between his method of explaining from his own experience and his urge to impart his view.

In each case, the forming of a relationship between the individual's association and the act of participation or communication draws the two together. Timothy forces the villagers to acknowledge his grief while they force him to temper it sufficiently to act with them. Neither Timothy nor the villagers becomes privy to each other's perspectives. Because there are limits on what they can know of each other, each can expand his perspective by partial accommodation of the other. Without such limits, each perspective would be severely narrowed. Timothy would have to deny his grief to be absorbed into the gaiety of the chase, and the villagers would have learned nothing new from having incorporated him. Similarly, the narrator's associations arise and depart from his visual relationship with the hunt. They help him to deal with otherwise baffling phenomena, such as Timothy's behavior. His explanations have no objective validity, but their private validity gives him the urge to communicate. Feeling that he has expanded his perspective through his observations, he wishes in turn to expand the perspectives of others.

The poem, then, deflects attention away from breaking down the limits surrounding what one can know of another's perspective to exploring how the limits can expand every perspective. Two invariable techniques guide the search. First, the integrity of the other's view is always assumed and respected. The poem corrects the villagers' seeming disregard for Timothy's feelings by having him received into the group on his own terms. It never allows the narrator's assumption of authority to claim knowledge he could not have. He presents his views of the hunt and of Timothy as his own observations and deductions. Secondly, the status of the other as object is strictly maintained. The relationships that expand perspectives cannot be established without the perceiver's assumption that he is interacting with something. Without his initiative to interpret, nothing happens. Hence, the poem makes Timothy silent, so that the narrator must stretch his faculties to accommodate him. (Timothy's speaking would not remove the need for the narrator's effort, but it would complicate the point at issue.) Even if Timothy exists only in the narrator's mind, the narrator must still define him as a recognizable object and then abide by his imputed integrity in order for his (the narrator's) perspective to expand. The two techniques check each other. The necessity of fidelity to the object as it is perceived prevents the perceiver from being lost in isolated meditation. Perception must proceed through relationships.

It follows that the greatest threat to perception is fixity of mind. Too much attachment to one's own perspective leads to a bullying of the object, such as would occur if the perspective in the first quotation proceeded unaltered. Too little attachment to it leads to an awe of the object, which would occur if the narrator lacked the confidence to draw on his own knowledge to explain Timothy.   In either case, relationship would fail. Perceivers ought to acknowledge that their views have only individual validity even as they act upon their veracity. If they forget that, they become too involved in protecting their former ideas or preserving new objects. In that condition, they cannot establish relationships, and therefore their perspectives cannot grow. The poem carefully balances the tension between the narrator's authority and the individuality of his views. Recognition of the narrator's position should send the external reader beyond the narrative point of view.

The poem challenges external readers to give up confidence in any one of the perspectives in the text and to rely instead on their own. It gives them only a suggested interpretation of Timothy's situation, but it makes the situation itself clearly a springboard for other considerations. If readers follow the poem carefully, they come away from it with a new interest in how people interact with each other in communities, an interest that can   make the empirical dilemma at least manageable and at best advantageous. The poem liberates readers from attachment to shared views by suggesting the potential virtues of the limits of individual experience. The poem threatens any reader who wants to receive universally valid knowledge from a privileged source.

Such a reader will feel betrayed by the inadequacy of any of the perspectives, especially the narrator's, and will retreat from the poem rather than face the failure of authority. Such a reader, of course, never learns of the alternative benefits the text raises.

Wordsworth's attention to "The Childless Father" suggests that it should serve as a paradigm for his other lyrical ballads, a designation supported by the similar demands made on the reader by more widely known lyrical ballads such as "We Are Seven." Like "The Childless Father," "We Are Seven" consists of a narrator's report of a conversation with a character—this time, a child—whose relationship with departed loved ones uniquely distinguishes her perspective. The child's inclusion of the deceased siblings among her brothers and sisters is incomprehensible to the narrator, who wants her to acknowledge the fact of their death. By making the two perspectives equivalent, this poem likewise directs the reader to consider what is known and communicated in the exchange. Indeed, attention to insight as contingent upon the individuality of perception recurs in pointed variations throughout Wordsworth's contributions to the collection. An examination of some of the more startling variations shows the extent of Wordsworth's concern. Wordsworth sometimes calls attention to the integrity of each individual's perception by creating characters with markedly unconventional views, and sometimes he does so by treating readers as characters themselves.

For variations involving deviant or altered perspectives, Wordsworth avails himself of the superstitious mind in "The Thorn," of the deficient mind in "The Idiot Boy," and, often, the undeveloped or unsocialized minds of children.[6] In "Anecdote for Fathers," for example, the child's evasive response calls for a revaluation of what appropriate questions and answers are.

The narrator-participant sets the scene of his walk with the boy (11. 1-8), then pays particular attention to reporting what he had been thinking about (11. 9-24). He had been comparing the pleasure he derived from his present location at Liswyn to that he felt at his former situation at Kilve. The four stanzas in which he does so suggest his associations to the reader.   Both instances of pleasure stem from a relationship with rustic nature during the spring.   Hence, the observation of the lambs playing in the current Liswyn spring (11. 17-10) call to mind the different but equally pleasing rusticity experienced at Kilve the previous spring (11. 10-12).

If the associations are clear to the reader, they are opaque to the narrator.   The stanzas arrange the associations randomly.   They show the narrator aware of himself as a thinking being but one who makes no attempt to understand or benefit from the associative process.   He moves from his thoughts—

> My thoughts on former pleasures ran;
>
> I thought of Kilve's delightful shore,
>
> Our pleasant home when spring began,
>
> A long, long year before. (11. 9-12)

—to his observations—

> A day it was when I could bear
>
> Some fond regrets to entertain;
>
> With so much happiness to spare,
>
> I could not feel a pain. (11. 13-16)

Then, from his observations—

> The green earth echoed to the feet
>
> Of lambs that bounded through the glade,

> From shade to sunshine, and as fleet
> From sunshine back to shade. (11. 17-20)

—he works back to his thoughts, without expanding his perspective—

> Birds warbled round me—and each trace
> Of inward sadness had its charm;
> Kilve, thought I, was a favoured place,
> And so is Liswyn farm. (11. 21-24)

He reaches an impasse. He only holds in tension the two pleasures, being none the richer for his observations and memories. Because he has established separate relationships with each scene, he sees each as equally pleasant. This leads him to believe that sadness in either one would be inappropriate. He fails to establish the further relationship with his conjunction of the two that would account for his regrets and sadness at leaving Kilve without denying the merits of Liswyn. He resorts to the poetically conventional device of pleasing melancholy to repress his thoughts. His feeble oxymorons suggest an effort to be satisfied with a troubling condition.

Since that convention is inadequate, the narrator seeks more immediate outside authority to explain his feelings—either to confirm the equal pleasures in a presumably more convincing way or to provide the missing link that will elevate the one over the other. He questions the source at hand, his young companion:

> "Now tell me, had you rather be,"
> I said and took him by the arm,
> "On Kilve's smooth shore, by the green sea,
> Or here at Liswyn farm?" (11. 29-32)

His plea for external confirmation would not seem at all strange if it were directed at a recognizably authoritative source. Because it is directed at a child, however, it inverts the usual hierarchy of authority. The obvious futility of appeal to this authority should prepare the reader to question the merit of other appeals to external authority.

The father insists on a reason for the child's arbitrary preference (11. 35-36). He himself has seemingly arbitrary feelings that he wants the child to help him understand. The child eventually accounts for his preference: "'At Kilve there was no weather-cock;/ And that's the reason why'" (11. 55-56). In Wolfson's words, the child has replied "merely by adapting something he sees to the syntax of his father's question" ("Speaker" 551). The emptiness of the statement and the meaning of the formula comment on the appeal to authority. It is doomed to yield only individual associations that cannot be communicated directly and that cannot represent a privileged perspective. The obvious failure of the straw authority figure throws the father back on his own resources, with which he can come to terms with his individual associations.

The poem does not reveal whether the father does so or not. His final statement asserts that he has learned something:

> O dearest, dearest boy! my heart
> For better lore would seldom yearn,
> Could I but teach the hundredth part
> Of what from thee I learn. (11. 57-60)

It does not indicate what he has learned. In fact, it does not indicate that he has learned, only that he thinks he has.[7] The situation in the poem parodies reliance on external authority. The individual sets up a figure and values its ideas. The early subtitle ("Shewing how the art of lying may be taught") and the added epigraph ("'*Retine vim istam, falsa enim dicam, si coges*'") calls attention to the "falsity" of the child's answer. The narrator recognizes this at some level, i.e., he knows that it does not fit his associations. But he does not necessarily recognize the inadequacy of external authority. He may as soon turn to a more recognizably privileged source as become self-reliant. The reader, of course, should see the way out of the narrator's predicament. "Anecdote for Fathers," then, prompts the reader to consider not the appropriateness of questioning a child too closely (as the child-rearing conventions from which the poem's repertoire is partly drawn might indicate) but the appropriateness of expecting universally valid explanations for individual associations.

Not only does Wordsworth often lead readers to a vantage from which to revalue the empirical dilemma by encouraging them to assess the limits of his characters' perspectives, he sometimes prompts them to self-consciousness about their activity. Readers of "Simon Lee," for example, must decide how the narrator's abdication affects them. The most remarkable—and problematic—feature of this lyrical ballad is its direct address of the reader. At a glance, this address seems an exaggerated transfer of authority from narrator to reader, but a transfer would more surely occur if the address ended the poem—or as much of it as the narrator was able to relate. The address, however, comes in the middle of the ballad. Having exhorted the reader to complete the tale, the narrator himself continues. Though the address reminds readers of their responsibility, it does not signal a simple transfer.

The address divides the ballad into two parts: a condensed biography of Simon Lee and an anecdote involving that character and the narrator. In the first part, the narrator assumes the familiar stance of the omniscient storyteller, the guardian and conveyor of folk culture. His "In the sweet shire of Cardigan" (1. 1) exudes an aura of "once-upon-a-time" or "long-ago-and-far-away." His present tense "dwells" (1. 3) might be an historical present, reinforcing his control of the material. His leisurely spinning of the yarn settles the in-text reader, for whose benefit he presumably exercises his skill, into a state of comfortable and expectant passivity.[8]

The poem compromises the narrator's authority before the first stanza has concluded. The narrator betrays his reliance on other's information: "'Tis said he once was tall." Like "The Childless Father," the poem calls attention to the limits surrounding one perspective's access to another. As the narrator of "The Childless Father" could not claim verifiable knowledge of Timothy's associations, the narrator of "Simon Lee" cannot claim verifiable knowledge of a past condition he did not observe. The scrupulous preservation of these limits should alert the external reader to the illusoriness of the narrator's authority. Instead of merely accepting the narrator's description of the huntsman, the reader should be examining it to ascertain the basis of the narrator's knowledge and the process by which he uses it.

In general, the narrator combines his observations of the present Simon Lee with hearsay about the former Simon Lee to create a composite portrait. For example, Simon Lee's observably flushed face becomes an emblem of his previous, healthy exertions (11. 5-8). The narrator tries to make the young Simon Lee increasingly vivid to his readers (11. 9-24). From his point of view, tale and audience are in his control. His apparent intention is to build up to a melodramatic climax. He makes his readers see a vigorous Simon Lee not present to their vision so that he can arouse their emotions toward the decrepit Simon Lee whom they can see, whom, in fact, the narrator directs them to see:

"But, oh the heavy change!—bereft/ Of health, strength, friends, and kindred, see!" (11. 25-26). That readers "see" Simon Lee in this way depends upon their having "seen" Simon Lee before in the way the narrator directed. The in-text reader is to be marvelling at the description and to have learned how to look at Simon Lee; the external reader should note that the portrait is the result of the narrator's artfully arranged associations.

The narrator's confidence in his control leads him to enlist the reader's participation, but the reader's independent eyes check his storytelling freedom. Having exhorted the reader to observe also, the narrator must refer to things the reader can confirm, or he loses his control. Hence, his description relies increasingly on physical details:

> And he is lean and he is sick;
>
> His body dwindled and awry,
>
> Rests upon ankles swoln and thick;
>
> His legs are thin and dry. (11. 33-36)

Moreover, the presence of his subject restricts the narrator to reporting Simon Lee's assessment of his condition or risking Simon Lee's correction:

> Few months of life has he in store
>
> As he to you will tell,
>
> For still, the more he works, the more
>
> Do his weak ankles swell. (11. 57-60)

Characteristically, this lyrical ballad assumes and respects the integrity of every perspective. The narrator has inadvertently brought himself to an impasse. By inviting his readers and his subject into the poem, he invokes perspectives that reveal the individuality of his own and undermine his omniscience. He cannot continue as he began without violating the other perspectives, and that the poem will not allow him to do so. So he states his predicament to the reader in a significantly modified vocative. Apart from the formulaic exclamations, he hardly addresses the readers at all. He reports his assessment of his readership, carefully qualified by "I perceive" and "I fear" (11. 61, 64). With a proliferation of subjunctives and conditionals, he speculates about what the reader might do under the circumstances or what he wishes the reader would do (11. 65-72). His posture is far different from that of his earlier address in which he sought to impose a particular vision upon the reader (11. 25-26).

"Simon Lee" allows its narrator openly to embrace individuality of perspective. The narrator does not invite the reader to replace him in his former position because he has realized its lack of validity. Instead, he suggests that readers use their own resources to give meaning to their surroundings—or, in the story-telling idiom, to make a tale of them. He then demonstrates his new orientation in the second part of the poem, which concerns Simon Lee and the narrator and does not attempt to present a particular view of Simon Lee. It can have no significance for the reader until each has interacted with it. Hence, it is not, as written, a tale. Because the written object can engage the reader, it can become a tale. The narrator's distinction between what is a tale and what is not is remarkably like Iser's distinction between a text (the written pages) and a work (the "actualization" of the text by the reader) (21). The narrator's interruption, then, redefines his stance, his reader's role, and his very idea of literature. The second part of the poem signals the narrator's new view most obviously by the replacement of the third person with the first. It emphasizes that the narrator now relies on his experience. He now relates that experience not to tell readers about Simon

Lee but to show them how he established a relationship with him and how that expanded his perspective.

The narrator's relationship with the huntsman depends upon his observation. He sees that Simon Lee cannot uproot the stump; he knows that he can; therefore, he helps him (11. 73-88). No longer the omniscient narrator, he does not have access to Simon Lee's emotions or knowledge of his former condition that might make help seem demeaning to him.[9] Because the narrator establishes a relationship with the character, he is shown something of the other's emotion. That reaction becomes in turn an object with which he interacts. He notes what he observes the reaction to be:

> The tears into his eyes were brought,
>
> And thanks and praises seemed to run
>
> So fast out of his heart, I thought
>
> They never would have done. (11. 89-92)

He associates the reaction he observes with other reactions he has been told about: "I've heard of hearts unkind, kind deeds/ With coldness still returning" (11. 93-94). His generalizations represent a search for a norm to explain the observed reaction. Although he does not play out the associations, his report implies that the reactions of those who have received charity provoke reactions in those who have given. The sets of reactions are assumed to be definable and predictable: a grateful recipient makes the actor happy; an ungrateful one makes him sad and cynical. The narrator cannot find a paradigm for Simon Lee's reaction and his own concomitant response: "Alas! the gratitude of men/ Hath oftener left me mourning" (11. 95-96). In drawing his conclusion and expressing it as a generalization, the narrator suggests that the other norms are generalizations from individual experience. When they are inadequate to experience, experience must alter them, not they experience.

The latter part of "Simon Lee" draws on truisms about charity for its repertoire and strategically puts them into a situation they cannot cover.[10] By allowing the narrator to experience their inadequacy, the poem goes beyond questioning a norm or norms to suggesting the process by which norms are questioned. The first part of the poem has prepared the narrator to participate in this process by having him accept limits on what he can know about another. These limits make it necessary for the narrator to establish an individual relationship with Simon Lee if he is to learn about him. By maintaining the necessity of approaching even another person as an object of perception, Wordsworth forces readers of "Simon Lee" to confront the disturbing idea that people are in fact isolated from each other. The poem, however, does not cast this circumstance as a dilemma. It shows that the circumstance merely obtains and that it can enhance perspectives both in and out of the text. Having seen the failure of the narrator's authority and the success of his individual associations, readers should be prepared to move beyond the narrator's generalization about his individual experience (generalization left exaggeratedly individual in the text) and reconstitute norms of behavior for themselves. Readers who can confront the limits of human relations in "Simon Lee" can confront the empirical dilemma with a new confidence in self-reliance.

Chapter 5

Lyrical Ballads: Complications

Not all of Wordsworth's lyrical ballads rely on the interaction of characters or on storytelling devices to nudge readers beyond any one perspective. Some poems in the collection are first-person monologues, but that form does not necessarily place them outside of Wordsworth's campaign. Indeed, it may place them at the heart of it, indicating the extent and intensity of Wordsworth's effort to solve the empirical dilemma through poetry. Although the invention of characters clearly suits Wordsworth's enterprise, it has the disadvantage of suggesting an underlying authorial omniscience. No matter how accomplished their strategies, the poems cannot prevent readers from thinking about the inventiveness of the author who formed all the perspectives—who shared all the views, as it were. In spite of their strategies, the poems may send contradictory messages to their readers. On one hand, they demonstrate the integrity of every perspective; on the other, they betray the master perspective of their author. Readers may take the latter intrusion as a sign that these poems can give them access to shared knowledge and, clinging to that hope, ignore the examination of perception the poems try to prompt.

Early reviews of *Lyrical Ballads* attest to readers' inclination to wrest an authoritative statement from characters' perspectives—and to be disappointed with the resultant view that they believe Wordsworth would have them share. Southey's and Burney's respective articles for the *Critical Review* and *Monthly Review* are cases in point. Southey objects to the exaggeration by which the perspectives are individuated: the narrator of "The Thorn" is too talkative; the acceptance of superstition in "Goody Blake and Harry Gill" is unqualified; the sympathy for the mentally deficient in "The Idiot Boy" is excessive. By singling out such features, Southey is reacting to a strategy that directs the reader away from adopting a perspective from the poems and toward evaluating the perspectives raised in and elicited by them. Southey's own judgment shows him that these are not authentic replications. He assumes, however, that they ought to be so, an assumption he indicates through his analogy to realistic painting: "The Idiot Boy"

> resembles a Flemish picture in the worthlessness of its design and
> the excellence of its execution. From Flemish artists we are
> satisfied with such pieces: who would not have lamented, if
> Corregio or Rafaelle had wasted their talents in painting Dutch
> boors or the humours of a Flemish wake?

Without the idea of perception to control the elements, Southey is left with a repertoire of eccentric, lower-class characters supposedly representing privileged attitudes.

Unable to share such views, Southey rejects them because they are not authentic representations, because they do not communicate the single perspective to which he is committed. He protects his belief that communication can be direct and that perspectives can he held in common by faulting *Lyrical Ballads* for not affirming it and by leaving open the possibility that the affirmation could have obtained had the volume portrayed other characters and other topics. Thus, he concludes:

> The "experiment," we think, has failed not because the language
> of conversation is little adapted to "the purposes of poetic
> pleasure," but because it has been tried upon uninteresting
> subjects.

In short, Southey seems to apprehend a strategy that allows the poems to offer an alternative to perception as replication, but his assumption about their purpose prevents him from exploring other possibilities.

Like Southey, Burney objects to exaggeration in *Lyrical Ballads*, but he devotes much space to demonstrating that the perspectives in the poems are not suitable for universal adoption. Two examples may suffice to illustrate his technique. "*The Female Vagrant* is an agonizing tale of individual wretchedness," he admits.

> . . . Yet, as it seems to stamp a general stigma on all military transactions, which were never more important in free countries than at the present period, it will perhaps be asked whether the hardships described never happen during revolution, or in a nation subdued?

Similarly, he notes that "the hardest heart must be softened into pity for [Goody Blake]"; nevertheless, he worries: "if all the poor are to help themselves, and supply their wants from the possessions of their neighbors, what imaginary wants and real anarchy would it not create?" The strategically exaggerated perspectives in the poems prevent Burney from fitting the repertoire back into the milieu from which it was shaped. Burney sees that the single views are incompatible with a communal ideal, but he does not use the views to question the idea. Instead, he uses the ideal to judge individual perception as detrimental to a valued order.

Using an analogy similar to Southey's, Burney indicates his assumption that *Lyrical Ballads* ought to contain authentic representations of collectively assimilable views:

> The author shall style his rustic delineations of low-life poetry, *if*
> *he pleases*, on the same principle as Butler is called a poet or
> Teniers a painter: but are the doggrel [sic] verses of the one equal
> to the sublime numbers of Milton, or are the Dutch boors of the
> other to be compared with the angels of Raphael or Guido?

Burney turns the failure of direct communication into the failure of *Lyrical Ballads* to effect it, and he protects the possibility that it can occur by calling on Wordsworth to write other poems "on more elevated subjects and in a more cheerful disposition," poems that would presumably uphold an ideal for readers to adopt.

As if in an effort to prevent authorial privilege from interfering with epistemological inquiry, Wordsworth seems to have experimented with forms that would allow him the greatest fidelity to an individual point of view. The first-person monologue is well-suited to the task.   Grammatically and rhetorically, it indicates a single—as distinct from a shared or privileged—perspective. Its necessarily personal dimension signals the limits of the speaker's perception. The complex of individuating factors that comprise a first-person utterance should decrease the temptations both to embrace the speaker's perspective and to root out an underlying authority.

The merits of the first-person monologue in Wordsworth's undertaking might best be shown by an analysis of "The Old Cumberland Beggar," a poem that, like "Simon Lee," draws its repertoire from charitable norms but that, unlike "Simon Lee," centers on first-person assertions. "The Old Cumberland Beggar" falls into three main sections: the narrator's observations of the beggar (11. 1-66); the narrator's polemic against those who find the beggar useless, together with his own assessment of the beggar's use (11. 67-161); and the narrator's peroration on what the beggar's disposition should be (11. 162-97). As the narrator moves from section to section, he becomes more involved in his own view and less interactive. At the outset, his direct use of the first person indicates that his report proceeds from his perspective ("I say," "Him from my childhood have I known," 11. 1, 22). By the second section of the poem his first-person qualifiers have become parenthetical ("Many, I believe, there are" 1. 133), and by the end, they disappear. The narrator's commitment to his view seems to make him forget that he is presenting his perspective and not an absolute truth. He becomes increasingly careless of the first-person qualifiers that made his utterance promise to report and effect relationships until he replaces them with exhortations that try to fix and impose a single attitude. The modulations in the narrative presentation should make readers aware of it as one speaker's view. Alerted to the inappropriateness of the authority assumed, readers should evaluate rather than accept the narrative perspective.

Evaluating the perspective requires careful attention to its nuances. The narrator does begin by establishing a relationship. He observes the beggar in one situation at one particular time--sitting on the stones, examining the orts, eating them, and feeding the birds (11. 1-21). Respecting the necessary limits and integrity of the object, the narrator scrupulously avoids presuming access to the beggar's perspective. The examination has to the narrator a "*look* of idle computation" (11. 11-12, emphasis added), but the narrator does not say that *is* the nature of the beggar's activity. The dropping of the crumbs appears accidental, and the narrator does not color it by deciding that the beggar is pleased by the kindness to the creatures or disappointed at his own loss.

Perhaps surprisingly, the narrator associates the stationary beggar he now sees with the itinerant beggar he has seen often. Still, he carefully respects the bounds of the relationship. He reports as fact only what is observable even as he recalls it from his memory, and his explicit reference to his childhood observations (1. 22) provides evidence for his generalizations. That the beggar travels, that he is solitary (1. 24), the narrator has seen repeatedly. That the beggar is helpless, the narrator infers from his appearance (11. 24-25). He deduces that if the beggar appears so to him, the beggar might also appear so to others, and he uses his inference to explain what he has observed of the Horseman's, the toll-gate keeper's, and the post-boy's behavior toward the beggar (11. 25-43). Thus, the narrator displays how his associations expand his perspective, how they help him make sense out of his environment. His respect for the boundaries of the perspective make it clearly his view.

The narrator violates the boundaries at line 54. His generalized memories of the beggar include one uncommonly keen and still appropriate observation about the beggar's posture: "On the ground/ His eyes are turned, and, as he moves along,/ *They* move along the ground . . ." (11. 45-47). Carried away by this observation, the narrator reports it as if it gave him access to the beggar's sight: ". . . seeing still,/ And seldom knowing that he sees" (11. 53-54). The narrator's claim to a knowledge he cannot have and his departure from his formerly careful method should alert the reader to be wary of the narrator's statements. The poem emphasizes the departure for the reader by having the narrator return briefly to the first method to reveal the connection he made between the visible, seated beggar and the remembered, itinerant beggar. Describing the beggar's habitual movement, he says:

> His staff trails with him; scarcely do his feet
> Disturb the summer dust; he is so still
> In look and motion, that the cottage curs,
> Ere he has passed the door, will turn away,
> Weary of barking at him. (11. 59-63)

Knowing that the seated beggar's stillness suggested his characteristically slow gait, the reader can now be sure that a relationship with the object triggered the narrator's association and should therefore be all the more startled by the narrator's change.

Significantly, the reintroduction of the first pattern of association refers back into the poem. When the narrator moves forward in the poem, he gets away from his original premises. His transition from his recollections of the beggar to his rhetorical address to the statesmen seems to turn, appropriately enough, on the idea of waste. He observes that the beggar is habitually left behind all traffic in the road, knows that useless things are left behind and useful things brought along, and realizes that such a pattern of association from observation might lead some to conclude that the beggar is useless, a conclusion that he knows certain statesmen have drawn. He takes it upon himself to correct the view by showing that observation of the beggar in other situations can lead to other associations and other conclusions. His eloquent explanation of how interaction with the beggar nurtures charity among the villagers and makes him supremely useful counters the opposite view power-fully and viably. It is built up from the narrator's observation of the interac-tions and casts the beggar as an object to the villagers, as he must be to them if they are to establish a relationship with him.[1]

The fault lies not in the narrator's view but in the presentation of it. He wants to replace the statesmen's view with his, a direct communication for which there is no precedent: "But deem not this Man useless—Statesmen!" (1. 67). He claims a greater validity for his perspective than for theirs, but he contradicts himself in doing so. Their perspective would be invalid if it had somehow disregarded the integrity of the object or the conditions of relationship. The narrator's transition has shown by what appropriate means the statesmen could have come to their conclusion; therefore, he undermines the authority he arrogates to himself by demonstrating in his very argument that others have as much or as little right to it as he. The narrator concludes the poem by generalizing his preferred view into a course of action that he expects others to accept and follow:

> Then let him pass, a blessing on his head!
> . . .
> May never *House*, misnamed of *Industry*,
> Make him a captive!
> . . .
> As in the eye of Nature he has lived,
> So in the eye of Nature let him die!
> (11. 162, 179-80, 196-97)

By the time readers confront these passages, they should be well-prepared to see them as enthusiastic expressions of one view. The eloquence and passion that deceive the narrator about his own authority vivify his individuality for his readers. They can consider not only how the narrator's attachment to his view leads him to close off avenues of experience but also how those barriers deprive him of continuing relationships and leave him insisting more and more on one idea.

The first-person monologue, then, challenges readers to an especially careful anatomy of the individual point of view. Appearing intermittently and variably among the poems with multiple characters, it allows Wordsworth and his readers to consider perception in as many aspects as possible. Sometimes, it even admits combinations, as in "The Forsaken Indian Woman," which gives the speaker a recognizable character identity.[2] The inclusion of the first-person monologue in the collection ought to check readers' tendency to disassemble the perspectives in the other poems, for readers should bring their experience of one piece to bear on their experience of others. The technique, however, is problematic. Crafting the single perspective remains as much an act of authorial license as manipulating interacting perspectives. The fictive persona, a product of its author's consciousness, threatens to compromise by textual existence the exclusivity of every view. Readers who note the persona's alterity from the poet can still hope to share the poet's knowledge. Readers who identify the persona with the poet face the frustration of trying to adopt an exaggeratedly individual and inadequate view, a frustration Wordsworth's first readers often displaced by criticizing the "egotism" they believed led him to impose such peculiar views on others.[3]

An effort to give credibility to the individual perspective may have been a factor in Wordsworth's turning to an autobiographical mode. If the individuality of perception invites identification of any persona with its author on the ground that all fictive views necessarily stem from the single perspective of their creator, it also invites a converse dissociation of even an autobiographical persona from its author on the ground that interpretations of the self are necessarily fictional.[4] Representing the individuality of perception through an autobiographical stance would allow Wordsworth to maintain a scrupulous fidelity to the integrity of every view. It would allow him to show readers that he works within the limits he would revalue, and it would encourage readers to see his perspective as personal rather than as privileged.

Evidence of Wordsworth's interest in the manipulation of an autobiographical persona appears in the statements he made about Burns's technique while defending that poet from an early biographer. According to Wordsworth, Burns "avail[ed] himself of his own character and situation in society, to construct out of them a poetic self,—introduced as a dramatic personage—for [a specific] purpose" (*Prose* 3: 125). Burns's "poetic character" is based on but separate from his "human character" (3: 121). Burns's effect comes from his readers' belief in the identity of the two characters:

> The momentous truth of . . . "One part must still be greatly dark,"
> &c. could not possibly be conveyed with such pathetic force by any
> poet that ever lived, speaking in his own voice, *unless it were felt*
> *that*, like Burns, he was a man who preached from the text of his
> own errors. (3: 125 emphasis added)

Wordsworth's interest in the autobiographical figure centers on its deliberate purpose. Purposive use becomes the criterion by which Wordsworth argues for the superiority of strategic revelation in Burns's poetry over gratuitous revelation in Currie's *Life of Burns*. He deplores Currie's work because he finds it to have amassed details without using them to illuminate the implied center of Burns's character around which they revolve:

> But the painful story, notwithstanding its minuteness, is incomplete
> —in essentials it is deficient; so that the most attentive and

sagacious reader cannot explain how a mind, so well established by knowledge, fell—and continued to fall, without power to prevent or retard its own ruin. (3: 119-20)

Like his remarks on genius, Wordsworth's statements about biography draw on and diverge from Johnsonian premises. In *Rambler* 60, Johnson explains the "task" of biography as the presentation of the subject's "real character," and he finds that it can accomplish this only if the biographer "select[s] the most important" specific details of the subject's life (*Works* 3: 322). He criticizes both biographers who catalogue only matters of public record and those who present public and private details exhaustively and indiscriminately. He exhorts the biographer to exercise his judgment with respect to the material known to him about his subject and to put it before his readers in such a way as to lead them to share his conclusion about the subject's "real character." Johnson thus defines the role of the biographer as that of active interpreter. Wordsworth follows Johnson in this conception of the role, as his indictment of Currie's failure as an interpreter shows. Moreover, he advises Gilbert Burns not to deny the data assembled by Currie but to supply the missing interpretive dimension (*Prose* 3: 118). Wishing a "plague on hunters after matter of fact" (3: 123), Wordsworth shares a Johnsonian abhorrence of the biographical catalogue. If Johnson objected to the catalogue approach as merely uninformative, Wordsworth feared it as potentially malicious, for in exempting the biographer from his interpretive responsibility, it gives him an excuse to contribute to mere sensationalism. Johnson's *Idler* 84 identifies "falsehood" with "useless truth," (*Works* 2: 262), and Wordsworth avows himself to be no lover of "knowledge independent of quality" (*Prose* 3: 123).

Wordsworth diverges from Johnson over the issue of unflattering revelations, a divergence that seems directly related to an insistence on the individuality of every perspective. Working from the primacy of purpose in biography, Johnson countenances the revelation of unflattering detail about a subject. As long as the information helps readers to grapple with the particular manifestation of human nature, the biographer is justified in placing society's need for knowledge above the individual's right to privacy (*Rambler* 60, *Works* 3: 323). Wordsworth acknowledges the validity of such a view within Johnson's bounds. If a biographer could seize and relate such information and surely further the general good, he should do so (*Prose* 3: 118-19). Wordsworth, however, challenges the premise within which Johnson's conclusion obtains. He denies the biographer's access to the "real character" of his subject, claiming that such access is always relative (and thus Gilbert Burns's intimacy makes him better suited than any Robert Curries to interpret Robert Burns's character), "but in no case" absolute (3: 118).

Johnson himself has doubts about the quality of a biographer's knowledge of his subject. In *Idler* 84, he writes: "What we collect by conjecture, and by conjecture only can one judge of another's motives or sentiments, is easily modified by fancy or by desire"; therefore, he supports autobiography because "the writer of his own life has at least the first qualification of an historian, the knowledge of the truth" (*Works* 2: 263). Despite awareness of the difficulties in ascertaining the subject's "real character," Johnson never gives up the idea that biography shows what is truly common to humans despite their variety, and he holds onto the idea of commonality as a means of access (3: 320). For Johnson, the biographer's impulse to overstep his place as interpreter and become creator—to add his individuality to that of the subject's and thus obscure the focus—is the principal obstacle to true knowledge of the subject and correct presentation of it, and he criticizes biographers who allow themselves "to conceal, if not to invent" (*Rambler* 60, 3: 323), who "hide the man, that [they] may produce a hero" (*Idler* 84, 2: 262). In short, Johnson requires the biographer to be active enough to analyze and interpret data but not so active as to enhance or contribute to it. The biographer who indulges in the latter modes no longer writes biography but fiction. Johnson explains the differences that he believes do and must exist between the two genres in *Idler* 84.

Wordsworth responds differently to his awareness of the uncertainty of knowledge of another. While Johnson seems troubled by it, Wordsworth seems accepting, and eventually, delighted. Johnson takes great pains to separate biography from fiction, but Wordsworth fosters the identification of the two forms:[5]

> Biography, though differing in some essentials from works of fiction, is nevertheless, like them, an *art*,—an art, the laws of which are determined by the imperfections of our nature, and the constitution of society. Truth is not here, as in the sciences, and in natural philosophy, to be sought without scruple, and promulgated for its own sake, upon the mere chance of its being serviceable; but only for obviously justifying purposes, moral or intellectual. (*Prose* 3: 121)

While Wordsworth's assessment of the limits human nature imposes on biography seems sober here, it really endorses the inventive capacity. The biographer's purpose—his active contribution—precedes even the decision to examine material for the project. In contrast, Johnson seems to require that a purpose be found given the material. Wordsworth can thus prefer what

"Horace *chooses* to communicate of himself and his friends" (3: 122 emphasis added) to any "records of the Sabine poet and his contemporaries, compounded upon the Boswellian plan" (3: 123). The former shows Horace's active intellect, while the latter does not necessarily surpass the ability to record. Moreover, Wordsworth suggests that a document of the Boswellian type might not necessarily have a purpose even if it did alter his view of classical civilization (3: 123). Wordsworth knows how his view of the classical world has served him and suspects that the thought it has fostered might be more valuable even if "inaccurate" than a random reordering of his ideas. Once again, the limits of perception foster rather than hinder the perceiver's experience.

The purposive use of personal revelations and the qualified access to another's character that animate the *Letter to a Friend of Robert Burns* likewise inform Wordsworth's private remarks about poetic personae. In general, he did not believe in monuments to poets because, he wrote to Mitchell in a letter dated April 21, 1819, their works should represent them to their readers (*MY* 2: 533-36). He was even against the publication of personal letters and agonized over the dilemma Lamb's posed. On December 16, 1835, he wrote to Henry Crabb Robinson:

> I have been very uneasy since I sent off the selection of Lamb's
> Letters, as by so doing I seem to sanction a practice, which I hold,
> for the most part, in utter detestation—viz—that of publishing the
> casual infusions (& most letters are nothing more) of men recently
> dead—I was much pleased to learn from the life of Mackintosh that
> Sir Jas Scarlet destroyed all letters but those upon business, I wish
> this to be done towards myself & I would do it towards others,

unless where I thought the Writer himself wished for their preservation. (Robinson, *Correspondence* 2: 288)

Wordsworth was equally reticent about self-revelation. A letter dated January 15, 1837 documents his resistance to Hall's idea of a biographical note of himself on the ground that, except for his birth and publications, his life represents "nothing that the world has to do with" (*LY* 2: 829).

Wordsworth's preoccupation with the manipulation of poetic identities invites speculation about his possible experimentation with such a technique in his own poetry.[6] As early as the composition of "Tintern Abbey," Wordsworth may have been experimenting with the construction of an autobiographical persona that would allow him punctilious observation of the limits of perception and thus greatly assist the enterprise of the *Lyrical Ballads*. Wordsworth's *Preface* distinguishes between poetry in which "the Poet speaks through the mouths of his characters" and poetry in which "the Poet speaks to us in his own person and character" (*Prose* 1: 142). In the context of his other comments on biographical revelation, the parallelism in the prefatory statement seems to hint at the complementarily between the two modes. In both, the poet manipulates personae. In the former, he uses one or more figures clearly other than himself. In the latter, he uses an autobiographical figure. Without denying the movingly confessional tone of the poem, one may consider "Tintern Abbey" as much a part of Wordsworth's campaign as his other contributions to *Lyrical Ballads*.[7]

The first twenty-two lines of "Tintern Abbey" actually show the persona's perspective taking shape. By "eavesdropping" on what at this point appears to be the speaker's soliloquy, the reader can witness the interplay between the individual's private cerebration and the objects of his thought that together issue in a perspective. The first object of the speaker's attention—"five years" (1. 1)—is not a feature of the natural setting but of human taxonomy. The speaker uses the abstract, artificial, and impersonal units of calendar time as devices for clarifying his perception, for he joins the common idea of years to his own idea of portions of those years as "long" (1. 2). Juxtaposing conventional time and a private sense of its passage so as to maintain the integrity of each, the speaker uses the convention to articulate his individual notion and his individual notion to inform the convention. The poem prepares the reader to see the speaker's perspective emerge through the relationships he establishes between common and independent concepts. The opening section develops by emphasizing such interaction as a primary source of ideas.

The mutually supportive relationship between conventional categories and private meaning that obtains in "five long winters" is strengthened by that phrase's inclusion of another aspect of time measurement, the seasons. Like years, summers and winters are artificial categories in general use, but they are more obviously and directly tied to natural phenomena. Since they stand for an aggregate of primarily affective natural occurrences, connotations of human interaction with the environment lie near their surfaces. As some prior relationship between observer and observed scene yielded these terms as meaningful concepts, so the speaker's sense of time and the convention of time measurement yield (or will yield as the poem unfolds) an articulable view. As his selection of one season as "long" indicates, the speaker does not turn to the seasons as fixed concepts in which to confine his thought but uses them to expand on the relationship he posited by remarking on the years. By having the speaker proceed in this way, the poem not only emphasizes the process by which the speaker's perspective will form but also suggests this process to underlie other acts of perception, even those—such as time measurement—that customarily represent shared ideas. In addition, the link between the seasons and the environment smooths the transition from the temporal meditation with which the speaker begins to the spatial observations with which he continues. Reference to the seasons focuses readers' attention on thought as the product of interaction and directs them to concentrate on that notion, retrospectively—with respect to the speaker's use of conventional measures—and prospectively—with respect to the speaker's use of landscape.

As the speaker makes an interpretive use of time measurement, so he makes an interpretive use of the physical environment. His reflections on the landscape do not convey a scientific or photographic view of it; rather, they concentrate on an individual significance. That view can emerge, however, only by a careful attention to the features observable to others. The speaker scrupulously reports his sensory activities: "I hear/ These waters" (11. 2-3); "I behold these steep and lofty cliffs" (1. 5). He identifies them as his own acts, yet he states them as acts of listening and seeing that others might also perform. The speaker then develops a unique view of the cliffs, one animated by his particular preoccupation with privacy: "I behold these steep and lofty cliffs,/ That on a wild secluded scene impress/ Thoughts of more seclusion" (11. 5-7). The statement departs not only from what other observers might conclude but even from what they might see, for cliffs do not impress thoughts.

In essence, the speaker sets up a frame for the communication of a common view, then frustrates the expectation. He substitutes a literal statement of what every view is—an individual perspective on an object that the perceiver usually assumes to be an accurate reflection, as this perceiver assumes that the cliffs impress certain thoughts. In some sense, of course, the cliffs *do* impress thoughts, for the speaker develops his sense of seclusion through his interaction with this scene. Even when informing his observations with his associations, the speaker never violates the integrity of his object. His reference to the cliffs demonstrates that individual views take form in context and not in the isolated mind, but it also shows that the context does not make the individual's perspective available for others' replication.

A few lines later, the speaker forms a view of the hedge-rows as he had formed a view of the cliffs. "I see/ These hedge-rows," he begins (11. 14-15). He follows the observation with a unique qualification, making them "hardly hedge-rows, [but] little lines/ Of sportive wood run wild" (11. 15-16). Besides reiterating and emphasizing the earlier point, the reference to the hedge-rows makes a clearer suggestion about the importance of context. Instead of immediately amalgamating his observation and association as he does in remarking on the cliffs, the speaker arrests the process. Between his observation of the hedge-rows and his resultant perspective on them, he inserts an indication of the individual perceiver beginning to act on his observation, of the perceiver realizing that the sight accessible to all is "hardly" sufficient for each.[8] Accepting that limit allows the speaker to develop and express the significance of the hedge-rows for him. By implication, a similar acceptance would allow similar freedom to other perceivers.

In addition to involving the speaker in present interaction with a scene, the opening section of "Tintern Abbey" makes that current relationship contingent upon a past one. The speaker not only reports his sensations and perceptions but repeatedly states that he is approaching a scene he has approached before. The first twenty-two lines seem to indicate that the speaker is duplicating his former perspective, but the remainder of the poem qualifies that impression.[9] From line 22 to line 57, the speaker explains the circumstances that inform the significance of his second encounter with this landscape. While away from the area, the speaker interacted with his memory of it and formed a particular perspective on it, one that balanced his perspective on his new environment. The associations of comfort, pleasure, and repose that the speaker derived from his recollections of the Tintern milieu functioned to reassure him that alternatives to the disturbing, unpleasant, and frantic new environment were available to him.

The speaker's interaction with his own memory shows that not even remembering involves replication of a perspective, for the associations with which the speaker later invests the scene differ from those with which he first approached it. Unable to duplicate his previous attitude, the speaker tries to explain it as fully as will serve to illustrate the contrast:

> For nature then
> (The coarser pleasures of my boyish days,
> And their glad animal movements all gone by)
> To me was all in all.—I cannot paint
> What then I was. The sounding cataract
> Haunted me like a passion: the tall rock,
> The mountain, and the deep and gloomy wood,
> Their colours and their forms, were then to me
> An appetite; a feeling and a love,
> That had no need of a remoter charm,
> By thought supplied, nor any interest
> Unborrowed from the eye. (11. 72-84)

Clearly, the expectations of rest and quiet that characterize the speaker's unique view of the landscape in the opening section come from his intervening experiences and not from his recollection of how the landscape used to impress him.

By making the speaker's former perspective inaccessible to him, the poem calls attention to perception as a dynamic relationship, not a replication or approximation of a "true" view. The landscape is not more accurately calming than stimulating, but it is validly one or the other for certain perceivers at certain times. To encourage readers to consider whether this variety may be advantageous, the poem has the speaker say that it is so. He comes to terms with the change in his perspective on the Tintern landscape not by ranking the relative accuracy of his new and old views but by giving preference to function over "truth":

> That time
> [when "nature . . . was all in all"] is past,
> And all its aching joys are now no more,
> And all its dizzy raptures. Not for this
> Faint I nor mourn nor murmur; other gifts
> Have followed; for such loss, I would believe,
> Abundant recompense. (11. 84-89)

Because he no longer expects objects to be "all in all," the speaker can find value in the perspective he had when he held such expectations and the perspective he has now that he does not. Seeing the individual and interactive nature of perception lets the speaker understand his own change and disposes him to continue to develop. His second experience of the landscape includes "pleasing thoughts/ That in this moment there is life and food/ For future years" (11. 63-65)—possibly because he has not had to reject a former mistaken self or a former illusory landscape. He is not embittered by the change:

> Therefore am I still
>
> A lover of the meadows and the woods,
>
> And mountains; and of all that we behold
>
> From this green earth; of all the mighty world
>
> Of eye, and ear,—both what they half create,
>
> And what perceive; well pleased to recognise
>
> In nature and the language of the sense,
>
> The anchor of my purest thoughts, the nurse,
>
> The guide, the guardian of my heart, and soul
>
> Of all my moral being. (11. 101-10)

In contrast to his description of his former attitude toward nature in terms simply of prevailing conditions ("aching joys" and "dizzy raptures," 11. 85-86), his description of his new attitude implies reciprocity. If he casts nature in the roles of "nurse," "guide," and "guardian," it follows that he casts himself in the roles responding to these nurturers. His emphasis has shifted from states of being to relationships.

With the revelation of an in-text listener at line 114, the poem explores yet another aspect of the speaker's perception. Having engaged him in interaction with phenomena and with his own memory, it now turns to his relationship with another person. Consistent with its presentation of the landscape and of the young speaker entirely from the current speaker's point of view, the poem shows only the speaker's conception of the listener he calls "Friend" and "Sister." Such a presentation does not deny her a capacity for independent perceptions of her own; rather, it emphasizes the fact that the speaker cannot share them. His view of her, like his view of the landscape and of his youth, depends upon his unique vision. His circumstances and experience lead him to align her appearance and behavior with his own former manner, which he is in the process of interpreting.

Though the speaker dwells on what he sees as her similarity to his former self (11. 116-20), he is as scrupulous in reporting this apprehension as his own perception as he had been in making the same qualification with respect to the landscape (11. 2, 5, 14): "I catch . . . and read" (11. 116-17); "I behold" (1. 119). Besides raising a parallel to the earlier part of the poem, this exactitude and emphasis follows logically from the speaker's stated rationale for addressing the listener. The speaker turns to her after he has decided that his new attitude does not require him to repudiate his previous one or to denigrate the natural objects that had figured in it (11. 101-10). As if worried by the abstractness of discovering his new perspective through interaction with memory, the speaker seems to look for tangible confirmation and to find it in his sister as he found thoughts impressing seclusion in the cliffs:

> Nor perchance,
> If I were not thus taught, should I the more
> Suffer my genial spirits to decay:
> For thou art with me . . .
>   and in thy voice I catch
> The language of my former heart, and read
> My former pleasures in the shooting lights
> Of thy wild eyes. (11. 110-19)

Continuing his speculations after he might have stopped, the speaker puts into practice the flexibility he has been contemplating. His new perspective influences his actions.

If the listener presents a challenge to the speaker's new-found flexibility, it is one to which he rises. His "prayer" (1. 121) seems less to express the hope that her view will come to replicate his than the hope that her maturation will demonstrate the compatibility of new perspectives with old. The "prayer" stems from the speaker's assumption "that Nature never did betray/ The heart that loved her" (11. 122-23), the same assumption informing his conclusion that he can remain a lover of nature despite his altered view (11. 101-10), that he need not see the old view as false nor the objects contributing to it as deceitful. Nature does not betray because it does not represent an ideal to which its perceivers should acquiesce. It does provide a means for perceivers' perspectives to form, and the speaker's prayer dwells on the hope that nature will afford such opportunity to the listener as it has to him.

Recalling his complex use of "impress" in his earlier reference to the cliffs impressing seclusion and his discovery of an implied reciprocity in his relationship with nature, the speaker's prayer teems with verbs similarly suggestive of perceptive interaction. It is nature's office to "lead," "inform," "impress," and "feed" (11. 124-27). If the personification is in a literal sense inaccurate, it is in a figurative sense exact. It stresses the importance of both perceiver and object in a relationship. Imputing activity to the object emphasizes the fact that the perceiver cannot proceed in isolation. Insofar as the perceiver's perspective is fostered by interacting with an object, the object might be said to educe the perspective.

The speaker's references to his listener's possible responses in a relationship with natural objects allow room for her independence. He hopes she will realize "that all which we behold/ Is full of blessings" (11. 133-34), an idea that suggests she will see the potential of all objects for contributing to intellectual development; he wants her mind to "be a mansion for all lovely forms" (1. 140), a wish that suggests she will possess the materials with which perspectives take shape and that the results will be pleasant for her. His open-mindedness is perhaps surprisingly confirmed by his most specific wish—that she be mindful of him:

> If solitude, or fear, or pain, or grief,
>
> Should be thy portion, with what healing thoughts
>
> Of tender joy wilt thou remember me,
>
> And these my exhortations! (11. 143-46)

As he develops this wish, he explains it to consist of recollection of their current conversation (11. 151-55) and particularly of the functional importance of the landscape and her presence for him (11. 155-59). In effect, he invites her to execute a future role reversal, to make her memory of him an object in a perceptive relationship that will foster a perspective to help her deal with a difficult situation as he now interacts with her to craft his view.

Perhaps Wordsworth posited the kinship between the speaker and listener and chose the personal mode for "Tintern Abbey" in order to enhance with affection the bond that obtains between them by the end of the poem. Though independent as perceivers, they are dependent upon each other for their future perceptions, a condition that emphasizes the complementarity between perceiver and perceived. The poem leaves the speaker asking for assurance that his new view is viable and makes the listener capable of providing that assurance only through her own independence and integrity. The poem brings them to the threshold of a new development but does not realize it; instead, it allows it to remain a pleasant possibility.

Despite the advantages of the autobiographical mode for a poet dedicated to observing the limits of perception, the technique remains open to interpretation as self-indulgent. Readers committed to consensus will not easily believe in the existence of a non-coercive perspective, and Wordsworth seems to have devoted his ensuing literary career to looking for a technique that would allow for a non-threatening and non-contradictory presentation of the individual point of view as a viable alternative to the cherished but chimerical ideal of shared knowledge. Privately, Wordsworth continued to mine the autobiographical vein in what became *The Prelude*;[10] publicly, he adapted the mode to the even more daring exaggeration of a personal view integral to his next major publication, the *Poems, in Two Volumes* of 1807.

Chapter 6
Categories and Sequences

The two volumes of poems Wordsworth published in 1807 show his increasing technical virtuosity and his continuing preoccuption with the empirical dilemma. The volumes consisted of lyrics, sonnets, and an ode. Some of the lyrics and sonnets were grouped in special ways while others were not. The first volume began with undesignated lyrics, but then presented some as "Poems Composed on a Tour, Chiefly on Foot"; similarly, it first presented some "miscellaneous" sonnets but followed them with a group "dedicated to Liberty." The second volume grouped thirteen lyrics under the category "Moods of my Own Mind," and this section represents a further development in Wordsworth's use of a personal stance to preserve the limits of perception. As his letter dated May 21, 1807 to Lady Beaumont indicates, he gave the section a unified aim:

> Turn to the "Moods of my own Mind." There is scarcely a Poem here of above thirty Lines, and very trifling these poems will appear to many; but, omitting to speak of them individually, do they not, taken collectively, fix the attention upon a subject eminently poetical, viz., the interest which objects in nature derive from the predominance of certain affections more or less permanent, more or less capable of salutary renewal in the mind of the being contemplating these objects? This is poetic, and essentially poetic, and why? because it is creative. (*MY* 1: 147)

The category makes the individuality of perception a *donnée* of the thirteen lyrics. It frees Wordsworth to use their limited space for a compressed presentation of an individual's associations, and it frees readers to concentrate on the function of the associations for the speakers' views. Examination of two of the lyrics should elucidate their pattern.

Though any of the thirteen lyrics could be singled out, "To the Cuckoo" clearly represents Wordsworth's technique.[1] The first two stanzas establish a relationship between the speaker and the cuckoo, a relationship that the rest of the poem develops and reflects on:

> O Blithe New-comer! I have heard,
>
> I hear thee and rejoice.
>
> O Cuckoo! shall I call thee Bird,
>
> Or but a wandering Voice?
>
>
> While I am lying on the grass
>
> Thy two fold shout I hear,
>
> From hill to hill it seems to pass,
>
> At once far off, and near.

These two stanzas define the condition of the experience. They depict it as an actual incident in which the speaker was in a particular attitude and setting ("lying on the grass") listening to a particular cuckoo. Bird and man pursue specific and characteristic activities, the bird singing and the man listening, and they play complementary roles, the bird's voice capturing the man's attention and the man responding ("I hear thee and rejoice"). The relationship depends upon the integrity of the object, yet it triggers an associative process that allows the speaker to move beyond the present situation.

The speaker isolates the voice of this one cuckoo as the characteristic that compels him in this situation. He notes that the sound of its voice is not unique to it but common to all cuckoos—other cuckoos that exist in other places at the same time and other cuckoos that have existed in the past. By means of the sound, he connects the cuckoo present to him in this time and place, together with his immediate occupation of listening and rejoicing, to other cuckoos absent from this specific scene but present to him at other times and places and to which he listened and responded with joy. The speaker's awareness of the commonalty allows the present cuckoo and the present incident to include past cuckoos and past incidents. The actual change in location of the source of the present cuckoo's sound as it flies invisibly "from hill to hill" becomes emblematic of the past experiences included in the present one, experiences that are, like the voice, "far off" (in the past) and "near" (present) and "seem" so "at once" by virtue of the intellectual connection.

Working from the literal nature of the cuckoo, the speaker evokes "a tale of visionary hours" (1. 12), "visionary" seeming a bit ironic since the past experiences he refers to were those he had as a child when he looked for a cuckoo that he could only hear:

> The same [cuckoo] whom in my school-boy days
> I listened to; that Cry
> Which made me look a thousand ways
> In bush, and tree, and sky.
>
> To seek thee did I often rove
> Through woods and on the green;
> And thou wert still a hope, a love;
> Still longed for, never seen. (11. 17-24)

Surprisingly, perhaps, the adult does not resume the search. Instead, he replicates the exclusively aural experience—"And I can listen to thee yet;/ Can lie upon the plain/ And listen" (11. 25-27). In doing so, he engages in a creative activity—"And I can listen . . . til I do beget/ That golden time again" (11. 27-28). His non-ironic "visionary hours" reanimate the whole happy and naive juvenile view of reality embodied in his relationship with the cuckoo. By concentrating on the one element common to past and present experiences— the sound of the voice—the speaker adds a current, adult experience of joy to the childhood experiences of the same that sprang from the single element:

> O blessed Bird! the earth we pace
> Again appears to be
> An unsubstantial, faery place;
> That is fit home for Thee! (11. 29-32)

The speaker does not lose his adult identity and perception and replace them with his youthful sensibilities; he remembers the past and makes use of it in the present for the future. Perhaps it is in tribute to this outcome that the cuckoo is heralded as "thrice welcome" (1. 13)—welcome for the present incident it brings about, for the evocation of the past it makes possible, and for the realization of a heightened perception the past and present together imply. As Woodring explains:

> When the cuckoo's cry makes the earth again seem an "unsub-
> stantial, faery place," it is not merely the child's sense of secure
> delight at the unknown that is restored, but faith that somewhere
> the adult will find for his spirit a substantial, permanent home.
> (*Wordsworth* 75)

The speaker benefits from interacting with the cuckoo not because he increases his knowledge of the cuckoo but because he increases his capacity as a perceiver. His activity "beget[s]" a world view that enables him to deal with change in himself and in his environment. It takes control of and orders reality.

If readers see "To the Cuckoo" as one example of how a mind orders reality, they take a step toward revaluing the limits of perception. The limits can no longer appear unqualifiedly disadvantageous to readers aware of how the limits foster their comprehension of the poem. As the cuckoo stands apart from the speaker, accessible only through the relationship the speaker establishes with it, so the poem stands apart from its reader, accessible only through interpretation. The poem's highly individuated point of view is as alien to the reader as is the cuckoo's song to the speaker. Reader and speaker make sense of the respective foreign objects by locating them among their other experiences of reality and assigning them meaningful functions. The process is empirical; the result, more of an enrichment than a dilemma.

Although Wordsworth proceeds by the same technique in the other twelve lyrics, he does not merely multiply one perspective.[2] He distinguishes the figures from each other, sometimes individuating them with disturbing characteristics. For example, the speaker in "Gipsies" is an insecure figure whose statements show, in effect, the process of stigmatization from the point of view of one executing it. He begins to establish a relationship with the Gipsies by concentrating on one observable characteristic, their fixity:

> Yet are they here the same unbroken knot
> Of human beings, in the self-same spot!
> Men, women, children, yea the frame

Of the whole spectacle the same! (11. 1-4)

He continues by contrasting the Gipsies' immobility with others' activity—his own (11. 9-12) and that which he imputes to the personified sun (1. 13), planet Venus (1. 14-16), moon (11. 17-21), and uncounted stars (11. 23-24). The development shows the speaker's anxiety to distance himself from the Gipsies and align himself with natural forces. Another observer might have construed the Gipsies' condition as symbolic of constancy and valued it as virtuous or, like Coleridge, assumed it to be restful and decided it to be deserved.[3] Something in this speaker's experience causes him to see it as "torpid" (1. 22) and judge it to be reprehensible.

The insistent contrasts with which the speaker characterizes the Gipsies as inert and unnatural and himself as active and natural suggest that he needs this perspective to justify himself in some way. A close look at his own activity reveals it as nebulously defined:

—Twelve hours, twelve bounteous hours
    are gone, while I
Have been a traveller under open sky,
    Much witnessing of change and cheer,
    Yet as I left I find them here! (11. 9-12)

The speaker has been mobile but not necessarily interactive. He has observed the activities of others but apparently not participated in them. In that case, the similarity between his situation and the Gipsies' could be developed as easily as the dissimilarity. The speaker's preconceived aversion to torpor closes off the former avenue to him and leads him to exploit the latter.

In order to protect his self-image, the speaker must assure himself that his life is active and meaningful. He accomplishes this by setting up a norm in nature that mirrors his own behavior. As he characterizes them, the heavenly bodies all exhibit the same pattern of moving and watching that the speaker executes on his twelve hour journey. Having manufactured this standard, the speaker labels the Gipsies as deviant from it:

> —oh better wrong and strife
> (By nature transient) than this torpid life;
> Life which the very stars reprove
> As on their silent tasks they move!
>
> (11. 21-24)

The imputation of purposiveness to the stars' appearance extends that value to the speaker's parallel behavior. The transference of disapproval from himself to the stars gives authority to his censure, making his opinion seem objective rather than compensatory.

The speaker's tactic succeeds in comforting him about his own behavior, for it allows him to pass from disapprobation to a kind of magnanimity. "In scorn I speak not" (1. 26) he states, after he has spoken scornfully. He continues: "—they are what their birth/ And breeding suffer them to be;/ Wild outcasts of society" (11. 26-28). His conclusion misses the mark with respect to fact but lands on target with respect to point of view. The status of outcast is not an absolute condition to which a group is born and bred. It is a role created for a group by a larger society in order to reinforce the coherence of the larger collective in some way. (Once the role has been created, of course, future members of the group can be born and bred to it in the sense that they cannot generally escape from it.) In order to make the sub-group functional, the larger society does not acknowledge the factitiousness of the deviant status or admit its own agency in crafting the role. The dominant society assumes the

deviant characteristics to be absolute faults which it does not share and from
which it must protect itself. If the dominant group is securely distanced from
the outcasts, its collective attitude toward them could be one of complacent
condescension, the attitude expressed in the conclusion by the speaker toward
the Gipsies.

The poem emphasizes the function for the speaker of his relationship
with the Gispies as object. Its presentation of his unqualified perspective
shows readers how the speaker reassures himself of his use in society, a
reassurance that lets security temper the speaker's judgment. But through the
single point of view, the poem also shows the illusoriness of the status the
speaker construes as absolute and alerts readers to the danger of merely
accepting the speaker's perspective. His unmistakable self-righteousness—like
the exaggerated optimism of the speaker in "To the Cuckoo"—erects a barrier
between him and readers that prevents them from becoming too involved with
the in-text perspective, encouraging them instead to bring their own perspectives to bear on the text. The poem lets readers step aside from the process
of labelling in which they would usually engage with the certainty of the
speaker and see it for what it is. The poem neither hides nor denies the
distasteful aspects of the process—the speaker's narrowness and the irrelevance
of the Gipsies' point of view. Rather, it reproduces them as conditions that
obtain and leaves it to readers to speculate further.

Paradoxically, the very provocativeness of "Gipsies" serves as a pledge
of good faith between Wordsworth and his readers. By acknowledging the
darker dimension of the individual point of view, he assures them that he is
not blind to the difficulties the limits of perception entail but commited
nonetheless to working with them to solve the empirical dilemma.

Furthermore, by juxtaposing this example of an individual perspective with others, Wordsworth shows that he is genuinely calling for an investigation of a new epistemology and not surreptitiously advocating idealization of the individual in lieu of idealization of consensus. The mutually qualifiying short forms that constitute "Moods of My Own Mind" ratify Wordsworth's pledge. Because of their undefined interdependence, Wordsworth can use the pieces to capture the range and complexity of individual perceptions without offering them as a comprehensive system. He thus fulfills the office of the poet, which is to make insight into the matter possible for readers, without usurping the office of the reader, which is to derive the consequences of the newly available material. "Moods of My Own Mind" provides readers with a starting point from which to examine how individuals interact with their environments—their social environments as well as their natural environments and their private mental environments. Conclusions drawn as a result of applications made in consequence of that examination fall outside the province of the poems, though they have their provenance in them. By qualifying the perspectives of the speakers in "To the Cuckoo," "Gipsies," and the other lyrics, and allowing them to qualify each other, readers of "Moods of My Own Mind" begin to see the full import of the limits of perception and gain the vantage they need to confront the empirical dilemma.

After publishing the 1807 volumes, Wordsworth worked on a more extensive scheme of categorization. In a letter dated May 5, 1809 to Coleridge, Wordsworth proposed a plan for a collected edition of his works in which the poems would be grouped so as to emphasize mental activity. This broad designation for the gist of the undertaking is faithful to the import with which Wordsworth seems to have packed the plan. Though comprised of apparently heterogeneous classes such as those relating to ages of human life and those relating to emotions, the categories share a preoccupation with aspects of perception. For example, the "Poems relating to Childhood" focus on the "dawn of the affections or faculties" (*MY* 1: 334). By approaching abstract thought processes through diverse human contexts—especially contexts, such as childhood, that readers would tend not to construe as representing an outlook they should replicate—Wordsworth ties perception to the circumstances of the perceiver. But the categorization does more than point out mental activity represented in the poems. According to Wordsworth's summary of his aims, it must also provoke readers to mental activity in relation to the poems:

> The principle of the arrangement is that . . . each poem should be
> so placed as to direct the Reader's attention by its position to its
> *primary* interest. (*MY* 1: 336)

From early in its history, then, Wordsworth's categorization had a dual emphasis on mental activity—on the range of it displayed in the poems and on the range of it stimulated by the poems. The scheme seems to be a compromise between the two problematic techniques of personal stance and characterized perspectives. Like Wordsworth's previous variations, the development of his categories suggests an attempt both to stay within the given limits of perception and to accommodate readers' objections to modes of representing those limits. Readers generally objected to "Moods of My Own Mind" as self-indulgent.[4] Wordsworth invented categories that could less easily be construed as egotistical.

Six years after its epistolary conception, Wordsworth's plan issued in an edition presenting his poems through a method of classification similar to the one detailed in the letter. Wordsworth's *Preface* to the 1815 edition identifies the classifications as an integral part of his poetic endeavor. In effect, it describes them as response-inviting structures designed to stimulate readers to explore perception through the poems. Thus, it aligns Wordsworth's activity in classifying the poems with his activity in writing them.[5] In both instances, he engaged in the invention of similar response-inviting structures. Like the categories proposed in the letter, the categories in the published edition are apparently various,[6] a variety that the *Preface* identifies as deliberate:

> Poems, apparently miscellaneous, may with propriety be arranged either with reference to the powers of mind *predominant* in the production of them; or to the mould in which they are cast; or, lastly to the subjects to which they relate. From each of these considerations, the following Poems have been divided into classes; which, that the work may more obviously correspond with the course of human life, and for the sake of exhibiting in it the three requisites of a legitimate whole, a beginning, a middle, and an end, have been also arranged, as far as it was possible, according to an order of time, commencing with Childhood, and terminating with Old Age, Death, and Immortality. (*Prose* 3: 28)

By employing a range of classes, Wordsworth discourages the idea that there is one absolutely desirable arrangement for the poems. This discouragement is built up from and reinforced on the level of the individual texts in the canon by Wordsworth's characterizing the classes as "predominantly" (and not perfectly) indicative of the pieces they contain. The diffuseness of the scheme allows it to suggest something of the poems' potential to readers, potential that readers must realize in their own ways, and it prevents it from offering an interpretation for readers collectively to embrace.

The subsumption of classes referring to intellection, genre, and topic within categories representing the idea of a "whole" and, specifically, the "whole" of human life, suggests an attempt to make the scheme display conditions of perceiving. As the 1809 letter shows, reference to time of life can be one way to individuate a perspective. The arrangement brings the spectrum of age-oriented categories, suggestive of perceivers, to bear on genre- and topic- oriented categories, suggestive of conventions and objects with which perceivers interact. Thus, the scheme reflects an aggregate of individual perceivers engaged in various cerebrations as developed in the separate poems.

Lest its layers of categories privilege the importance of the perceiver over the integrity of the object, certain qualifications balance its striation. The age-oriented structure that implies individual contributions to perception is itself informed by preconceptions. It is most obviously restricted by the conventional idea that a "whole" is necessary and desirable, a conventionality that Wordsworth's use of "requisites" and "legitimate" emphasizes. In addition, the age categories are themselves conventions, the products of customary labelling of people. The same overarching structure that represents individuation is itself disturbingly bound by convention.

That the apparent contradiction is deliberate and awaiting readers' attention is supported by the appearance of "Immortality" among the age categories. The concept of immortality stems from more than the observation of physical characteristics by which the other markers for times of life may be defined. It requires certain philosophical assumptions. The equivalency posited between the immortality category and the age categories calls for a reexamination of all categories—such as those of age and completeness—taken for granted in everyday use. If one such concept, immortality, rests on complex premises about which not everyone would agree, then other symbols of shared ideas may be likewise less uniform than unthinking use supposes. This condition does not unfit categories for individual use; it merely unsuits them to replace individual with group experience.

Allocation of individual and group claims in the taxonomic structure suggests that categories arise from individual perceptions to serve specific purposes of clarifying and representing and, once expressed, remain as a store of experience to govern other perceptions. The structure, like the act of perceiving it represents, is predicated on the dynamics of its components. The scheme embodies perception as an infinitely occurring interaction between perceivers and their posited objects.

As if reiterating that the categorization does not purport to be a comprehensive view of human life to which passive assent is solicited, the *Preface* presents the classifications as primarily thought-provoking:

> I trust . . . the arrangement will serve as a commentary unosten-
> tatiously directing [the reader's] attention to my purposes, both
> particular and general. (*Prose* 3: 28)

Having already pointed out the multiplicity of the groupings, Wordsworth continues to dwell on their fluidity:

> But, as I wish to guard against the possibility of misleading by this
> classification, it is proper first to remind the Reader, that certain
> poems are placed according to the powers of mind, in the Author's
> conception, predominant in the production of them; *predominant*,
> which implies the exertion of other faculties in less degree. Where
> there is more imagination than fancy in a poem, it is placed under
> the head of imagination, and *vice versa*. Both the above classes

> might without impropriety have been enlarged from that consisting
> of "Poems founded on the Affections;" as might this latter from
> those, and from the class "proceeding from Sentiment and
> Reflection." The most striking characteristics of each piece,
> mutual illustration, variety, and proportion, have governed me
> throughout. (3: 28-29)

Insisting merely on the predominance of characteristics, expounding upon the possible reshaping of categories, and alluding to the potential of each class to qualify another, Wordsworth seems determined to raise his readers' curiosity sufficiently to force them to engage with each text and with the canon in order to satisfy it. Even if readers are tempted to cede their judgments to a perspective in a particular poem, they should be nudged out of contentment with that view by the necessity of relating it to the larger structure.

With the 1815 volumes, Wordsworth comes closer than ever before to the heart of the philosophical issue. The 1815 edition evidences an explicit preoccupation with perception not only in its categorization but also in its *Preface*, which contains Wordsworth's longest statement about the imagination. By directly addressing one of the most pressing philosophical concepts of his era (Engell 6), Wordsworth locates his work within the theoretical controversy. Characteristically, Wordsworth's treatment of imagination departs from the dominant trend of making that faculty a means to transcend the limits of individual natures;[7] Wordsworth's treatment concentrates on the imagination's capacity to exploit those very limits.

Wordsworth's imagination effects relationships between a perceiver and a given object of his perception in a way that maintains the integrity of both perceiver and object. Wordsworth explains:

These processes of imagination are carried on either by conferring additional properties upon an object, or abstracting from it some of those which it actually possesses, and thus enabling it to re-act upon the mind which hath performed the process, like a new existence. (*Prose* 3: 32)

Exercise of the imagination gives the perceiver an expanded understanding of the object, one so much enriched that the object seems to be a "new existence." That new appearance depends upon the relationship, upon the action of the mind upon the object and the reaction of the object upon the mind.

The relationship begins because of the perceiver's individual experience. Without some unique vision, the perceiver would have no source of properties to confer and no disposition to seize on a quality to abstract. In short, the perceiver would have no means of seeing the object as significant. He would be reduced to hoping to see the object as others see or saw it, an impossibility on at least two counts—first of all, because perspectives cannot be completely shared, and secondly, because no one else could have achieved a significant view of the object unless this perceiver is abnormal. Alternatively, all perceivers would have to have the same view of the object, a view that it somehow absolutely requires. Given the inadequacy of all these shared plans, individuality can be construed as a source of knowledge.

Just as the relationship cannot obtain without the integrity of the perceiver, so it cannot obtain without the integrity of the object. Without the integrity of the object, the perceiver has no new element to consider, nothing to spur him beyond the view he already has. This circumstance may account for a certain paradox in Wordsworth's depiction of the imagination. As Owen points out, Wordsworth sometimes portrays the imagination as passive, as if he "conceived of a recipient faculty which . . . takes in the external environment" ("Imaginations" 220).   Owen's method of using Coleridge's theory of imagination as a "control" (321) leads him to explain Wordsworth's conception as justifiably confused (222), but a method beginning with Wordsworth's theory in its own right might arrive at a more purposive interpretation.   If the imagination is the faculty of relationship, then it must accord equal importance to projecting impressions onto an object and receiving them from it.   Consequently, the faculty might be represented in active and passive modes so as to indicate the complementarity.

Wordsworth's prefatory remarks on imagination not only alert readers to the conception of that faculty figuring in some of the poems but also dispose them to engage their own imaginations.   As Owen additionally notes, Wordsworth seems not to "discriminate between the functions of Imagination in acts of commonplace perception . . . and of aesthetic creation" ("Imaginations" 222).   Owen concedes that Wordsworth's indiscrimination may indicate that "he is intent on elevating the act of perception, the meaningful interrelation of man's mind with the environment, to the status of artistic creation" (222); nevertheless, he concludes that the indiscrimation is a flaw in Wordsworth's theory.   Again, this conclusion seems to stem from Coleridge's "control."   It would, in fact, be inconsistent of Wordsworth to make perceiving and imagining, reading and writing, activities of different orders and values.[8] In contrast, it is perfectly consistent of him to send readers into the 1815 edition with the assurance that their activity is as legitimate and vital as his, that their activity, in essence, completes his.

If Wordsworth's theory of imagination is not very thoroughly expounded in the *Preface*, it may be because he did not see the privileging of this faculty as the ultimate way to address his concerns. He seems rather to have included it as a topical reference that might help his readers to understand the larger issue of perception of which it is a part. It would have been consistent of him to resist making the matter of perception contingent upon the technical aspects of faculty psychology that so often complicated his contemporaries' theories of imagination.[9] Wordsworth's treatment suggests that perception can be—but need not be—understood in terms of the operation of the imagination. By locating that faculty among other concentrations in his categorization, he leaves open the possibility that readers can become self-conscious about their mental activity without embracing a theory.

By all indications, the edition of 1815 was not a mere editing of old work but a shaping of something new. Policies against noticing reappearances of previously published work kept the volumes off reviewers' desks (Hayden 91) and no doubt played a role in the neglect the edition suffered; however, the slighting of the categorization by those who did remark on the edition cannot have been likewise fortuitous. Most tellingly, the writer for the *Quarterly Review* addressed the *Preface* and the *Essay, Supplementary* for the stated purpose of reiterating old differences with Wordsworth and did not even directly mention the arrangement of the poems. Thus alerted to readers' continuing suspicions of epistemological self-reliance, Wordsworth seems to have redirected his efforts. His later work does not so much provoke readers' responses as obviate their defences by reassuring them that valuing individuation does not require repudiating all forms, systems, conventions and publications with the engaging potential of mutually qualifying short forms, Wordsworth enlisted the sonnet sequence in his campaign.

The genre is well-suited to the task. The separation and concision of each sonnet within a sequence conduces easily to presentation of a compressed point of view without implying an overly personal dimension. Thus, the sonnet resists the taint of egotism to which other attempts at distancing the lyric—such as that of "Moods of my Own Mind"—were predisposed.[10] The flexible structure of the sequence allows for the suggestion of a controlling consciousness beneath seemingly random perceptions without including connections that imply an authoritative view. Thus, it throws readers back on their own resources to unify the poems. Finally, the juxtaposition of sonnets within the sequence accommodates replication of the associative quality of thought and individuation of perspective.

In adition to generic advantages, the sonnet and the sonnet sequence offered Wordsworth a way to concentrate on the relations produced in consequence of the limits of perception. Wordsworth's careful incorporation of the traditional form into his own poetics shows the coexistence of independent thought with inherited and widely-accepted ideas. As Lee M. Johnson's study details, Wordsworth reached back through a century of disfavor to revive the sonnet.[11] Upon doing so, he followed Milton in preferring the Petrarchan to the Shakespearean style and went beyond Milton to the greater integration of the volta with which he (Wordsworth) is traditionally credited. Wordsworth's independent contribution to the form calls to mind his statement in the *Essay, Supplementary to the Preface* of 1815 that every original writer draws from and adds to tradition as he finds it.[12] More broadly, it shows that the limits of perception rely on received ideas, requiring only that

that the limits of perception rely on received ideas, requiring only that perceivers recognize such ideas for what they are, i.e., agreed upon means of ordering and articulating a given aspect of reality. Neither intrinsically good nor bad, they are potentially useful. They benefit individuals who make them objects in a perceptual relationship; they stifle those who surrender independent judgment to them. Individuals may ultimately decide to preserve a given system or convention. As long as it is a thoughtful decision, it does not compromise their integrity. An emphasis on the use of familiar concepts counteracts fear of individual perception as isolating by suggesting that a new understanding of community should follow from a genuine examination of the new epistemology.

Wordsworth wrote two complete sonnet sequences, *The River Duddon* and *Ecclesiastical Sonnets* (although the latter was first published as *Ecclesiastical Sketches*, with the sonnets in the company of other poems).[13] Of the form of *Ecclesiastical Sonnets*, Wordsworth explains:

> For the convenience of passing from one point of the subject to another without shocks of abruptness, this work has taken the shape of a series of Sonnets: but the Reader, it is to be hoped, will find that the pictures are often so closely connected as to have jointly the effect of passages of a poem in a form of stanza to which there is no objection but one that bears upon the Poet only—its difficulty. (*Poetical Works* 3: 557)

Although the phrasing is common, it is suggestive in light of the rest of the canon. That Wordsworth hopes the reader will find the poems connected calls to mind the reader's role in the work. In addition, it confirms the absence of a perspective in the poem to convey those connections by authority. The reader can connect them, of course, because of the poet's strategy, but the strategy is not a perspective in the text.

Study of either sequence would be rewarding, but for purposes of economy I confine myself to one. I address *Ecclesiastical Sonnets* because of its unusual repertoire. *The River Duddon* draws its repertoire from rustic nature, as do many of Wordsworth's poems; *Ecclesiastical Sonnets* draws its repertoire from church history, an unprecedented source in the canon. That church history is the repertoire and not the subject of the sequence should be clear from the first sonnet, which compares this sequence to the earlier one. Wordsworth had traced the course of a physical river; now he would trace the course of an intellectual one. In drawing attention to the metaphor of the stream, the first sonnet encourages readers to recall how Wordsworth used the literal stream in *The River Duddon*. Clearly, the stream itself was not the point at issue.

Wordsworth had prefaced the earlier sequence with a note calling attention to a convention of descriptive poetry and to the variety of uses the river trope could serve:

> The power of waters over the minds of Poets has been acknowl-
> edged from the earliest ages;—through the "flumina amem
> sylvasque inglorius" of Virgil down to the sublime apostrophe to
> the great rivers of the earth, by Armstrong, and the simple
> ejaculation of Burns. (*Poetical Works* 3: 504)

The vehicle of the river had been a constant that had never fused the tenors in these various poems, just as his (Wordsworth's) own use of it would not compromise Coleridge's plans for "The Brook" (*Poetical Works* 3: 503). Wordsworth addresses the vehicle at some length but never the tenors, for deriving those is the office of each reader. If the poet inserts systematic explanations into his own kind of writing, he robs it of the unique characteristics that enable it to expand readers' perspectives. Wordsworth seems to be pushing readers toward realization of this point in his attention to the river metaphors and to the poetic license of claiming that the survey of the river was accomplished in one day:

> No one believes or is desired to believe, that those Poems were
> actually composed within such limits of time; nor was there any
> reason why a prose statement should acquaint the reader with the
> plain fact to the disturbance of poetic credibility. (*Poetical Works*
> 3: 503)

On one level, this introduction to Wordsworth's long preoccupaton with the subject frees him from accusations of poaching on Coleridge's territory; on another and more important one, it directs readers to take the river as the repertoire and not the subject of the poem and disposes them to consider the purpose for which the trope has been employed.

The reference in *Ecclesiastical Sonnets* to *The River Duddon*, then, should send readers into the new sequence with the idea that something underlies the literal or ostensible subject of the sequence. The analogy it makes between the two sequences should overcome the temptation to assume that a conceptual repertoire is somehow different from a phenomenal one. Twenty years before the appearance of this sequence, Dorothy Wordsworth had explained in the form of general advice to Mary and Sara Hutchinson the poem that became "Resolution and Independence": "above all, never think that [Wordsworth] writes for no reason but merely because a thing happened" (*EY* 367). Clearly Wordsworth did not write about church history merely because it happened.

The Fenwick Note attests to a subordination of fact to effort. It records Wordsworth's apology for the lack of documentation to support the story that Pope Alexander publically humiliated the Emperor Barbarossa and includes his instructions to readers to "substitute for it an undeniable truth not less fitted for my purpose, namely, the penance inflicted by Gregory the Seventh upon the Emperor Henry the Fourth" (*Poetical Works* 3: 557).

Wordsworth's purpose has been variously construed. Gates argues that "through selection, misapprehension, and limited symbolism," Wordsworth systematically misrepresented events in order "to illustrate morality [rather] than to give a realistic account of the church's politico-ecclesiastical history" (129). More broadly, Lee M. Johnson posits that Wordsworth saw history subsumed by mutability (145-46). Alternatively, Wordsworth's purpose in *Ecclesiastical Sonnets* can be located with respect to the empirical dilemma. Drawing on a topic as tightly bound up with belief as is church history, Wordsworth makes a deliberate challenge to independent thought. He extends the idea that familiar concepts can be independently examined even to the area of religion while he raises the possiblity that community can exist only through individual relationships, a possibility he makes comforting by representing it in the constant symbol of Anglicanism.

Wordsworth's idea of individual perception seems to have informed his ideas about religious institutions more than religious beliefs seem to have affected his notion of perception. His prose statements on the Catholic Relief Question, collected by Christopher Wordsworth in the *Memoirs*, indicate that he feared Roman Catholicism because it repressed the individual and that he endorsed the Church of England because it protected the individual: Romanism . . . by its slavish spirit, makes the people more manageable. . . . It is essentially at enmity with light and knowledge" (2: 139-41). In contrast, Wordsworth wrote: "The Church of England as to the point of private judgment, standing between the two extremes of Popery and Dissent, is entitled to heartfelt reverence" (2: 142). Wordsworth's concern for individual freedom within the community is perhaps best illustrated by the following passage:

> It is, we trust, the intention of Providence that the Church of Rome should in due time disappear; and *come what may of the Church of England*, we have the satisfaction of knowing, that in defending a government resting upon a Protestant basis, . . . we are working for the welfare of human kind, and supporting whatever there is of dignity in our frail nature. (2: 150 emphasis added)[14]

Even if Wordsworth were personally committed to the Church of England, the nature of his poetic campaign makes it unlikely that he would have written *Ecclesiastical Sonnets* merely to endorse the Church as an institution. He is more likely to have begun with fundamental concerns, which he could manifest through reference to institutions that touch on them.

In essence, *Ecclesiastical Sonnets* explores the effects of belief. The repertoire of the poem, church history, in reality encompasses thousands of individuals in numerous locales. In the new context of the poem, it is reduced to the control of the persona who surveys it to make sense of it. From the beginning, individual judgment is privileged. The view of church history that the persona presents through the poem focuses on the struggle of individual belief against group-imposed substitutes. The Church of England represents the former; pagan rites, Papal abuses, and Protestant extremisms variously represent the latter. The poem does not endorse a set of beliefs so much as it holds up the individual act of faith as a good, celebrates the benefits of exercising it, and shows the consequences of surrendering it.

The poem does not systematically examine the nature of the objects of faith just as earlier poems do not theorize about the nature of objects apart from the way they are perceived. The objects are subordinate to the process of growing in relation to them. Readers need not adopt a view of Anglicanism from the poems just as they need not assent to any view of a landscape or character.[15] In fact, readers' religious convictions could interfere with their appreciation of the poems if faith makes them reluctant to subject their beliefs to the theme-and-horizon structure of reading. One is reminded of Wordsworth's statement in the *Essay, Supplementary to the Preface* of 1815 that "men who read from religious or moral inclination, even when the subject is of that kind which they approve," somehow miss the point of poetry (*Prose* 3: 64-65). The reader of *Ecclesiastical Sonnets* above all must become increasingly adept at recognizing systematic encroachments upon individual judgment and prevailing against them.

After the introductory sonnet, the sequence takes up the matter of church history with a series of questions about who first brought Christianity to England. For a sequence detailing church history, this is a weak beginning; for a sequence addressing individual belief, a strong one. It deflects attention away from the church as a massive and externally defined institution and directs the reader to think about it in fundamental terms. The sonnet depicts the putative founders as engaged in natural activity. In some way, they contribute to the courses of active waters that represent their faith: "Did holy Paul a while in Britain dwell,/ And call the Fountain forth by miracle,/ And with dread signs the nascent stream invest?" (11. 6-8). Or, did "some of humbler name" first begin "to guard/ The precious Current they had taught to flow?" (11. 13-14). The founders are recognized by their activity, not by fixed identity. Their faith is defined as a vital principle, not an institution. The founding of the church consists in the establishment of a relationship between individual believers and the source of faith as object. If the sonnet cannot supply its readers' historical curiosity, it can shift their interest from fact to concept. It prompts a reconsideration of the founding of the church in the individual act of faith rather than in the erection of buildings or the regularization of practice.[16] In those terms, the identity of the founders becomes irrelevant, subsumed by the relationship on which both perceiver and object depend.

Consistently throughout *Ecclesiastical Sonnets*, Wordsworth uses natural imagery to represent the "true"—i.e. appropriately individual and relational—faith and alienation from or aberration of the environment to show impediments to it. The sequence follows the struggle of individual belief to maintain its integrity. The pattern first emerges in the third sonnet, the "Trepidation of the Druids." In contrast to the fluidity of the early Christian organization, Druidism appears fixedly institutionalized. It has a hierarchy and a division of labor, as evidenced by references to the "Arch-druid" (1.1), the "Augurs" (1. 3), and the "Bard" (1.8). It is highly ritualistic, a characteristic on which the sonnet dwells. It first captures the Druids at "the mystic ring/ Where Augurs stand, the Future questioning" (11. 2-3) and continues:

> Slowly the cormorant aims her heavy flight,
> Portending ruin to each baleful rite
> That, in the lapse of ages, hath crept o'er
> Diluvian truths, and patriarchal lore. (11. 4-7)

The portrait of Druidism is not one of inherent evil but of religion *manqué*. Apparently, it gained ascendency over a more basic way of making sense out of the environment, a way represented by "Diluvian truths, and patriarchal lore."

Reference to the flood should summon from the reader's horizon all the references to active waters from the previous sonnet. Its appearance here with "truths" should reinforce its position as signifying a good. The plurality of "truths" stemming from one source in turn reinforces the individuality of belief. "Patriarchal lore" emphasizes the human, interactive dimension. The "lore" is something developed and guarded by fathers, i.e., with human effort and in human relationships. "Lore" itself signifies knowledge gained in a student-teacher relationship, again, through human interaction.[17]   The Druids now stand alienated from this natural and basic approach to reality. They have replaced patriarchal relationships with artificial ones, and they seek knowledge through a "mystic ring" instead of from the environment and the human community. The sonnet emphasizes their alienation by showing their obliviousness to birds: a sea-mew "screams round the Arch-druid's brow" (1. 1); a cormorant forebodes their doom (11. 4-5). Ironically, a note points out that the sea-mew was "an emblem of those traditions connected with the Deluge" (*Poetical Works* 3: 342). It now calls unheeded. The cormorant, it is also noted, "was a bird of bad omen" (3: 342). The natural object has been superseded by an arbitrary, superstitious significance. No interaction occurs between the birds and Druids. The Druids have become too intent on ritualistic behavior, which they have divorced from the environment, to engage in it. This attachment leads the Bard to dismiss non-ritualistic Christianity as unthreatening: "Haughty the Bard: can these meek doctrines blight/ His transports? wither his heroic strains?" (11. 8-9). Druidism, then, appears as a consequence of allowing institutional ritual and form to displace more individual and basic orientations toward reality.

The sequence does not allow such artificialities lasting ascendency, and the third sonnet ends with the Roman conquest of the Druids opening the way for Christianity. The succession is more a matter of the re-emergence of "Diluvian truths and patriarchal lore," of the impulse of individual faith, than of the replacement of one system by another. The first part of the sonnet carefully shows the crack in the foundation of Druidism itself. The revelation prepares the "all shall be fulfilled" (1. 10) with which the poem signals the Roman conquest. The Romans, then, appear to be agents of the natural consequences attached to the condition into which Druidism has fallen. The sonnet even reinforces such an interpretation formally. It has an uncharacteristically sharp division into two parts—the first on the impending fall of the Druids, the second on the Roman enactment of it. Wrenching the reader from the Bard's complacency to the impartial action, the volta is abrupt, but it is delayed until line ten. The extension of the octet carries the Druids' point of view over into the sestet of the Roman action and suggests their responsibility for their own downfall. That Druidism could not last in such a state pays a nice compliment to the vitality of the individual act of perception, for which the replacement of Druidism by Christianity is just one figure.

Having seized on the history of the church as the surfacing of perception as individual and relational, the sequence repeats the pattern at the two major cruces in its trope's development: the threat to individual faith posed by Roman Catholicism and the threat to individual faith posed by Protestant extremisms. The first of the three parts of *Ecclesiastical Sonnets* builds to the climax of "Papal Dominion," and in its last sonnet describes Roman Catholicism as an inversion of natural order: "Unless to Peter's Chair the viewless wind/ Must come and ask permission when to blow,/ What further empire would it have?" (11. 1-3). The sonnet chooses a man-made, common, and functional object as a symbol of the church and emphasizes how out of proportion things have become when it can aspire to dominate natural forces. Moreover, the object has betrayed its own function. It should be a tool for human use, but this tool's aberrant use is threatening to effect alienation instead of relationship. As in the case of the sonnet on the Druids, this sonnet prepares the Church's downfall as an inevitability of it own making. As the Druids departed from "patriarchal lore," so the Church has departed from its role as a help to individual acts of faith.

This sonnet develops by showing the Church selectively appropriating natural forces to itself to turn against individuals: "Resist!—the thunder quails thee!" (1. 9). By the end of the sonnet, the Chair and the Roman Catholic Church are opposed to "the ancient thrones of Christendom" (1. 11), emphasizing the difference between control exercised in cooperation with natural and individual conditions and control effected as if by "a magic wand" (1. 12). The Church has become as oblivious to the environment as the Druids at the "mystic ring." In fact, the Church obviates all possibility of relationship by putting "our world . . . in [the Pope's] hand" (1. 14). The assimilation of the object signals the impossiblity of perception. The sonnet leaves the Church—but not individual faith—self-defeated.

The sequence draws out the resurgence of individual faith until several sonnets into the second section. In part, the delay allows the sonnets to explore nuances of the topic. The climax of "Papal Dominion" had not been achieved abruptly. It had been built up through previous sonnets. For example, the one immediately preceding it had shown the Pope treading on the Emperor, robbing him of "even the common dignity of man!" (xxxviii.8). It emphasizes the antagonism toward the individual and the environment that culminates in the megalomania of the last sonnet. Alienation is again emphasized in the sonnet that introduces the Reformation as the resurfacing of individual and interactive perception. Sonnet II.xi on transubstantiation uses that doctrine as a symbol of unnaturalness to which it opposes the naturalness of individual faith.

Transubstantiation is singled out to exemplify "rites that trample on the soul and sense" (1. 14). Its effect is described:

> And, while the *Host* is raised, its elevation
> An awe and supernatural horror breeds;
> And all the people bow their heads, like reeds
> To a soft breeze, in lowly adoration. (11. 5-8)

Consistent with the Church's appropriation of natural elements from Sonnet I.xxxix, this sonnet turns to that imagery to describe the effect on the people; however, the imagistic inaptness calls attention to the impossibility and inappropriateness of the Church's position. Reeds respond cooperatively to a soft breeze; they are not reduced, diminished, or trampled upon by it as these worshippers are by the practice. The very incongruity of the imagery parodies the Church's point of view, which would take the comparison seriously.[18] The simile, however, replaces the people in a potentially interactive posture which prepares and is fulfilled in Valdo's independent response (1. 9). The sonnet locates Valdo and his fellow dissenters appropriately among natural scenes: "On the banks of Rhone . . . 'Mid woods and wilds, on Nature's craggy throne" (11. 9, 13). This harmony with nature replaces the Church's desired control over it; Valdo's act of teaching (1. 10) replaces the Church's elaborate ritual. In effect, the sequence again suggests a return to "Diluvian truths and patriarchal lore" and shows a second triumph of individual perception.

In general, the sequence describes the Reformation in terms of a reintegration of human and natural aims. Sonnet II.xxi, "Dissolution of the Monasteries," shows the buildings that had tyrannized over humans within and landscape without reclaimed by nature:

> The tapers shall be quenched, the belfries mute,
>
> And, 'mid their choirs unroofed by selfish rage,
>
> The warbling wren shall find a leafy cage;
>
> The gadding bramble hang her purple fruit;
>
> And the green lizard and the gilded newt
>
> Lead unmolested lives, and die of age. (11. 3-8)

The next sonnet compares a nun re-entering the world to Iris, using the personification to suggest the fullness of interaction between individual and environment. Even Sonnet II.xxix, "Translation of the Bible," takes pains to locate individual faith among other natural, daily activities:

> And he who guides the plough, or wields the crook,
>
> With understanding spirit now may look
>
> Upon her records, listen to her song,
>
> And sift her laws—much wondering that the wrong,
>
> Which Faith has suffered, Heaven could calmly brook. (11. 4-8)

In keeping with the precedent established by the appearance of Valdo (II.xi), other Reformers are placed in natural settings. Sonnet II.xxxvii compares its titular "English Reformers in Exile" to "birds escaped the fowler's net" (1.1). But the sequence does not simply value the Reformation as a good. The good is the individual act of faith, and the Reformation is positive only insofar as it conduces to it. It brings its own set of problems that are potentially as damaging as Druidism or Roman Catholicism. Sonnet II.xxviii warily notes that "with the spiritual sovereignty transferred/ Unto itself, the Crown assumes a voice/ Of reckless mastery, hitherto unknown" (11. 12-14). As the Reformers betray their commitment to individual faith for interest in imposing their versions of religion on others, the previously healthy natural imagery turns morbid. Of the English Reformers in exile, Sonnet II.xxxvii observes: "their union is beset/ With speculative notions rashly sown,/ Whence thickly-sprouting growth of poisonous weeds" (11. 8-10). Instead of helping others to realize their perceptions, the Reformers are impeding their activity, and the sonnet concludes: "How enviably blest/ Is he who can, by help of grace, enthrone/ The peace of God within his single breast!" Like Druidism and Roman Catholicism, institutionalized Protestantism has grown away from "Diluvian truths and patriarchal lore," and Sonnet II.xli shows its alienation in by now familiar terms:

> Men, who have ceased to reverence, soon defy
> Their forefathers; lo! sects and formed, and split
> With morbid restlessness:—the ecstatic fit
> Spreads wide; though special mysteries multiply
> The Saints must govern is their common cry. (11. 1-5)

In keeping with the diffuseness of the situation, *Ecclesiastical Sonnets* does not raise the sequence to a third climax over the Reformation problems but continues into the third and final section with the suggestion of the need for individual effort and caution. It finds Anglicanism to be most conducive to the exercise of it (III.iv, "Latitudinarianism"), but it notes how fragile that condition is (III.x, "Obligations of Civil to Religious Liberty"). The sequence celebrates the Church of England not as such but as a symbolic manifestation of a theoretically ideal condition—a community in which individual belief is not compromised.[19] The conception of individual faith had been non-isolating from the first. The founders were brought together by the integrity of their individual acts of faith. Although it is easy to neglect in finding the main pattern of the sequence, the importance of community to individual faith is never overlooked. In fact, Wordsworth may have chosen the ecclesiastical repertoire in order to emphasize that individual perception is not solipsistic.

Describing this perfectly balanced condition is one of the challenges of the sequence. Sonnet I.ii on the founders does it by suggesting the church as an activity, not an institution. The sequence does not introduce Christian rites until I.vii, which depicts the survivors of the first wave of persecutions and martyrdoms pursuing "their holy rites with vocal gratitude:/ And solemn ceremonials they ordain/ To celebrate their deliverance" (11. 7-9). Unlike Druidic or Papal rituals, which substitute for a more basic approach to reality, these rites are initiated for purposes apart from the act of faith itself. These bring believers together in harmony and leave the question of belief to its appropriate place. Hence, these do not interfere with the relationship of faith, which the sonnet indicates by introducing the believers' rites with a natural simile: "As, when a storm hath ceased, the birds regain/ Their cheerfulness, and busily retrim/ Their nests, or chant a gratulating hymn" (11. 1-3).

Other sonnets see institutions as beneficial though not in the way they are intended to be. For example, Sonnet I.xxiv passes over as doubtful (1. 8) the idea that monasticism "obtains/ From heaven a *general* blessing" (11. 4-5);

instead, it concentrates on the effect of such a belief upon some individuals. It posits the idea as the functional object in a relationship with certain perceivers and notes:

> The Sensual think with reverence of the palms
>
> Which the chaste Votaries seek, beyond the grave;
>
> If penance be redeemable, thence alms
>
> Flow to the poor, and freedom to the slave;
>
> And if full oft the Sanctuary save
>
> Lives black with guilt, ferocity it calms.

(11. 9-14)

"The Sensual" expand their perspectives by pondering the idea, and sometimes they act for the practical good of others. Without community, human interaction is limited; therefore, it cannot be discarded because it can threaten individuals. Its dangers must be worked around because isolation is equally impoverishing. Commitment to individuality in community underlies Wordsworth's sympathetic portrayal of Laud (II.xlv), whose emphasis on "external publick worship" Wordsworth quotes and praises in a note (*Poetical Works* 3: 568), and likely informs Sonnet II.xxvi: "Not utterly unworthy to endure/ Was the supremacy of crafty Rome" (11. 1-2).

As it explores through church history the dimensions of communal existence and individual integrity, *Ecclesiastical Sonnets* focuses its readers' attention on the interdependence of the two. It presents no conclusion to them, but it does enable them to abandon their defences against isolation by placing individuality at the heart of a cherished institution.[20] *Ecclesiastical Sonnets*, then, appears among Wordsworth's other uses of mutually qualifying short forms as his most accomplished celebration of the limits of perception.

Chapter 7

Assembling *The Recluse*

Instead of saying "farewell to all small poems" in 1803 as Coleridge thought or hoped Wordsworth had (*Anima Poetae* 30), Wordsworth clearly continued to explore the strengths of mutually qualifying short forms, which he presented to his readers in his numerous volumes. He may even have experimented with a short form pattern for *The Recluse*. His discussion with Henry Nelson Coleridge of an abandoned plan in terms of "parts" suggests a poem consisting of juxtaposed pieces,[1] and it recalls the conception of *The Recluse* he had stated in a letter dated March 6, 1798 to Tobin: "My object is to give pictures of Nature, Man, and Society" (*EY* 212). As de Selincourt points out in his commentary to the *Poetical Works*, the letter shows that Wordsworth had his own notion of *The Recluse* and that it was markedly different from Coleridge's plan for "a philosophical discourse delivered authoritatively from the mouth of the poet" (5: 368). Coleridge may have introduced Wordsworth to the project, but Wordsworth assimilated it into his own poetics before proceeding with it and proceeded with it only as far as his own fundamental principles would allow.

Wordsworth could not have written a poem that presents an all-inclusive perspective for the reader to receive without giving up his inquiry into the value of epistemological self-reliance. He seems to have interpreted *The Recluse* as a widely inclusive poem rather than as a poem from an all-inclusive perspective. As such, it promised to be the *sine qua non* of his campaign. In *The Recluse*, Wordsworth could demonstrate exhaustively how the limits of perception facilitate the interaction of all human society. In addition, he could show how literature uniquely conduces to understanding and exploiting perception and interaction by modifying existing genres even more daringly than he had done in *Lyrical Ballads*: he could try to preserve long narrative forms in the absence of an authoritative point of view on which they traditionally depend.

If *The Reculse* fell short of its grandest promise when it issued in *The Excursion*, it enhanced Wordsworth's "campaign" nonetheless. Surveying Wordsworth's predecessors, Lyon emphasizes that *The Recluse* "was to have marked the creation of a new literary genre" and notes that *The Excursion* manages to blend at least four existing forms: "the long blank-verse didactic poem; the philosophical dialogue; the short verse narrative of humble life; . . . and the funeral elegy" (29-31).[2] That *The Excursion* is surely a formal amalgam may be the result of using form as repertoire. *The Excursion* calls to mind various narrative styles that, in their familiar contexts, would be unified by a privileged view. The new context replaces textual authority with "pictures" or "*views* of Man, Nature, and Society" (*Prose* 3: 5 emphasis added), which the reader must unify.[3] The modified long form still sustains relationships among the perspectives. It contains them and allows them to interact, but it does not compromise their individuality. In some sense, it becomes a formal representation of perceptual limits. Characters in the work, like perceivers in the world, interact because of the barriers; the interaction defines something different from separate poems or separate perceivers and objects; the narrative is empty, the relationship void, apart form its components. Neither the form of the poem nor the concept of perception allows for the absolute value of a character's view or a perceiver's perspective outside of an individual relationship. Even if aesthetically cumbersome, the form enacts the condition it demonstrates among the characters.

Perhaps Wordsworth first chose to acquaint readers with the idea of *The Recluse* through *The Excursion* because of the greater ease with which perspectives can be seen to qualify each other when recognizable characters are present. Or, perhaps he wished to avoid another confrontation over the personal stance that *The Recluse* would inevitably provoke if Wordsworth followed his announced intention of making it "consist chiefly of meditations in the author's own person" (Prose 3:6). For whatever reason, Wordsworth carved out "the intermediate part" of *The Recluse* as *The Excursion*, in which "the intervention of characters speaking is employed" (3: 6). *The Excursion* details how its four principle personae interact with their environment, with their accumulated thoughts, and with each other. The process by which they build up their views and by which their views color their succeeding thoughts and actions is the central concern of the work. The absolute value of any perspective apart from its perceiver is not at issue.[4] The use of the four serves as a device to prevent the reader from seizing on any one view as a cynosure. It diffuses the authority among personae and suggests that whatever value there is inheres in each relationship between perceiver and object.

The short *Preface* to *The Excursion* that places it in the context of *The Recluse* also delineates the author's and readers' roles:

It is not the Author's intention formally to announce a system
. . . if he shall succeed in conveying to the mind clear thought,
lively images, and strong feelings, the Reader will have no
difficulty in extracting the system for himself. (*Prose* 3: 6)

Leaving no room for doubt about the necessity of reader participation, the *Preface* defines Wordsworth's work as the strategic deployment of perspectives, from which readers are to derive meaning. Readers of *The Excursion*, as surely as readers of "Simon Lee," must "make a tale" from the incidents brought to their notice.

Readers of *The Excursion*, in fact, come to the poem through numerous incidents, for as Lyon points out, *The Excursion* consists of "22 short stories, . . . 7 about the living and 15 about the dead. One is related by the Poet, 2 by the Wanderer, 2 by the Solitary, and 17 by the Pastor" (46). The narrative loosely contains the mutually qualifying stories or "pictures" (as Wordsworth's early letter terms them) much as categories contain mutually qualifying short forms in Wordsworth's other works. The Pastor's graveyard "pictures," then, appear not so much as "interpolated tales" as multiple examples of the "picturing" technique of the entire poem. Examination of the Pastor's procedure and his role within the poem might elucidate the whole. The Poet opens Book VI, in which the Pastor's recitation begins, by praising "the State and Church of England" (11. 1-41) and placing the Pastor within its idealized tradition (11.42-87). He thus signals to the reader on what role-playing the Pastor's discourse depends. The Pastor undertakes his task in response to the Solitary's cry for knowledge: "Give us, for our abstractions, solid facts;/ For our disputes, plain pictures" (V.637-38). The Solitary voices a human and appropriate impulse to understand another's view. The Pastor cannot provide absolute data, "perspectiveless" information. He can give only his view of the objects. He proceeds, of course, as if his perspective were accurate, as, for him, it is.

The opening encomium indicates that the Pastor's belief system will color his view of any object. In responding to the Solitary, he assumes the role of teacher assigned to him within that system. By marking the boundaries of the Pastor's perspective, the poem takes it out of the context of church and state in which it stands unchallenged and puts it into a new one in which it is only one orientation toward the environment. With the Pastor's world so neatly circumscribed before him, the reader should attend less to what the Pastor says than to how the Pastor brings his accumulated perspective to bear on his relationship with each new object. Delivered as it is by the Poet, the encomium makes economic use of the perspectives in the poem. It fulfills the obligation of the Poet as narrator to guide the reader into the poem's context, and it emphasizes the nature of the Poet as character. He here assumes the role of the bard whose age-old function is to reinforce community values. He slips from his familiar first person to a distant third, indicating his wearing of the mask: "The Poet, fostering for his native land/ Such hope, entreats that servants may abound . . ." (VI.42-43). His role-playing reveals the authorial perspective for what it is, i.e., one conventional way to order reality, just as his statements likewise define the pastoral perspective. The exposition prepares the reader to consider not just the ensuing portraits but their painter as well.

In painting his portraits, the Pastor answers the Solitary's question but in different terms than he (the Pastor) thinks. His perspective compels him to believe that he is directly communicating real knowledge; his discourse demonstrates that he is articulating his view. As his audience listens to him, the characters relate to each figure drawn in an individual way, a way on which their own accumulated perspectives clearly bear. This pattern of interaction appears most explicitly with respect to the story of the two politically opposite exiles—"flaming Jacobite/ And sullen Hanoverian" (VI.458-59)—who form a peculiar alliance and leave a joint monument (VI.391-521).

The Pastor relates this story—as he relates all of them—to illustrate his ethical system, which he offers as "the mine of real life" (V.630). As the

Pastor tells it, the ruin of each figure's ambition turns his attention from worldly to heavenly rewards. Realizing the illusoriness of all the former, whether couched in Jacobite or Hanoverian terms, creates an identity between the enemies and effects a kind of truce. The worldly values that fueled their hatred are replaced by other-worldly values that temper their passion. Their epitaph provides something of a formula for achieving contentment in misfortune:

> Time flies; it is his melancholy task
>
> To bring, and bear away, delusive hopes,
>
> And re-produce the troubles he destroys.
>
> But while his blindness thus is occupied,
>
> Discerning mortal! do thou serve the will
>
> Of Time's eternal Master, and that peace,
>
> Which the world wants, shall be for thee
>
> confirmed! (VI.515-21)

The Pastor builds the story to climax with the epitaph. He has manipulated the story so as to direct his audience to it and have them "gather" the intended "appropriate sense" (VI.513-14). His technique depends on his assumption that he can and should give them a perspective to adopt. Could the audience share his view, they would see "the mine of real life" in the Christian eternity and adjust their interpretations of the ruin and association of these two accordingly. The thwarting of their ambitions would seem fortunate circumstances that enabled them to realize better goals.

The story is the result of the Pastor's relationship with the figures as objects, of his beliefs reanimating their lives. Given different accumulated ideas, a different perception of the two figures results—as the Solitary's exclamations show. While he acknowledges the Pastor's point (VI.522-26), the more humanistic cynosure of his classical orientation leads him to ponder rather than accept the Pastor's view (VI.528-57).[5] For him, the pair's legacy consists not in the peace that comes from seeing all earthly cares subsumed by divine benevolence but in the peace that comes from knowing all mortals are united against a common enemy, fate. He aligns the Jacobite and Hanoverian with Prometheus and Tantalus (VI.539, 543) and concludes:

> Amid the groves, under the shadowy hills,
> The generations are prepared; the pangs,
> The internal pangs, are ready; the dread
>   strife
> Of poor humanity's afflicted will
> Struggling in vain with ruthless destiny.
>
> (VI.553-57)

His interpretation shows perception proceeding by individual relationship. He has engaged with the Pastor's story but not surrendered himself to the Pastor's judgment.[6] The Solitary's remarks bring the narrative to a deadlock. Although the Solitary has remained independent of the Pastor's views, he has not been acting fully as an individual. He counters Christianity with Classicism, system with system. His approach has a dual effect in the poem. For one thing, it reins in the Pastor's perspective. The Pastor's use of the epitaph had been a ploy to assimilate authority to his view, to incorporate the presumably privileged perspective of the object itself into his account. The impossibility of doing so should be obvious to the reader, but the poem throws it into relief by having the Solitary repeat it in different terms. He calls upon classical precedent to shore up his interpretation. Both Pastor and Solitary are merely invoking other individuals' views that fall within the confines of given systems. Neither can invest them with authority. The reader thus should see that systems are widely maintained conventions that have no authority apart from their individual voices. What the Solitary's approach gains for itself in qualifying the Pastor's interpretation, it loses in equally qualifying its own. It betrays the desire to receive absolute knowledge from some outside source that had first prompted the Solitary's request. In effect, the Solitary's approach directs the reader toward questioning the merits of systematic thought.

Having brought the narrative to an impasse, the poem shows how systematic thought deals with alternative views. Working from the premise of its own validity, it denies the validity of other interpretations, but it tries to recast those alternatives in its own mold and assimilate them into the given system. Thus the Pastor proceeds:

> "Though," said the Pastor in answer,
>   "these be terms
>   Which a divine philosophy rejects,
>   We, whose established and unfailing trust
>   Is in controlling Providence, admit
>   That, through all stations, human life abounds
>   With mysteries. . . .
>   Our system is not fashioned to preclude
>   That sympathy which you for others ask."
>   (VI. 558-63, 567-68)

The Pastor avoids the Solitary's challenge to address the tragic vicissitudes of life by suggesting the indifference toward benevolent Providence that such an emphasis implies (VI.569-79). The reader does not learn the outcome of the

Pastor's attempt, for the Wanderer interrupts him. The reader does learn, however, to recognize the Pastor's technique. The demonstration of it over twenty lines should be sufficient to alert him to its strengths and inevitability within the Pastor's view and to its invalidity without it.

Two things redirect the narrative—The Wanderer's and the Narrator's interruptions (VI.579-88; 599-644). Each responds to immediately preceding comments rather than directly to the point at issue, and the characteristic concerns of each prompt each response. Thus, their statements demonstrate that the colloquy proceeds by association, and they indicate something of the nature of that process. The Wanderer and Narrator interact with the Pastor's and Solitary's words as objects because their accumulated perspectives sensitize them to the words' potential. For instance, the Wanderer's characteristic commitment to "social man" (IV.261) moves him to arrest the Pastor's embarrassing defence of his avoidance of the miserable as theme: "Ah! do not think,/ . . . Wish could be ours that you . . ./ Should breathe a word tending to violate/ Your own pure spirit" (VI.579-84).[7] His statement calls for respect of the Pastor's perspective as the Pastor's perspective and suggests that some means can be found to accommodate both Pastor and Solitary. His plea does not make him a privileged spokesman on behalf of individual perception. He does not now come to respect fully the Solitary's point of view. Indeed, he does not in the poem ever come to do so. He can, however, suggest accommodation from the decorum of the situation, from the fact that the Pastor is speaking at their request and that it is inappropriate to solicit his view merely to challenge it. This is the interpretation the Solitary seems to put on his comments, with his potentially sarcastic: "True . . . be it far/ From us to infringe the laws of charity" (VI. 589-90). The Wanderer's and the Solitary's short exchange about tolerance and kind judgment (VI.584-93) ostensibly refers to an attitude toward the buried figures, but it is pregnant with applicability to their own situation.

The Wanderer's intervention alone fails to start the narrative again, for the Solitary, still desiring a "perspectiveless" and invariable explanation, turns from accommodation to reiteration of his point:

> " . . . but if the thing we seek
> Be genuine knowledge, bear we then in mind
> How, from his lofty throne, the sun can fling
> Colours as bright on exhalations bred
> By weedy pool or pestilential swamp,
> As by the rivulet sparkling where it runs,
> Or the pellucid lake. (VI.593-99)

The natural imagery engages the Poet-Narrator's characteristic sensibility to a scene and prompts his remarks on the nature and use of objects.[8] He begins by focusing attention on what can be observed of an object and builds to the effect of observation as of central importance. He counters the Solitary's dismay at the sun shining on evil as well as good with the observation that those concepts are not present in the scene. He respects the limits of the object and literally describes the green, hilly, nearly monument-less graveyard (VI.605-10). His notion that it does not tempt the perceiver "to exceed the truth" (VI.601) refers to the consistent limits of the object that must be preserved for one to interact with it. That it does not refer to the absolute value of the object is supported by his continuation about the buried Dalesmen. He separates memory of them from the scene as arising from relationships established with them as people, not relationships established with the scene (VI.610-15). What can come from relationship with the scene (or some such scene) he develops through associations.

The dearth of tombstones in the present cemetery allows for relatively unrestricted interaction with the scene. For example, the Narrator's conclusion that the Dalesmen "trust . . . to oral record" (VI.610, 612) for their monuments results from his interaction with the scene as object. It reflects an expectation that memory is desired, an expectation stemming perhaps from his professional involvement with the preserving, written word, and an expectation challenged by the nearly anonymous object before him. The object prompts the Narrator to expand his idea of what constitutes an epitaph and leads him to a new definition of it as a habit of mind rather than a piece of writing (VI.614-15). That this idea is a function of his perspective and not a verifiable part of the scene is preserved by the Narrator's immediate introduction of another interpretation of the nearly monument-less expanse (VI.620-23). Having established a productive relationship with the scene, the narrator makes his associations in turn the object of a relationship and concentrates on the effect of it as its chief good. The Narrator associates from the scarcity of monuments in the present scene to the profusion of them in others he has seen. He does not consider whether the epitaphs give a truly just and appropriate summary of the individuals' lives; instead, he notes that he is soothed by the sentiments they express, accurately or not. As he expanded his definition of epitaphs in the earlier lines, so here he revalues his idea of their use. They serve not to preserve a particular memory but to preserve generous thoughts and habits often threatened by other scenes. Providing *"one* Enclosure where the voice that speaks/ In envy or detraction is not heard" (VI.638-39), they facilitate the balance of human emotion. Thus, the Narrator moves the colloquy away from its fixation on the value of the object to concentration on its effect.

The Narrator's deft demonstration of how perception occurs through interaction with an object and how it is individual does not make his a privileged perspective in the poem. He gives no indication of understanding the process he enacts. He presents his redefinitions to correct the Solitary's interpretation of the scene. Like the Wanderer's, his is a partial perspective. Only the reader can constitute a whole by putting the poem's perspectives together. The partiality of the perspectives serves in-text and out-of-text ends. Within the poem, it allows the characters to give a genuine enactment of the perceptual process. They operate within the bounds of their assumptions. For the reader looking into the text, the partiality shows the dangers of mistaking an individual perspective for a universal truth. To move beyond a search for a view to adopt to a reliance on his own deductions, the reader must see the strengths and weaknesses of the characters' perspectives, display of which would be hampered by an omniscient participant.

Since self-knowledge is a prize for the reader, the Narrator's intervention moves the colloquy forward again not because the characters learn from the discussion what the reader can but because the Pastor seizes upon the Narrator's redefinitions. He takes them for encouragement to tell his stories in order to arouse noble human feelings (VI.645-60). This provides the sought-for way to assimilate the Solitary's challenge into his system. He can now choose seemingly tragic examples because he will use them to educe feelings appropriate to his interpretation (VI.660-74). With the impasse reached at the conclusion of the exiles' portrait circumvented, the narrative can proceed to the next story.

Even consideration of this one segment of the portrait section can suggest how the "picturing" technique works in the poem as a whole. As the Pastor's presentation is introduced by the Poet-Narrator, who indicates what ideas control the Pastor's view of the objects he encounters, so each character is introduced by another character, the Wanderer by the Narrator, the Solitary by the Wanderer, who indicates the predominant nature of the other's view. The introductions give one character's point of view on another. They do not replace each character's later elaboration of his own story, and they are not inconsistent with the outward circumstances of the later statements. They focus the reader's attention on the fact of each character's perception and on the nature of that perception as interaction with an object. The exception to this pattern, the Narrator who opens the poem without another's introduction, still maintains the emphasis on perception. He begins by describing his relationship with the landscape and shows that there is no such thing as a "perspectiveless" presentation of an object.[9]

As the characters achieve a broader range and greater articulation of their individual perspectives by interacting with the Pastor's portraits, so they arrive at a similar result by interacting with each other in the larger poem. The campaign to reform the Solitary serves as an abstract portrait that stimulates all of them (including the Solitary) to heightened perceptual awareness, which is more lasting than a "conversion." In fact, a "conversion" that would involve the Solitary in adopting another's view would be inimical to genuine perception. The portrait section, then, shows in concentration how the poem as a whole proceeds—by the juxtaposition and interplay of perspectives.

The conclusion of the portrait section likewise resembles the conclusion of the poem. By the end of the last portrait, the four have exhausted systematic investigation. That they have broadened but not altered their perspectives is evidenced by the Wanderer's summary. Predictably, he accommodates all of their characteristic concerns. He calls them "pathetic records" that lead to "reverence for the dust of Man" in recognition of the Solitary's humanism (VII.1053, 1057); "words of heartfelt truth,/ Tending to patience when affliction strikes;/ To hope and love," in recognition of the Narrator's interest in effect (VII.1054-56). To the statement about emotion, he adds the idea that the portraits tend "to confident repose/ In God" in recognition of the Pastor's beliefs (VII.1057), and he performs the act of accommodation from his own disposition (VII.1051-57).

By the end of the final picnic, each character has in some way reiterated his dominant concern. The Wanderer has conjured a Utopian vision (IX.1-415). If his celebration of an *"active* Principle" (IX.3) tempts the reader to identify the Wanderer's view with Wordsworth's, his expectation that a perfect—and therefore static—condition can and should be enacted (IX.293-415) prevents the error. The Wanderer is expatiating upon his now heightened confidence in "social man." The poem emphasizes the fact that this is his view and not a privileged view by having the Pastor's wife note its illusoriness:

> While he is speaking, I have power to see
> Even as he sees; but when his voice hath
>   ceased,
> Then, with a sigh, sometimes I feel, as now,
> That combinations so serene and bright
> Cannot be lasting in a world like ours. (IX.465-69)

Her distance from even a view she admires confirms the Utopian scheme as an imposed system, the product of ideal "British Law-givers" (IX.399) and ironically inimical to independent thought despite its focus on education. The Poet again concentrates on the effect of the scene (IX.503-44); the Pastor prays (IX.614-745). The Solitary interjects alternate views (IX.138-52; 550-58), which are either assimilated or ignored. Finally, but cordially, he separates from the group (IX.750-83).

In each case, the inappropriateness of the initial objective has been demonstrated. The portraits have not provided real knowledge; the Solitary has not been converted. But in each case, a redirection has also been suggested. Before his summary, the Wanderer interacts with the last portrait and draws a parallel between Sir Alfred Irthing and himself that carries forward past the finality of the summary and into the next book. His conclusion asserts what has been the pattern of interaction with the portraits. Each character could expand his own perspective by individual relationship with them, but none could productively exchange his dominant concerns. Throughout the poem, the Solitary has maintained his integrity. He must embark on his own course, one that grows out of his interaction with others and not out of adoption of their views or substitution of alternate systems. If he reenters the poem or a sequel as promised (IX.784-96), it must be on terms of individual growth, the terms in which the Wanderer carries the poem past the portraits and into the next book.

The Excursion may be incomplete, but it is not necessarily inconclusive.[10] Readers see the failure of direct communication and the inadequacy of systematic thought, but they also see the potential of individual interaction. The partiality of each in-text perspective replicates the individual views of every perceiver. Their individuality does not prevent them from learning from each other, but it does prevent the usurpation and imposition of ideas. From the partiality of each perspective, readers must formulate a whole new view of systematic thought. Even if Wordsworth had shown the reform of the Solitary, it would not have changed the purpose of the poem or the reader's role. Wordsworth would not necessarily have shown—and is not likely to have shown—the Solitary adopting another's view. He might rather have shown the Solitary changing his life by means of his own relationships. Wordsworth might have decided that such a demonstration was superfluous or that it would interfere with the reader's activity. Existing as a series of juxtaposed, interrelated, and mutually qualifying perspectives, *The Excursion* stands as an experiment in adapting narrative form and systematic inquiry to non-authoritative conditions.

The Excursion, then, is a philosophical poem, but it is one that challenges the idea of philosophical authority and completeness. Instead of proposing a new and full system for readers to adopt, it stimulates them to greater self-reliance. Such a poem is consistent with Wordsworth's commitment to individual integrity and inimical to Coleridge's commitment to a new and all-inclusive *magnum opus*.[11] In a sense, Wordsworth did give *The Recluse* back to Coleridge, as Kenneth Johnston argues, but he seems more to have presented it to him transformed into *The Excursion* than to have "abandoned the idea" (xxi). *The Excursion* stands as Wordsworth's comment on the condition of systematic philosophy. Given the nature of that comment, *The Recluse*, as Coleridge conceived it, cannot exist. But perhaps the Wordsworthian *Recluse* can and does exist. Several arguments for its reality have been advanced. For example, Kroeber maintains "that *Home at Grasmere* is *The Recluse*" (*Romantic Landscape* 117). He states that the truncation of *The Recluse* to one book is "formally appropriate to the poet's ambition" (117) and finds that the resultant work epitomizes the interdependence of the individual and his environment. Thus it captures and manifests the essence of *The Recluse* (117-31). Alternatively, Kenneth Johnson claims that "*The Recluse* exists . . . as a coherent though incomplete body of interrelated texts . . . susceptible of constructive reading" (xi). His thesis opens up the possibility of the reader's completing *The Recluse* by assembling separate texts into the structure.

Johnston deduces the reader's activity through attention to how Wordsworth's prose places his poetry with respect to *The Recluse*. Wordsworth thought, and exhorted his readers to think, of his canon as a collection of mutually supportive units. The *Preface* to *The Excursion* advances this conception most graphically, comparing the poems to the parts of a Gothic church, with the "minor Pieces" clustered like "little cells, oratories, and sepulchral recesses" around the body of *The Recluse* (*Prose* 3: 5-6). The reader's potential role may be confirmed by the preoccupation with individual perception evident in the poetry itself. As a body of poems that explores the nuances of perception, Wordsworth's canon redesigns the philosophical poem to suit a new understanding of thought. As philosophy is not a repository of ideas external to individual perspectives, so *The Recluse* is not a structure external to Wordsworth's other poems. Without its cells, oratories, and sepulchral recesses, the Gothic church is not the Gothic church. The structure exists through its elements, not independently of them.

Construing *The Recluse* in this way suggests that the canon not only treats perception as a subject but represents it in form through Wordsworth's preference for short, juxtaposed pieces, a preference incorporated even into his use of the traditional long narrative. If the canon were indeed a metaphor,

its tenor would be the act of perceiving; its vehicle, the objects or ideas
perceived, such as rustic nature, social norms, religious beliefs or literary genre.
The care and consistency with which the poems place their objects or ideas in
unexpected arrays and prompt the reader to look at them in a new light
suggest that Wordsworth was offering poetry as a mode of discourse that could
succeed in areas where philosophy had failed.[12]   Such an idea has an
Aristotelian precedent, but Wordsworth does more than locate literature
between the abstraction of philosophy and the specificity of history. He tries
to define its unique role in the individual's acquisition of knowledge. If his
endeavor seems to have yielded more questions than answers, it may be
because it finds provocativeness to be the essence of that role. *The Recluse*,
then, provides something of a test case of authorial provocation and reader
response. Having exhorted his readers to consider his poems together,
Wordsworth leaves them to build *The Recluse* from the wealth of materials in
the canon.

Readers who do assemble the canon build an impressive if asymmetrical
structure, for the materials display the positive features of epistemological
self-reliance a bit ostentatiously. While Wordsworth's unflinching looks at the
darker side of relationships—in "Gipsies," for example—demonstrate his
awareness of the unpleasant dimensions of individual views, his unflagging
determination to examine the function of such views suggests a hope that the
advantages of the condition might predominate. Wordsworth's use of mutually
qualifying short forms saves him from the self-contradiction of offering
individuality as a good and marks his enterprise as the opening of a debate
rather than the imposition of a theory; nevertheless, he is unlikely to have
begun such an enterprise without a hypothesis that individuality is in fact a

good and a desire to have readers confirm it. He is thus in a frustrating position. Having committed himself to directing this inquiry through literary discourse, he had to relinquish control of his readers' responses, though not the direction of them. If he were really to discover the consequences of accepting perceptual limits, he would have to face the possibility that readers would show him the difficulties inherent in the orientation. Since readers' combativeness and subterfuge seemed always to qualify the reader-writer relationship Wordsworth was proposing to realize the functional relationships in his texts, he tried various ways to shape the space for readers' views to the positive dimensions of individual perception.

Wordsworth and his readers seem inextricably entangled in the empirical dilemma he set out to solve. Their entrapment does not so much invite criticism of either Wordsworth's ability to perform the task he gave himself or his readers' competence to meet his challenge as suggest the circularity of the dilemma itself. Wordsworth's campaign took shape in response to the demands of a consensual ideal dominant in his culture. His readers' reactions likewise took shape in that milieu. If Wordsworth and his readers were both formed in the softly but surely determining matrix of their cultural moment, Wordsworth's campaign for individual integrity may ironically bear out nothing so much as Stanley Fish's claim that there are truly no individuals but only socially conditioned interpreters (182-83). The nature of the empirical dilemma may compromise Wordsworth's campaign in the long run, but it does not necessarily indicate the failure of his effort in his cultural moment. Wordsworth did expedite—and perhaps set in motion—the examination of individual perception that is still in process.

The struggle to comprehend Wordsworth documented in the reviews attests to the fact that he at least interfered with unthinking acceptance of consensus. Appropriately enough if *The Excursion* is taken as an emblem of the canon, reviews of that work exhibit the dominant trends in contemporary reactions. Some reviewers—most notably Francis Jeffrey and William Hazlitt—found the *The Excursion* as innovative as the strategically radical *Lyrical Ballads* or "Moods of My Own Mind" and objected to suffering another unusual and uniquely Wordsworthian poem.[13] Other reviewers found the strategies subtle and were generally content to extract the repertoire from the poem as reviewers of Wordsworth's loco-descriptive work had done and reviewers of his sonnets would do. For example, the articles in the *British Critic* and the *Eclectic Review* concentrate on the uplifting effects of the love of nature evident in *The Excursion*, but they worry that the portrayal of such effects might mislead readers into valuing nature as ethically sufficient. They "save" the work by taking love of nature out of the poetic context, in which it helps to delineate a perspective, and placing it into the context of revealed religion, in which it serves to lead people toward the common tenets of belief. The dominant culture could not assimilate Wordsworth; it had to coopt him, incorporating the individual poet into the consensual ideal. The ascendency of Wordsworth's reputation follows the trajectory of the reviews drawn by Klancher. Wordsworth's reviewers use interpretation of his poetry, as their colleagues use the devices Klancher identifies, to ensure that "innumerable acts of reading . . . produce a centralized intellect" (60). Paradoxically, the cooptation of Wordsworth weakened the consensual ideal, letting into the dominant structure an element it could contain but not defuse.

If Wordsworth's contemporaries had merely embraced his work, they would have strengthened the hold of the consensual ideal. Such a response would indicate that Wordsworth's work did not stimulate readers at all, that it facilitated the very sharing of perspectives that Wordsworth questioned. On the contrary Wordsworth's challenge provoked elaborate defences of the shared ideal, defences that revealed it as supportable only by force of will and prodigality of intellectual resources. As readers found consensus less viable, they achieved the detachment from it that would enable them to examine it critically and to consider alternatives. Wordsworth's challenge tilled the intellectual soil in which would grow the realization that perceptions cannot be shared, a realization that attained its own intellectual hegemony the consequences of which are only now coming into view.[14] It remains for Wordsworth's continuing readership to analyze fully the significance of the statuses assigned to him by his changing historical audiences and to become more self-conscious about his current canonicity. Assembling *The Recluse* may provide a metaphor for the effort to turn from the sufficiency to the function of the text.

Notes

Chapter 1: The Empirical Dilemma

[1]For comments on Locke's relation to Scholasticism, see Gibson 40-41, 182-204 and Yolton 26-27.

[2]Yolton 97-98 points out that Locke's method—not his terminology—was new (Kenneth MacLean 32-33 even finds previous uses of the famous phrase *tabula rasa*.) Hobbes may have been the first empiricist, but Locke became the more influential figure, making empiricism truly what Willey has termed "the Locke tradition" (296). In the "Foreword" to his edition of *An Essay Concerning Human Understanding*, Nidditch defends Locke's ascendency partly on the ground that Locke was the first empiricist to make epistemology his primary concern (ix).

[3]Locke's purpose was to identify what people can know certainly, so, strictly speaking, other considerations were outside the scope he set for himself (Gibson 2-9). *Cf.* Yolton: Locke knew that his way "leads to a restriction of knowledge" but thought that speculative matters could be made to follow from certain ones closely enough to compensate for the limits (26).

[4]Alexander claims only that his analysis "makes Locke's view look a little less foolish than it is usually made to look" (19).

[5]For specific examples, see Yolton 99-113. Though the "Stillingfleet Controversy" should not be reduced to one issue, the Bishop may nevertheless be singled out as the most prominent objector to Locke's potential isolationism insofar as his criticism of Locke centered on the barrier of substance.

[6]Parenthetical references to Berkeley are to his section numbers. I use "Introduction" to distinguish his "Introduction" from "Part I" but omit "Part

I" before referring to sections of his main text since the absence of a second part makes such designation unnecessary.

[7]Not all commentators agree. Hay, for example, argues that Berkeley's approach further isolates the perceiver within his particular apprehension. Whether Berkeley adheres to or departs from reality has been and continues to be a crux dividing commentators into "realist" and "idealist" camps. See Moore and Stace.

[8]Bracken, whose translation of the review I cite, gives the original text in an appendix. Since he approaches Berkeley as a realist, Bracken maintains that there is no connection between Berkeley's and Malebranche's positions. Alternatively, Luce argues that Berkeley is in fact derivative from Malebranche.

[9]The infinitive is incomplete in Wesley's text. The context makes it clear that he is approving the admission.

[10]As Cragg explains in his introduction, Volume 11 of the Oxford Wesley collects the texts of "An Earnest Appeal to Men of Reason and Religion" and "A Farther Appeal" together with numerous letters in which Wesley explicitly aimed to define his doctrine and defend his practice (*Works* 11: ix).

[11]See especially *Works* 11: 111-16 for reference to the *Thirty-Nine Articles*.

[12]Yates' chapter on "the validity of an inner sense of certainty" confirms the fundamentally ambiguous and unverifiable nature of the concept (210-18).

[13]Hempton identifies anomie as at least a contributing factor in the Methodist struggle for a separate identity. On the evolution of Methodist independence he observes: "Wesley's ambivalent attitude toward the Church of England could not have lasted forever, and his followers had to pick up the cheque for his renowned 'flexibility'" (59).

[14]Shepherd analyzes the pervasive effects of Methodism on literature.

[15] Volume 11 of the Oxford Wesley includes the text of Wesley's "Letter to the Rev. Mr. Horne" (*Works* 11: 443-58), together with commentary and quotation of the pertinent part of Horne's sermon (*Work* 11: 437-40).

[16] Though Shaftesbury's published writings are usually held to be directed against Hobbes, they attack the self-interest principle in any manifestation. The passage cited here, for example, generalizes about "the philosophy or philosophers of our days" (1: 81). Shaftesbury's private writings show that he implicated Locke in the system he attacks. See *Life, Letters* 403, 414.

[17] Engell's history of the imagination credits Smith with the fullest use of the concept (149).

[18] See Hume, "Dissertation on the Passions" 164-65 and *Treatise of Human Nature* 198, 265-68 (III.ii.2 and II.5).

[19] Bromwich identifies Hazlitt's *Essay* as an argument against egoism (47-57). The persistence of this issue into the nineteenth century, along with its diffusion beyond the discipline of philosophy, suggests the usefulness of examining the empirical dilemma exclusive of the philosophy of Kant. Although German thought became increasingly accessible to English minds, its availability failed to loosen the grip of the dilemma. (See Wellek for a history of the intellectual exchange.) In light of the pattern, I omit abstracted consideration of whether or not Kant provided a viable alternative to empiricism in favor of refocused attention on contemporary perceptions (supported by many later philosophers, Gibson 312-14) that he did not.

[20] See especially Hazlitt's writings on "gusto," (*Works* 4: 68-80).

[21] Engell explains that the distinction at issue here is one between sympathy with people and empathy with objects. Though conceptually present in English thought as early as the eighteenth century, the distinction in

terminology entered the language much later (157-60). The *O.E.D. Supplement* lists the first known use of "empathy" in 1904.

[22]Johnson often addresses the accomplishments of poets with reference to their success at conveying a universal perspective. His *Preface to Shakespeare*, for example, expounds upon the importance of such an achievement: "Nothing can please many, and please long, but just representations of general nature" (*Works* 7: 59). The following quotation from *Rasselas* may be Johnson's most famous statement advocating universality:

> "The business of a poet . . . is to examine not the individual, but
> the species; to remark general properties and large appearances;
> he does not number the streaks of the tulip, or describe the
> different shades of the verdure of the forest." (*Works* 1: 22)

It should be remembered, however, that the latter words are those of a character in a work of fiction and not those of Johnson in a work of criticism.

Reference to Johnson's works, except *Rasselas*, are to the Yale edition. Reference to *Rasselas*, not yet completed as a Yale volume, are to the Oxford edition.

[23]The hierarchizing of audiences is especially apparent in Klancher's explanation of how radical writing defined both dominated and dominating classes.

[24]Klancher frequently points out the instability of periodical audiences in spite of efforts to fix them (75, 148).

Chapter 2: Wordsworth's Response

[1]Exceptions are David Simpson's *Wordsworth and the Figurings of the Real*, which borrows German philosophy to shed light on the "figurative"

quality of Wordsworth's poetry and uses its theoretical analogies to draw socio-political conclusions, and Keith G. Thomas's *Wordsworth and Philosophy: Empiricism and Transcendentalism in the Poetry*, which argues that Wordsworth tried and failed to move from the former to the latter orientation.

[2]Hence, the approach does not simply extend William Galperin's pioneering article, which analyzes part of *The Excursion* in Iser's terms, nor does it follow Michael Riffaterre's equally pioneering article, which applies a method to Wordsworth's work without concern for its compatibility with Wordsworth's own thought. It comes closer in spirit to generalizing from a suggestion of Gene W. Ruoff that "the edition of 1815 represents in a surprisingly complete and sophisticated manner . . . [the notions of] reader response criticism" ("Critical Implications" 81); it explores the territory that Willard Spiegelman delimits as nearby but outside the bailiwick in which he "deal[s] with Wordsworth's characteristic uses of reading as a metonymy for perception, growth, and control" (226 n.4).

Iser's emphasis on how reading develops the individual human being and his ability to distinguish between the common elements of the text that all readers see together and the individual applications that all readers make separately bring his theory closer to Wordsworth's stated aims than, for example, the extreme subjectivism of Norman Holland or the extreme collectivism of Stanley Fish. For other possible implications, however, see pp. 187-89 of this study.

[3]Wolfgang Iser, *The Act of Reading*, p. 50. Further references, parenthetical within the text, are to this work. Iser's earlier book, *The Implied Reader*, concentrates on analysis of specific texts and does not lend itself easily to the comparison proposed here; his most recent work, *Prospecting: From*

Reader Response to Literary Anthropology, marshalls his previously established paradigms to align literary studies with the social sciences as disciplines jointly engaged in analyzing human communication (61). Answering Iser's call to literary studies to discover how particular texts take particular readers beyond points of view dominant in their present realities (263), my study examines how Wordsworth's texts generate alternatives to a consensual ideal otherwise privileged in his reader's experience. In applying Iser's theory to poetry— instead of to novels, with which he deals almost exclusively in his early work—I have followed up on his suggestion that his theory may be extended to other genres (*Act* 87), a suggestion he himself develops in *Prospecting* (54-55).

[4]See, for example, Berg 259-62.

[5]For analysis of Berkeley's egoism, see the previous chapter; for analysis of Wordsworth's egotism, see John Jones' *The Egotistical Sublime*, which is to date the only full-length study of Wordsworth's "egotism," though references to it teem in other contexts. Jones argues that Wordsworth's "egotism" is the backbone of his poetry because it informs his attention to the "singleness" of every object and enables his poetry to portray all natural things as "a partnership in harmony" (29-32; 54-110). Though I am indebted to Jones, my hypothesis differs from his. Jones begins with Wordsworth's "egotism" as a reality of his character; I posit it as something imputed to Wordsworth by others.

[6]In the first two volumes of *The Romantics Reviewed*, Reiman catalogues one hundred twenty-five contemporary reviews of Wordsworth's work. In the interest of discovering the dominant mode of reviewers' initial reactions, I have discounted the two pieces from 1835 and 1842, substituting the *Edinburgh Review*'s article on Southey's *Thalaba* (1802) and the *Monthly Review*'s article

on Coleridge's *Biographia Literaria* (1819), both of which deal extensively with Wordsworth.

[7]Criticism of Wordsworth's subjects in particular can be found in the following: *Annual Review*, 1807 poems; *Augustan Review, Excursion; Le Beau Monde*, 1807; *British Lady's Magazine, Peter Bell; British Review, Memorials of a Tour on the Continent; Champion, White Doe, Peter Bell; Edinburgh Monthly Magazine, Peter Bell; Edinburgh Review*, 1807, *Excursion, Memorials; Fireside Magazine, Waggoner; General Weekly Register, Ecclesiastical Sketches; Literary and Statistical Magazine, Peter Bell, Waggoner, Memorials, Ecclesiastical Sketches; London Magazine, River Duddon; Monthly Review*, 1815 poems, *Waggoner; New London Review, Lyrical Ballads; Satirist*, 1807; *Theatrical Inquisitor, Waggoner*.

[8]See Wordsworth's letters to Heraud (Nov. 23, 1830, *LY* 1: 537), Hamilton (Jan. 4, 1838, *LY* 2: 910), and Moxon (April 10, 1845, *LY* 3: 1248).

[9]Iser separates literary from theoretical writing. The former, for example, contributes to "the realization of human potentials, and these can only be brought to light by literature, not by systematic discourse" (76).

[10]I propose this theory of strategic accommodation as an alternative to theories explaining Wordsworth's stylistic variety as indicative of a "decline." "Decline" theories range widely, as a glance at a few confirms: Sperry attributes the "decline" to Wordsworth's fixity of mind, an inability to take up new ideas after he had fully explored what he learned from Coleridge (43-47); Hamilton interprets it as an act of psychic self-preservation, for he sees Wordsworth as a potential schizophrenic who exaggeratedly located himself within society, specifically religious society, to protect the mental health continued independence would threaten (375-77); Friedman explains it as evidence of Wordsworth's need to attach himself to a socially and economically

stable system to compensate for his divided and unstable sense of self (296-97); Reiman accounts for it as an indication that Wordsworth solved the emotional problems, especially with respect to his feelings for his sister, out of which his early poetry sprang ("Poetry" 144). Although the range of opinions is far-flung, all are underpinned by a view of Wordsworth consciously or unconsciously fulfilling his own needs over those of his readers, saving himself and sacrificing his poetry. Wordsworth may still have derived any or all of the above personal gratifications from his writings while nevertheless varying his style from at least partially deliberate and reader-oriented motives.

Though generally accepted, "decline" theories have opponents, among whom Ferguson may be most vocal. She argues for "the nearly astonishing consistency in Wordsworth's poetry," stating:

> It may be that Wordsworth's famous "decline" itself resulted from the asceticism of his poetics, but that asceticism was pronounced from the outset of his poetic career. One cannot, it seems to me, appeal to explanations of a change in method to account for his decline; the difference between poems of the different periods are ones of degree rather than kind. (xv)

[11]For detailed examination of Young and Wordsworth, see Siskin.

[12]*Rambler* 137 (*Works* 4: 362); Owen and Smyser note the parallel in a slightly different context (*Prose* 3: 104).

[13]In fairness to Colville, I add that the inconsistency obtains only with respect to Wordsworth's conscious aims. Insofar as Wordsworth values and privileges individual response, he imparts it as a good to his readers and hence approaches a self-defeating situation. See the concluding pages of this study.

[14]I am grateful to the Coleridge Estate and the Harry Ransom Humanities

Research Center, The University of Texas at Austin, for access to these loose leaves on which Henry Nelson Coleridge reports a conversation of Wordsworth's. For the published text, see "Table-Talk by William Wordsworth" in Samuel Taylor Coleridge, *Table Talk* 1: 549-50.

[15]In telling Henry Nelson Coleridge that "it is impossible to reconcile the exact truth with poetry," Wordsworth does not necessarily contradict the assertion that the "object [of poetry] is truth" he added to the *Preface* to *Lyrical Ballads* in 1802 (*Prose* 1: 139). The manuscript statement seems to refer to an actuality of fact or morality of point of view displayed in poems. The 1802 statement seems to refer to the significance a reader carries away from the poems, for the passage describes truth in active terms as

> not individual and local, but general, and operative; not standing
> upon external testimony, but carried alive into the heart by
> passion; truth which is its own testimony, which gives competence
> and confidence to the tribunal to which it appeals, and receives
> them from the same tribunal. (*Prose* 1: 139)

To "individual and local" Wordsworth opposes not "general and universal" but "general and *operative*." His terminology suggests that he is contrasting an undesirably single and confined perspective taken as "true" with a preferable multiplicity of individually crafted perceptions. Moreover, his distinction between truth that stands on "external testimony" and "truth which is its own testimony" seems to describe a contrast between passive assent and active response. Hence, the "exact" truth of the manuscript and the "operative" truth of the *Preface* can be construed as representing two different concepts consistently opposed in Wordsworth's usage.

[16]*Cf.* Shairp (2) and Arnold (89).

[17]The cooptation begun in the reviews culminates in Arnold's edition. Arnold works from the premise that "poetry is the perfect speech of man, that in which he comes nearest to being able to utter the truth" (94). A number of absolutes follow from Arnold's position. "Conditions immutably fixed by the laws of poetic beauty and poetic truth" determine the value of forms of writing, and "some kinds of poetry are in themselves lower kinds than others" (101-03). Similarly fixed conditions determine the value of the writer, for a great poet is one accomplished at infusing his works with "moral ideas," i.e., guides about "how to live" (103-04). An overarching control—a nation's opinion being checked by the rest of the civilized world—even determines the value of a writer's reputation (92-93). Such standards prevent the ascendency of "private judgment," of which Arnold is extremely distrustful: "it is so easy to feel pride and satisfaction in one's own things, so hard to make sure that one is right in feeling it" (93). Arnold intends to put Wordsworth in a position to be recognized as a great poet by the civilized world; hence, he concentrates on aligning Wordsworth with the requisite conditions of that status.

Pursuing this aim, Arnold dismantles the Wordsworth canon in a search for "profound truth of subject" and profound "truth of execution" (116). He finds evidence of the former in those works that he believes inculcate one world view, those that capture "the joy offered to us in nature, . . . in the simple primary affections and duties" and show it to be "accessible universally" (112). He finds evidence of the latter in those works that have "no style," those that seem as if "Nature . . . wrote [Wordsworth's] poem for him" (114). Arnold's distrust of individual effort makes him unwilling to give Wordsworth credit for his achievement. He attributes Wordsworth's greatness to "inspiration," to a "not ourselves" element entering into human endeavor (112).

Having established Wordsworth's conformity to absolute poetic standards, Arnold proposes a means to make that conformity apparent to the civilized world. He selects "the best" portions (those evidencing conformity) of Wordsworth's canon and reorganizes them "more naturally," according to genre instead of according to mental faculties as Wordsworth had done (98-101). He believes that his method will ensure Wordsworth's reputation, which Wordsworth himself failed to do through his inability to distinguish his good work from his bad (99). Ironically, Arnold claims that Wordsworth wrote his best work between 1798 and 1808, the decade in which Wordsworth produced his most apparently individualistic work and in which his reviewers railed most vehemently against his "egotism."

By praising this early work for its conformity and universality, Arnold performs a quintessential act of cooptation and reassures himself and his contemporaries that they share an ascertainable view. Arnold's influence was so great that Raleigh could consider selection and evaluation of Wordsworth as a *fait accompli* and announce heightened appreciation of the inherited Wordsworth as the goal of twentieth-century criticism (1-2).

[18]Perhaps the most influential work privileging the early Wordsworth is that of Jonathan Wordsworth, who first made *The Ruined Cottage* available to readers. Following his lead, a new edition of Wordsworth's works was begun, having as its aim the presentation of the works in their earliest forms. As Parrish points out, the Cornell Wordsworth can

> make it possible . . . to follow the maturation of [Wordsworth's]
> poetic genius, and to honor his lifelong concern about his poems
> by bringing equivalent care to the reading and study of them.
> ("Worst" 91)

Privileging Wordsworth's early work, however, sometimes seems at odds with investigating his "lifelong concern about his poems." For example, Gill expresses concern over the fact that many poems in the Cornell Wordsworth owe their existence as such to editorial reconstruction and not to authorial execution (185-90). Gill does not impugn the right of editors to examine manuscripts and to decide

> either that [a given poem] had come to rest at a certain state of
> completeness, which would have been publishable had circum-
> stances permitted, or that the poem was still developing but that
> the interim state is too important to be suppressed. (186)

He does, however, insist that readers must be helped to see the resultant text clearly as "a creation of modern scholarship" (187). Gill's plea has been answered by the recent publication of *Romantic Texts and Contexts*, in which Reiman includes his balanced assessment of the advantages and dangers of the Cornell Wordsworth. If readers approach Wordsworth's poetic variety mindful of his theoretical consistency and of his empirical inheritance, they can return to the Cornell edition not only with a new understanding of why modern readers tend to prefer the early poems but with a new base—the persistent concern with individual perception—from which to examine how and why Wordsworth revised.

[19]As McGann maintains, modern readers have an incomplete understanding of previous texts unless they make an effort to grasp the historical conditions that inform them (56). *Cf.* Jauss, who argues that readers cannot completely grasp the current significance of a text or understand the current needs it satisfies unless they distinguish these from prior significances and satisfactions derived from it (28-32).

Chapter 3: The Dilemma and Wordsworth's Poetry: *An Evening Walk*

[1]Most attention has attached a biographical significance to the two early works. Notable exceptions are Hartman and Ramsey. Hartman reads *An Evening Walk* as a "poem issuing from the mind of someone interested in the mind, and especially the mind of a poet" (*Poetry* 90). He traces in it not only "the poet's revolt against artificial eyes and ears" but also his attention to presenting the scene as it is perceived rather than replicating it as it is found: "his realism . . . is a kind of surrealism; it appropriates nature-facts" (100). Ramsey claims that Wordsworth's early works "shed light on the psychological questions which challenged him early in his career . . . [and] give us in latency the states of consciousness which nurtured his better works" (376). Ramsey reads *An Evening Walk* as a failed but important attempt "to face head-on the problem of duality which its precursors generally ignored or else regarded as an issue of no consequence to poetry" (385).

[2]References to Wordsworth's poetry are to the Oxford edition, which is most respectful of Wordsworth's deliberations. The poems chosen range from 1793 to 1822, in an attempt to establish that Wordsworth's preoccupation with perception and his attention to his reader transcend—and possibly even account for—his stylistic varitey. Although this approach does not pretend that it can or should reduce the poetry to a body without contradiction or variety, it does argue for greater-than-usual attention to the continuity of Wordsworth's work.

[3]Carl Woodring, "The New Sublimity in 'Tintern Abbey,'" shows Wordsworth redirecting readers' expectations about what aesthetic categories designate. Wordsworth's ability to do so might have developed from an earlier awareness of the superficialities and limitations of preconceived systems generally.

[4]This conclusion is consonant with Wallace Jackson's explanation of how late eighteenth-century poets usually manipulate readers' emotions. They depict

> qualities or states of mind by endowing them circumstantially, by offering the emblems of an affective presence. . . . The figure is detached from its germinating occasion, from its causal relation to the psychology of the speaker. (125)

The concentrated figure is impressed on the reader, with the intention of usurping causal relationships and conveying emotional experience (125-27). The effect is "built up from the outside" (125). The emphasis is on the isolated emotional state, which additional figures may be created to enforce (127). Jackson says that Wordsworth and Coleridge depart from their predecessors in their method of building up from "inside" (125) and in their

> interest in the time-fragments separating discrete emotional states, those formative moments that inhabit the interlude between completed sequences. (127)

As repeated references to a specific and original source of an emotional state, Wordsworth's place names run counter to the customary approach of presenting carefully contrived emblems of a quality and suggest an intention other than imitation behind *An Evening Walk*.

[5]In Iser's terms, which I use freely, these might fall under the "perspective of character." Describing most clearly a condition of prose fiction, Iser states: "Generally speaking, there are four perspectives through which the pattern of the repertoire first emerges: that of the narrator, that of the characters, that of the plot, and that marked out for the reader" (96). Iser himself views these flexibly. He notes that not all texts use all four (96) and

that texts do not mark them off from each other (113). Since the most important point is the interaction of different perspectives and since the perspectives clearly need not be those of speakers present, my extension of the theory is a small liberty that does not violate its integrity.

[6]Jonathan Ramsey notes the near absence of the addressee:

Dorothy Wordsworth is simply *a* person addressed by the poet, not a figure incorporated into the poem's psychology, and so she resolves none of Wordsworth's ambivalence by her special presence but remains the silent recipient of his testimonial. (380 emphasis added)

[7]Recall the exposition in the preceding chapter.

[8]In a different context, Karl Kroeber remarks on the variety of Wordsworth's descriptions: Wordsworth "even compares (by superimposing) a scene with itself, and, in *Peele Castle*, compares a real scene with its painted representation" (*Romantic Landscape* 80). Kroeber stresses that such flexibility can come only from a definition of a scene "as the interaction of scene and viewer, as the coalescence of subject and object, as an *experience*" (80). John Beer also suggests that what Wordsworth depicts in his poetry and how he presents it is informed by a particular notion of perception. Wordsworth focuses on things according to a principle of "Kairos," or significant time, as opposed to one of "Chronos," or merely time passing (*Time* 30). The dependence of the object on the mind makes Wordsworth's poems partly "psychoscapes" (17).

[9]This interpretation owes much to John Jones, who first argued that "relationship" (his term, which I borrow) is a central concept in Wordsworth. Jones reads Wordsworth's work as a "private effort in the traditions of western

thinking" (198-99). Although Jones takes some trouble to place it with respect to the "public context" (198) of Western epistemology (27-47), finding Wordsworth closest to Spinoza (36), he insists that it represents no revolutionary thought on Wordsworth's part:

> What is a thing? How is one thing related to other things? Wordsworth would not have framed his questions in quite the way he did, had he not grown up in the eighteenth century, nor would his metaphysical enquiry have been thus childlike in its unembarassment had he possessed the intellectual selfconsciousness of a philosopher. This very innocence lends importance to his inherited forms of thought: it allowed him to give general assent to the assumptions of the age. He accepted the problem as it had been stated by the eighteenth century: in doubt or in extremity he did not, like Coleridge, attempt restatement. Rather, he persisted in the old questions; and hence the monotony of his genius. (34)

That Wordsworth worked unthinkingly within an eighteenth-century tradition is not the only conclusion that can be drawn from Jones's identification of Wordsworth's interest in old—or, more exactly, unanswered—questions. Wordsworth seems more to return to the question of individuation because known theories failed to describe perception as he experienced it and as he heard and read others did than because he was a philosophical innocent. Wordsworth does not explicitly address the issue of solipsism. That avoidance may indicate—but does not necessarily indicate—an exaggerated fear of the issue. It is more likely to be deliberate because in all Wordsworth's attention to the particular boundaries of objects, he never affirms that they must in "reality" exist in some fixed and independent condition apart from the perceiver. On the contrary, he revels in the lack of fixity. Wordsworth notes that their seeming externality is an unavoidable condition of perception and allows that inevitability to give a "factual" status to externality. If Wordsworth kicks the stone, it is not to refute the Bishop. It is more likely to see what happens. Whether or not the stone exists, the activity, the relationship obtains, and the perceiver benefits in some way from it. Wordsworth thus shifts inquiry away from an inevitable condition to a process involving it and a result stemming from it.

[10]Wordsworth thus appropriates the eighteenth-century technique for his own purposes. See above, note 4 to this chapter.

[11]"Literalness is the necessary preface to [Wordsworth's] genius. Everything, for him, was what it was, and it was not anything else. . . . In its being so he saw it as somehow self-guaranteeing" (Jones 15-16); Havens uses Coleridge's term to lament Wordsworth's "matter-of-factness," a condition he attributes to Wordsworth's "difficulty . . . in distinguishing the essential from the accidental" (11-14). Neither Jones nor Havens ascribes the characteristic to artistic or intellectual intention, and neither separates its function in Wordsworth's poetry from its possibly personal origin and consequences.

[12]Since the poems have been customarily associated with each other, a significant body of early responses to either independently cannot be efficiently isolated.

[13]Sharp assumes that the meeting took place after Holcroft reviewed the poems ("Principle" 74, n. 5). Mark Reed's *Chronology* gives no date for their first meeting, and in a letter to me dated April 8, 1986, he confirmed the unavailability of that information.

Chapter 4: *Lyrical Ballads*: **Genre, Paradigm, Variations**

[1]For a study of Wordsworth as a "supreme artificer" in his use of genre, see Curran ("Wordsworth").

[2]My analysis concerns itself only with how Wordsworth's contributions to *Lyrical Ballads* show his characteristic concerns. Stephen Prickett, in *Wordsworth and Coleridge: The Lyrical Ballads*, has argued that Wordsworth's and Coleridge's poems together unify the project, a position consistent with his earlier statements about Wordsworth's dependence on Coleridge (*Coleridge and Wordsworth: the Poetry of Growth*) and with which many concur. Beer, for example, argues that Wordsworth became "humanized" through his relationships with Coleridge and Dorothy Wordsworth (*Human Heart* xiii). My analysis, however, follows Parrish (*Art* 34-79) in accepting the fundamental incompatibility of Wordsworth's and Coleridge's views and credits Wordsworth with having kept his own goals in mind throughout the partnership. Emphasizing Wordsworth's independence in no way detracts from Coleridge's importance in other contexts.

[3]Wolfson (*Questioning*) and Swingle identify a similar technique, which they separately analyze in terms of a preference for investigation over declaration, as characteristic of Wordsworth.

[4]As Manning observes with respect to "Poor Susan" (351), it is surprising that work Wordsworth singled out as representative seems to have received less critical attention than many undesignated pieces in the collection (351). For particular comments on "The Childless Father," see Garner (187-88), Harson (139), and Beatty (207).

[5]In the *Preface* to *Lyrical Ballads*, Wordsworth addresses the importance of "the perception of similitude in dissimilitude," toward which poetry helps

the mind. He calls it "the great spring of the activity of our minds and their chief feeder" (*Prose* 1: 148).

[6]For studies addressing "The Thorn" and "The Idiot Boy" as poems in which the portrayal of deviance provokes revaluation of the "normative," see Bewell's articles and also Kroeber's remarks on "The Thorn" in "Beyond the Imaginable" (200-05).

[7]In Bialostosky's reading, the father has not even this much assurance. He is, rather, in the process of making an anecdote out of a confrontation with his son in order to understand the conflict (112). In that context, the final statement is itself something of a lie. The fiction either substitutes the illusion that the father has learned something for the fact that he has not, or it allows some superficial lesson to usurp the place of more appropriate learning. Freely interpreted, Bialostosky's reading likewise sees the narrator in search of confirmation or clarification of his thoughts. Bialostosky posits that the father's question does not ask for a geographical preference but for some statement of the son's preference for being with him. The father thus solicits the son's reassurance about the security of their relationship, a reassurance that could obtain only through shared perspectives (109-12).

[8]*Cf.* Griffin, who remarks on the "formulaic phrasing" of the first part of the poem and the pointed assumption of a storyteller's stance (392). In analyzing "Simon Lee," I refer to the revised (or as de Selincourt says, the "final" [Wordsworth, *Poetical Works* 4: 413]) version. If the revised text still shows attention to association, it emphasizes the continuity of Wordsworth's aims. Griffin carefully points out the seemingly greater ineptitude of the 1798 narrator, who, in the first part of the poem, "sets down what he knows about Simon in a jumble, mixing personal observations with hearsay and history, the

present with the past"; Griffin generalizes: "the revision gains most . . . from a clean separation of past from present times" (399-400). I suggest that the earlier incompetence weakens the effect of the abdication, making it seem to stem from the narrator's frustration at a task beyond his ability rather than from realizing that the task itself is of dubious value. The revision allows for the opposite effect.

[9]*Cf.* Rzepka, who points out the narrator's concentration on his own reactions (53).

[10]Perhaps this point suggests how Mayo arrived at his still controversial conclusion that *Lyrical Ballads* is an essentially conventional example of magazine verse from Wordsworth's time (486). At least all of the conventional elements that Mayo lists (492-507) indisputably appear in the poems; however, they are not necessarily endorsed in the contexts of the poems.

Chapter 5: *Lyrical Ballads*: Complications

[1]Averill raises but does not pursue the appearance of the beggar as an object: "The analogy between the old nearly blind man and a parish registry tends to turn the beggar into a piece of writing" (127). Spiegelman draws positive inferences from that circumstance, referring to the beggar as "a 'record,' a history in which the community can read its past offices of charity" (24).

[2]Wordsworth included first-person poems in both the 1798 and 1800 editions of *Lyrical Ballads*, with the "Lines" poems being especially representative of a more personal technique in both cases. Of the monologues I have singled out, "The Complaint of a Forsaken Indian Woman" appeared in both editions; "The Old Cumberland Beggar" was added in 1800. The variety

evident from the first suggests Wordsworth's own commitment to investigating perception from all possible poetic angles. That Wordsworth chose to add to the next edition, along with his *Preface*, such an exemplary display of the limited view through the first-person monologue as "The Old Cumberland Beggar" offers may also reflect his sensitivity to readers' difficulties in sorting out characters' perspectives.

[3]Both Johnson's *Dictionary* and the *O.E.D.* support a sense of "peculiar" as encompassing the ideas that the views at issue are personal and characteristic of an individual alone; that they stand apart from and in contrast to the views of a group; and that they are therefore of questionable merit. The notion of Wordsworth's writing as "peculiar" begins in articles from the *Analytical, Critical,* and *Monthly Reviews*, which criticize the loco-descriptive pieces for somehow taking a wrong angle of vision on familiar scenes and thereby turning their potential clarity into actual obscurity. It persists in reviews of *Lyrical Ballads*. The critic for the *New London Review* joins Burney and Southey in wishing that Wordsworth had chosen to write about subjects of interest to his audience instead of only to himself. The relatively mild tone in which most reviewers of *Lyrical Ballads* couch their criticisms should not mask the fact that they resist or ignore the issue of individual perception in the poems.

Lyrical Ballads received ten major periodical reviews, if one counts the separate reviews of the second edition, a distinction made by only two journals (the *Monthly Mirror* and the *British Critic*). In both instances, the second reviews seem to have been undertaken for the purpose of expatiating upon the judgment made in the first. Of these ten reviews, four reject *Lyrical Ballads* (the *Critical Review*, the *Monthly Magazine* the *Monthly Review*, and the *New*

London Review). The remaining six clearly coopt the poems into the service of other concerns. The notice in the *Analytical Review* and both notices in the *Monthly Mirror* praise *Lyrical Ballads* for departing from the fashion of melancholy. These reviewers advocate an adoption of what they see as the dominantly cheerful tone of *Lyrical Ballads* as a substitute for the melancholic fashion they dislike. The second notice in the *Monthly Mirror* raises objections to any poems or parts of poems that might verge on melancholy. The paragraph in the *Antijacobin Review* and both notices in the *British Critic* praise *Lyrical Ballads* out of ethnocentrism. The author of the second review for the *British Critic* accepts *Lyrical Ballads* because it is a native production, a fact he uses to excuse those parts of it in which he finds "obscurity" or in which Wordsworth "sometimes goes too far in his pursuit of simplicity."

[4]For arguments supporting both extremes see, respectively, Jay and de Man.

[5]That Wordsworth, pondering biographical theory, might have entertained this idea is supported by Lyons' explicit statement and defense of such a position, which, he maintains, accounts for and follows from the symbiotic development of biography and the novel.

[6]Golden, in fact, reads Wordsworth's poetry in terms of its display of interaction between projected selves; however, he does not address the technique as part of a theoretical enterprise. He posits only two generalized "selves" (100-01) and allows the possibility that they help Wordsworth to deal with aspects of his personality that dominate his development (100-48). More recently, Pfau has pointed out that Wordsworth's autobiographical figure more often refers to a linguistic than a conscious existence and has called for greater

attention to intentionality in light of Wordsworth's apparent sensitivity to the *"ideal* dependency of consciousness on language" (510).

[7]Although it is more customary to consider "Tintern Abbey" apart from the *Lyrical Ballads*, some readers also find it congruous with the other poems. Wolfson, for example, sees a question and answer pattern of the *Lyrical Ballads* culminate in "Tintern Abbey," in which one speaker is "able to express opposition within a single, urgently sustained utterance" ("Speaker" 549).

[8]McFarland also reads this passage as the genesis of a perception:

> It is almost as though Wordsworth's "hedge-rows, hardly hedge-rows, little lines/ Of sportive wood run wild" were produced exactly to illustrate Rousseau's reveristic annulment of "the point of separation between fictions and realities." The "hedge-rows" are realities of present vision, the "little lines of sportive wood run wild" are fictions arising from the reality, and the equivocating word "hardly" bridges the line of separation between the two. (255)

[9]If and how the speaker reproduces his earlier view is a crux of the poem admitting of many interpretations. For example, Rzepka argues that the speaker succeeds in doing so for himself—"By putting himself back in its [sic] last known place, Wordsworth reinhabits the self of five years ago" (86)—while Hartman argues that the does so vicariously—"He believes that his former self may be revived or continued by his sister" (*Poetry* 286). Since the text seems to exploit the gulf between the speaker's two experiences of the scene, attention to the relationship between the two may be the most fruitful line of inquiry. Woodring opens such a path by remarking that the earlier experience

"returns with compound interest" to the speaker in his later circumstances (*Wordsworth* 60).

[10]Because I am most concerned with what Wordsdworth offered his readership, I have excluded *The Prelude* from this study. Wordsworth seems to have conceived *The Prelude* as part of his poetic campaign: its preoccupation with perception has been generally acknowledged (albeit not agreed upon) since Lindenberger analyzed its "rhetoric of interaction" (41); its intricately manipulated autobiographical details may be easily seen as a "repertoire," especially in light of Geoffery Jackson's theory that *The Prelude* is a public work "addressed to a multiplicity of unspecified readers" (227). Wordsworth, however, did not build his canon around the autobiographical poem. After finishing the first full version of *The Prelude* in 1805, Wordsworth withheld it from his readers, preparing for them instead two volumes of short, juxtaposed poems. His publication pattern suggests a dissatisfaction with the personal narrative mode as a means of challenging readers to perceptual self-reliance and a renewed interest in interactive perspectives as more conducive to reader engagement.

Since Wordsworth repeatedly revised the unpublished poem, he may have not so much rejected the autobiographical mode as doubted the effectiveness of his strategies to direct readers' attention to the issue of perception underpinning the personal details. Continued rewriting of *The Prelude* notwithstanding, Wordsworth's statements about the poem clearly indicate that he subordinated it to his other work. His references to it as a "tributary" (*EY* 454) and an "ante-chapel" (*Prose* 3:5) place it in the context of his other endeavors and foreground his commitment to his poetic campaign. Work more clearly involving his readership was more important to him. (For remarks on *The Recluse* in relation to Wordsworth's campaign, see Chapter 7 of this study.)

Wordsworth's position on *The Prelude* should caution readers who now have access to it against turning it into his major work. Later readers may achieve a greater understanding of Wordsworth's enterprise by resisting the temptation to privilege the poem on his own life in favor of grappling with what Wordsworth privileged for his readers.

Chapter 6: Categories and Sequences

[1]Garber refers to "To the Cuckoo" to illustrate Wordsworth's "object-consciousness" (xi) as distinct from Keats's or Shelley's (61-63). In a separate article, I address Wordsworth's and Keats's different expectations about individual perception, illustrated especially by "To the Cuckoo" and "Ode to a Nightingale," as informing Keats's idea of Wordsworth's "egotism."

[2]The thirteen lyrics in the first edition were, in order: "To a Butterfly" ("Stay Near Me"), "The Sun Has Long Been Set," "O Nightingale, Thou Surely Art," "My Heart Leaps Up," "The Cock is Crowing," "The Small Celandine" ("There is a Flower"), "I Wandered Lonely," "Who Fancied What a Pretty Sight," "The Sparrow's Nest," "Gipsies," "To the Cuckoo," "To a Butterfly" ("I've Watched You Now"), "It is No Spirit Who From Heaven." Perhaps the inclusion of two poems on the same topic—the butterfly—suggests a pointed interest in the different perceivers. The speaker in the first "Butterfly" lyric begins as a happy and secure individual whose perceptual relationship with the butterfly awakens him to alternative approaches to nature; the speaker in the second "Butterfly" lyric begins in poignant confusion and seems especially in need of the comfort he derives from his perceptual

relationship with the butterfly. The ways in which these thirteen poems might qualify each other seem inexhaustable, yet Wordsworth invites even further juxtaposition and comparison by adding a note directing the reader to see the first of the two volumes for another poem on the celandine ("Pansies, Lilies"). Indeed, every poem in the volumes might be examined fruitfully in terms of its position with respect to every other, an interdependence Curran analyzes in "Multum in Parvo." For detailed treatment of the importance of reading individual works in the context of the volumes in which they appear, see Fraistat's "Introduction" to *Poems in Their Place* as well as his earlier book.

³In Chapter 22 of *Biographia Literaria*, Coleridge criticizes the speaker of "Gipsies," whom he indentifies with the poet, in these terms:

> The poet, without seeming to reflect that the poor tawny wan-
> derers might probably have been tramping for weeks together
> through road and lane, over moor and mountain, and consequently
> must have been right glad to rest themselves, their children and
> cattle, for one whole day; and overlooking the obvious truth, that
> such repose might be quite as necessary for *them*, as a walk of the
> same continuance was pleasing or healthful for the more fortunate
> poet; expresses his indignation in a series of lines, the diction and
> imagery of which would have been rather above, than below the
> mark, had they been applied to the immense empire of China
> improgressive for thirty centuries. (2: 137)

Taking Coleridge's remarks as a springboard, Ferry counters by arguing that Wordsworth does not write "a poetry which *evaluates* the world according to a reasonable and common sense set of attitudes, [but] a poetry which *makes use* of the world for other purposes" (7). Coleridge's rejection is consonant with the basic divergence between his and Wordsworth's views more apparent in their different conceptions of *The Recluse*. (See below, Chapter 7.) Ferry's acceptance calls attention to the importance of the object perceived *as object* in Wordsworth's poetry, and opens the way for my own and other recent readings of the exaggeration in "Gipsies" as pointedly revealing its speaker's insecurity—in either political (Simpson, *Wordsworth's Historical Imagination* 22-55) or aesthetic (Kelley 160-62) contexts.

[4]All reviewers objected to "Moods of My Own Mind." Identifying Wordsworth with all of his personae, they criticized him especially for being more interested in how his mind might have unique ideas than in how he might receive and develop the ideas available to him from the poetic tradition. For example, the *Critical Review* exhorted him to learn from books instead of from "the moods of his own mind," to turn to others so as to escape "the infatuation of self-conceit"; the *Edinburgh Review* concluded that such writing could arise only "from the self-illusion of a mind of extraordinary sensibility habituated to solitary meditation"; the *Satirist* rails against his "swelling self-sufficiency"; the *Annual Review* pronounced him "arrogant" for thinking he had discovered subjects and feelings greater than any discovered by Virgil and Milton and labelled him "dangerous to public taste."

[5]Interest in Wordsworth's categorization is only just coming of age. Ferguson, Ruoff, Ross, Herman, and Briesmaster have followed Scoggins' ground-breaking work (which remains the only book-length study exclusively concerned with Wordsworth's categorizations and even it privileges two of them) with provocative analyses and speculations.

[6]Ross details Wordsworth's taxonomy not only in the 1815 edition but in the 1809 letter to Coleridge and in subsequent editions.

[7]See above, pp. 22-26.

[8]Recall Wordsworth's indiscrimination between "poets" and "men," (*Prose* 1:138), of which this issue seems to be a parallel.

[9]Coleridge's drawing attention (in Chapter 13 of *Biographia Literaria*) to the inacessibility of the issue stands out in contrast.

[10]For a different view of the "impersonal" tone of Wordsworth's later poetry, see Perkins, especially pp. 227-29. Perkins argues that Wordsworth's later "impersonal" poetry contrasts with his early "intimate" or sincere poetry because Wordsworth later substitutes reliance on traditional institutions for reliance on individual experience as a means to truth.

[11]After considering the eighteenth-century neglect of the form, Johnson shows Wordsworth not merely reestablishing it but combining and advancing the two extant conceptions of it. By the end of the seventeenth century, the sonnet could be construed either as a subordinate part of a sequence, which Sidney most representatively exploited, or as a "self-sufficient form," which Milton invented (15-16). Johnson posits that Wordsworth planned "a Miltonic sequence," i.e., a sequence in which each individual sonnet would not have to yield any of its own strength and integrity to become part of the whole (36). Although Johnson is dubious about the possible success of such a project and opines that it violates "the aesthetics of the Miltonic sonnet" (38), he still credits Wordsworth for "his most distinctive and original contribution to the history of the form" (173). Johnson argues that the constancy of the sonnet in Wordsworth's canon ought to qualify "our sense of 'decline'" (9), and his singular study supports efforts to see persistent concerns in all of Wordsworth's work. Although Johnson's is the only book entirely on Wordsworth's sonnets,

interest in the sonnets, and specifically *Ecclesiastical Sonnets*, may be growing. For example Palumbo has recently identified an integrated pattern of self-assertion and communal commitment especially in *Ecclesiastical Sonnets* I.xxi, xxii, and xxiii. One hopes that additional studies will follow in response to Curran's call (*Poetic Form*) for greater attention to the importance of genre in all Romantic writing.

[12]Insofar as Wordsworth's relation to Milton and the sonnet shares some of the characteristics of his relation to Young, Johnson, and literary theory (noted above, pp. 46-50), it strengthens the bond between his practices and declarations.

[13]Lee M. Johnson notes that the various collections of "Tour" poems are not genuine sequences but attaches no particular significance to that fact except to state that Wordsworth uses them "as a reflection of his state of mind," a use that lets him "moralize" too much in them (30-32). It is possible, nevertheless, that Wordsworth attempted a deliberate controverting of the assumption of an external unifying idea, a controverting represented by the irregularity of the form. *Memorials of a Tour on the Continent*, a series of juxtaposed poems of mixed genre, some of which are sonnets, might easily have been a sonnet sequence, and that it is not so seems more than accidental. In a sense, the work picks up the thread of presenting an individual view of objects seen on a journey that Wordsworth began to spin with *An Evening Walk*. These poems are "memorials" in the sense that they are testaments of an individual's interaction with the scenes. For example, the first poem memorializes a highly unexpected and individual sight form the tour—the fish-women at Calais.

The dedication to the "Fellow-travellers" with which the work begins indicates that it does not mean to replicate an unmediated view:

> Dear Fellow-travellers! think not that
>   the Muse,
> To You presenting these memorial Lays,
> Can hope the general eye thereon would gaze,
> As on a mirror that gives back the hues
> Of living Nature. (11. 1-5)

It also indicates that it does not offer its persona's view for adoption, for it presses the addressees to contribute their own perspectives to the verse:

> Ye only can supply
> The life, the truth, the beauty: she
>   [the Muse] confides
> In that enjoyment which with You abides,
> Trusts to your love and vivid memory;
> Thus far contented, that for You her verse
> Shall lack not power the "meeting soul
>   to pierce!" (11. 9-14)

Wordsworth's exaggerated sustenance of the Muse throughout the dedicatory sonnet distances the perspective in the poem from his personal view, and it suggests that the distance be extended to the other figures mentioned. The Fellow-travellers are not necessaarily persons who accompanied Wordsworth on his tour; they may be Fellow-travellers of the Muse, i.e., readers. They are not to supplement the poems with their recollections of the same scenes but to bring all their recollections to bear on the poems, establishing a relationship with them as the persona did with the objects he memorializes. *Memorials of a Tour on the Continent*, then, relies on reader response rather than the convention of the sequence to unify the poems.

[14]Woodring notes that Wordsworth's opposition to Catholic Relief stems partly from "his belief in Anglo-Saxon liberty versus Papal dominion" (*Politics* 130).

[15]They would, in fact, find it difficult to do so. Boulger notes that "there is little of specific religious or dogmatic matters in these poems," which are "by no means doctrinaire in [their] acceptance of the establishment" (388-387). In trying to extract what doctrinal points there are in the sonnets, Boulger identifies an emphasis on "the Holy Spirit or inner light as the ultimate religious authority in man" that seems at odds with "Anglican dogmas of the Trinity and of authority" (389). Wordsworth's religion, insofar as it can be pinned down, is more often associated with radical Protestantism and its emphasis on the individual act of belief than with established Anglicanism. See especially Brantley's first book. Watson even finds it more productive to analyze Wordsworth's religion in terms of "fundamental and primitive patterns of belief" (ix) than in terms of organized religion. More schematically, Hodgson traces Wordsworth's progress toward orthodoxy in terms of a struggle with the moralities implied by "iconic" and "emblematic" views of nature.

[16]Gates maintains that Wordsworth comes to such a conclusion during the course of working out the sonnets:

> In the end . . . for Protestant Wordsworth both the sacraments and "Faith" became a personal matter, ministered to but not completed by the Church. And in the end, Christian history, unlike politico-ecclesiastical history, became the history of the individual soul. (131)

It seems to me that the emphasis is present from the beginning.

[17]The *Oxford English Dictionary* shows an interesting development in the history of "lore." Uses of the term to signify a codified body of knowledge apart from the activities of investigating or communicating it—such as "Doctrines, precepts, ordinances"; "a form of doctrine, a creed, religion"; "a rule of behavior" (2b, c, d)—seem to have become obsolete before 1600. Uses that persist into the nineteenth century tie "lore" to the activity of ascertaining and conveying knowledge. For example:

> The act of teaching; the condition of being taught; instruction, tuition, education. In particularized use, a piece of teaching or instruction; a lesson. (1)

Or:

> That which is taught; (*a person's*) doctrine or teaching; applied chiefly to religious doctrine but used also with reference to moral principles. (2, emphasis added)

Coleridge's "Nightingale" (1. 41) and Scott's *The Last Minstrel* (I.viii) appear respectively among the first and second set of examples. Apparently, the active emphasis was especially common in northern England, for that region is given as using the compound "larefather" for "schoolmaster" or "instructor" (6). The citation comes from *A Provincial Glossary with a Collection of Local Proverbs*, edited by Francis Grose, 1790.

Samuel Johnson confirms the human and active emphasis. The corrected edition of the *Dictionary* defines "lore" as "Lesson; doctrine; instruction." Though Johnson's etymologies are not linguistically sound, this one gives a clue to the connotations of the term for him. He explains it as derived from a Saxon verb meaning "to learn."

[18]Perhaps this interpretation may be strengthened by recalling that Wordsworth had begun one of the "Sonnets Dedicated to Liberty," one on bowing to Napoleon, with the lines: "Is it a reed that's shaken by the wind,/ Or what is it that ye go forth to see?" His parodic use of reed imagery in the later sonnet seems all the more pointed for the precedent.

[19]Palumbo also notes the idealization of Wordsworth's historical referents, whether based in ecclesiastical, political, or biographical reality.

[20]The "conclusion" added in 1827 helps readers insofar as its reference back to the stream metaphor should induce them to pull the first and second sonnets, with contexts, from their horizons. Beyond that, it spurs readers to further activity, for it expresses the speaker's wish to see the effect of the composition (11. 13-14). The later additions to the sequence—on Christianity in America and on particular sacraments and ceremonies—are likewise in keeping with the main preoccupation of the sequence: American Christianity came about to protect the individual act of faith, and hence it repeats a familiar pattern. The approach to church practices is not doctrinal but undertakes to show the effect of such practices on individuals.

The strategic subtlety of Wordsworth's later work seems to have produced the same effect as the strategic subtlety of his earliest work: it allows readers to extract the repertoire. Reviewers tended to acknowledge the merit of a turn to traditional form and patriotic topic while dwelling on the resultant contrast to Wordsworth's earlier innovativeness. They perpetuate suspicion of individuality by lengthly recapitulations of Wordsworth's earlier "peculiarities" and look for persistence of them even in his reformed work. For example, the *Literary Gazette*'s reviewer of *Ecclesiastical Sketches* finds many of the pieces obscure and attributes that circumstance to Wordsworth's persistent privileging of his own interests over his readers'; according to *The Censor*, Wordsworth is becoming fashionable because he "has corrected some of the obliquities of his taste and abated many of the peculiarities of his composition," but he will never be "popular" because of the "extreme personal character" of his work. It seems that Wordsworth's technical spiral produced a circular response.

Chapter 7: Assembling *The Recluse*

[1]Recall the manuscript quoted in Chapter Two ("There were to be two other parts to *The Recluse* . . ."), and compare the published *Preface* announcing *The Excursion* as a "portion" of *The Recluse* and including what became *The Prelude* among the projected parts (*Prose* 3: 5). Wordsworth's emphasis on his work in terms of "parts," "portions," and "divisions" suggests that he habitually saw an assemblage of discrete pieces as the optimum form of his canon. References to *The Prelude* here reinforce a sense of the autobiographical mode as one among many in the enterprise.

[2]The genre of *The Excursion* has never been exactly defined. Less eclectically than Lyon, Hartman (*Poetry* 296-97) and Patterson see it as a revival of the georgic. Curran analyzes it in terms of an apotheosis of the pastoral tradition (*Poetic Form* 103-06).

[3]Lyon notes that in *The Excursion*, "the truth is not spoken exclusively by one character but is divided among them all." He does not develop the significance of the point beyond the fact that it distinguishes *The Excursion* from most other philosophical dialogues (35), but Thomas pursues the issue in a specific comparison to Berkeley's form (150-52). In a different context, Frances Ferguson maintains that "the 'conversational' scheme for *The*

Excursion was devised both to raise and to explore the nature of the poet's authority" (208).

[4]*Cf.* Spiegelman: "The ideas of the four main characters are not so important as the means of presenting them or as the dramatic functions they perform within the text" (214). For a different view, see Bostetter, who argues that Wordsworth uses the characters to deduce a surrogate principle of truth to replace the truth of human harmony with nature in which he had lost faith and ultimately suppresses the Solitary's doubt in favor of the Wanderer's and Pastor's hope (66-81).

[5]The Solitary's biography (Book III) indicates his basically humanistic outlook. Though disillusioned, he still looks to humanity for the greatest good and the greatest evil. In fact, he wants his confidence in humanity restored and mistakenly seeks this end from the Pastor. He even includes his desired result in his request, which concludes:

> Some by your records, may our doubts be solved;
>
> And so, *not searching higher*, we may learn
>
> *To prize the breath we share with human kind;*
>
> *And look upon the dust of man with awe.*

(V.654-57; my emphasis 65, Wordsworth's 656-57)

[6]Though he seems to imply the existence of verifiable "truth" in the situation, Galperin makes a similar point about the differences among the characters' views. He notes an "insuperable gulf between what each perceives to be the facts of life and the 'solid facts' themselves" (202) and illustrates it through their perspectives on the story of the childless couple (202-05).

[7]In general, the Wanderer clings to a divine Benevolence, hoping that

it will subsume all contradictions (IV.10-30). Hence, he looks for unifying means in all situations. The Wanderer demonstrates this orientation in minor and major ways. On a small scale, he praises rural funerary rites because of the "bond of brotherhood" they effect even among passing strangers (II.562). More centrally, he believes that the Solitary can be restored by finding a broader principle than he has previously known:

> If tired with systems, each in its degree
> Substantial, and all crumbling in their turn,
> Let him build systems of his own, and smile
> At the fond work, demolished with a touch;
> If unreligious, let him be at once,
> Among ten thousand innocents, enrolled
> A pupil in the many-chambered school,
> Where superstition weaves her airy dreams.
>   (IV.603-10)

[8]The narrator has been preoccupied with the effects of a natural scene from the opening of the poem. He moves quickly from the observable features of the situation—"'Twas summer, and the sun had mounted high"—to the way in which the scene impresses him—"Southward the landscape indistinctly glared/ Through a pale steam" (I.1-3). He develops the introduction through his associations, drawing from his accumulated perspective knowledge of the conditions under which the atmosphere in which he now finds himself could be enjoyable (I.9-17). He then contrasts that speculative state with the elements of the present situation that make the "same" atmosphere unpleasant to him (I.17-25). The opening lines not only demonstrate a process

of individual association but also indicate that the value of the object with which the perceiver interacts lies in the relationship between the two and does not inhere separately in either.

[9]McInerney points out "that everything shown [in *The Excursion*] is seen through a frame," as if the poem provided "arenas for perception" (191). He argues that attention to the frame is necessary for deducing the system as Wordsworth directed (191) and for understanding that the idea of perception at issue is perception as "a performance that creates textuality" (188).

[10]A range of interpretations about the end of *The Excursion* exists. Bostetter (13) and Woodring (*Wordsworth* 182) find it incomplete because it does not show the Solitary's promised conversion. Smith maintains that it finishes "dramatically and open-endedly" to show that "the Solitary's recovery . . . will come from within himself or not at all" (171-72). Smith does not emphasize the implications of this situation for the reader as much as he might. At the opposite extreme, Galperin celebrates the end as "a matter of choice" for the reader (213), and Spiegelman sees it as "deliberately unresolved" in tribute to the "excursive power" of the mind (214).

[11]Parrish (34-79) and Johnston (xvi-xxi) address the fundamental incompatibility of Wordsworth's and Coleridge's ideas.

[12]This proposition owes much to McGann's argument that all Romantic poetry manifests a confidence in literature to lead readers to knowledge that philosophy, religion, and other forms of systemtatic thought had failed to provide (70), but it calls for a narrower discrimination among the poets' confidences in literature. For example, Coleridge places quite a burden on literature, yet his trust seems to hope for a consensus that distinguishes it from

Wordsworth's. My present scope permits examination only of Wordsworth's approach, but a longer study might well anatomize how competing Romantic poetics arose in the context of the empirical dilemma.

[13]Jeffrey's review begins: "This will never do."

[14]The pattern seems to describe a full circle back to Locke, but modern privileging of individual autonomy in consequence of epistemological self-reliance ignores Locke's exhortation to humility in consequence of it. Analyses of individualism in Western culture are beyond citation. I confine my referent to recent literary critical efforts, such as those of Bleich, Culler, Fish, and Tompkins, to discover the assumptions that govern individual interpretations. Interest in factors that shape the individual shows itself in Wordsworth criticism perhaps most noticeably in the work of those scholars—Galperin, Griffin, Geoffrey Jackson, to name just a few—who depart from the convention of identifying Wordsworth with his personae and explore the interplay of the personae in Wordsworth's work.

Works Cited

Alexander, Peter. "Locke on Substance in General." [2 parts] *Ratio* 22 (1980): 91-105 and *Ratio* 23 (1981): 1-19.

Arnold, Matthew. "Wordsworth." Vol. 4 of *The Complete Works of Matthew Arnold.* 15 vols. New York: AMS Press, 1970.

Averill, James. *Wordsworth and the Poetry of Human Suffering.* Ithaca: Cornell Univ. Press, 1980.

Bailey, Nathan. *An Universal Etymological English Dictionary.* 1721. Rev. ed. Edinburgh: Neill and Co., 1789.

Bate, Walter Jackson. *From Classic to Romantic: Premises of Taste in Eighteenth-Century England.* Cambridge: Harvard Univ. Press, 1946.

Beatty, Arthur. *William Wordsworth: His Doctrine and Art in Their Historical Relations.* 1922. Madison, Wisconsin: Univ. of Wisconsin Press, 1962.

Beer, John. *Wordsworth and the Human Heart.* New York: Columbia Univ. Press, 1978.

———. *Wordsworth in Time.* London and Boston: Faber and Faber, 1979.

Berg, Temma F. "Psychologies of Reading." *Tracing Literary Theory.* Edited by Joseph Natoli. Urbana and Chicago: Univ. of Illinois Press, 1987. 248-77.

Berkeley, George. *A Treatise Concerning the Principles of Human Knowledge.* Vol. 2 of *The Works of George Berkeley Bishop of Cloyne.* Edited by A. A. Luce and T. E. Jessop. 9 vols. London and New York: T. Nelson, 1948-57.

Bewell, Alan J. "A 'Word Scarce Said': Hysteria and Witchcraft in Wordsworth's 'Experimental' Poetry of 1797-1798." *ELH* 53 (1986): 357-90.

_____. "Wordsworth's Primal Scene: Retrospective Tales of Idiots, Wild Children, and Savages." *ELH* 50 (1983): 321-46.

Bialostosky, Don H. *Making Tales: The Poetics of Wordsworth's Narrative Experiments.* Chicago and London: Univ. of Chicago Press, 1984.

Bleich, David. "Epistemological Assumptions in the Study of Response." *Reader-Response Criticism: From Formalism to Post-Structuralism.* Edited by Jane P. Tompkins. Baltimore and London: The Johns Hopkins Univ. Press, 1980. 134-63.

Bostetter, Edward. *The Romantic Ventriloquists.* Seattle: Univ. of Washington Press, 1963.

Boulger, James D. *The Calvinist Temper in English Poetry.* The Hague, Paris, and New York: Mouton Publishers, 1980.

Boswell, James. *Boswell's Life of Johnson Together with Boswell's Journal of a Tour to the Hebrides and Johnson's Diary of a Journey into North Wales.* Edited by G. B. Hill. Rev. and Enl. by L. F. Powell. 6 vols. Oxford: Oxford Univ. Press, 1934-50.

Bracken, Harry M. *The Early Reception of Berkeley's Immaterialism 1710-1733.* Rev. Ed. The Hague: Martinus Nijhoff, 1965.

Brantley, Richard E. *Locke, Wesley, and the Method of English Romanticism.* Gainesville, Florida: Univ. Presses of Florida, 1984.

_____. Wordsworth's "Natural Methodism." New Haven: Yale Univ. Press, 1975.

Briesmaster, Allan. "Wordsworth as a Teacher of 'Thought.'" *The Wordsworth Circle* 11 (1980): 19-23.

Bromwich, David. *Hazlitt: The Mind of a Critic.* Oxford and New York: Oxford Univ. Press, 1983.

Chandler, James K. *Wordsworth's Second Nature: A Study of the Poetry and Politics*. Chicago and London: Univ. of Chicago Press, 1984.

Coleridge, Samuel Taylor. *Anima Poetae from the Unpublished Note-Books of Samuel Taylor Coleridge*. Edited by Ernest Hartley Coleridge. Boston and New York: Houghton, Mifflin and Co., 1895.

——. *Biographia Literaria*. Edited by James Engell and Walter Jackson Bate. 2 vols. Vol. 7 of *The Collected Works of Samuel Taylor Coleridge*. Edited by Kathleen Coburn. 16 vols. London: Routledge and Kegan Paul; Princeton: Princeton Univ. Press, 1983.

——. *The Notebooks of Samuel Taylor Coleridge*. Edited by Kathleen Coburn. 3 vols. Princeton: Princeton Univ. Press, 1957-73.

——. *Table Talk*. Edited by Carl Woodring. 2 vols. Vol. 14 of *The Collected Works of Samuel Taylor Coleridge*. Edited by Kathleen Coburn. 16 vols. London: Routledge and Kegan Paul; Princeton: Princeton Univ. Press, 1990.

Colville, Derek. *The Teaching of Wordsworth*. American University Studies: Series IV, English Language and Literature 7. New York and Bern: Peter Lang, 1984.

Cowper, William. *Cowper: Verse and Letters*. Selected and Edited by Brian Spiller. 2 vols. Cambridge: Harvard Univ. Press, 1968.

——. *The Works of William Cowper*. Edited by Robert Southey. 11 vols. 1836. New York: AMS Press, 1971.

Cox, Stephen D. *"The Stranger Within Thee": Concepts of the Self in Late Eighteenth-Century Literature*. Pittsburgh: Univ. of Pittsburgh Press, 1980.

Cruttwell, Patrick. "Wordsworth, the Public, and the People." *Sewanee Review* 64 (1956): 71-80.

Culler, Jonathan. "Literary Competence." *Reader-Response Criticism: From Formalism to Post-Structuralism.* Edited by Jane P. Tompkins. Baltimore and London: The Johns Hopkins Univ. Press, 1980. 101-17.

Curran, Stuart. "Multum in Parvo: Wordsworth's *Poems, in Two Volumes* of 1807." *Poems in their Place: The Intertextuality and Order of Poetic Collections.* Edited by Neil Fraistat. Chapel Hill and London: Univ. of North Carolina Press, 1986. 234-53.

____. *Poetic Form and British Romanticism.* Oxford and New York: Oxford Univ. Press, 1986.

____. "Wordsworth and the Forms of Poetry." *The Age of William Wordsworth: Critical Essays on the Romantic Tradition.* Edited by Kenneth R. Johnston and Gene W. Ruoff. New Brunswick and London: Rutgers Univ. Press, 1987. 115-32.

de Man, Paul. "Autobiography as De-Facement." *The Rhetoric of Romanticism.* New York: Columbia Univ. Press, 1984. 67-81.

De Quincey, Thomas. *Recollections of the Lake Poets.* Edited with an Intro. by Edward Sackville-West. London: John Lehmann, Ltd., 1948.

Dyer, John. *Grongar Hill.* Edited with an Intro. by Richard C. Boys. Baltimore: Johns Hopkins Univ. Press, 1941.

Engell, James. *The Creative Imagination: Enlightenment to Romanticism.* Cambridge and London: Harvard Univ. Press, 1981.

Ferguson, Frances. *Wordsworth: Language as Counter-Spirit.* New Haven and London: Yale Univ. Press, 1977.

Ferry, David. *The Limits of Mortality: An Essay on Wordsworth's Major Poems.* Middletown, Connecticut: Wesleyan Univ. Press, 1959.

Fish, Stanley E. "Interpreting the *Variorum*." *Reader-Response Criticism: From Formalism to Post-Structuralism*. Edited by Jane P. Tompkins. Baltimore and London: The Johns Hopkins Univ. Press, 1980. 164-184.

Fraistat, Neil. "Introduction: The Place of the Book and the Book as Place." *Poems in Their Place: The Intertextuality and Order of Poetic Collections*. Edited by Neil Fraistat. Chapel Hill and London: Univ. of North Carolina Press, 1986. 3-17.

———. *The Poem and the Book: Interpreting Collections of Romantic Poetry*. Chapel Hill and London: Univ. of North Carolina Press, 1985.

Friedman, Michael H. *The Making of a Tory Humanist: William Wordsworth and the Idea of Community*. New York: Columbia Univ. Press, 1979.

Fussell, Paul. *Samuel Johnson and the Life of Writing*. New York and London: W. W. Norton and Co., 1971.

Galperin, William. "'Imperfect While Unshared': The Role of the Implied Reader in Wordsworth's 'Excursion.'" *Criticism* 22 (1980): 193-213.

Garber, Frederick. *Wordsworth and the Poetry of Encounter*. Urbana, Chicago, and London: Univ. of Illinois Press, 1971.

Garner, Margaret. "The Anapestic Lyrical Ballads: New Sympathies." *The Wordsworth Circle* 13 (1982): 183-88.

Gates, Barbara T. "Wordsworth's Mirror of Morality: Distortions of Church History." *The Wordsworth Circle* 12 (1981): 129-32.

Gibson, James. *Locke's Theory of Knowledge and its Historical Relations*. 1917. Cambridge: Cambridge Univ. Press, 1960.

Gill, Stephen. "Wordsworth's Poems: The Question of Text." *Review of English Studies* 34 (1983): 172-90.

Golden, Morris. *The Self Observed: Swift, Johnson, Wordsworth*. Baltimore and London: Johns Hopkins Univ. Press, 1972.

Goldsmith, Oliver. *Collected Works*. Edited by Arthur Friedman. 5 vols. Oxford: Clarendon-Oxford Univ. Press, 1966.

Gray, Thomas. *The Complete Poems of Thomas Gray*. Edited by H. W. Starr and J. R. Hendrickson. Oxford: Clarendon-Oxford Univ. Press, 1966.

Grean, Stanley. *Shaftesbury's Philosophy of Religion and Ethics*. Athens, Ohio: Ohio Univ. Press, 1967.

Greene, Donald. "Augustinianism and Empiricism: A Note on Eighteenth-Century English Intellectual History." *Eighteenth-Century Studies* 1 (1967): 33-68.

Griffin, Andrew L. "Wordsworth and the Problem of Imaginative Story: The Case of 'Simon Lee.'" *PMLA* 92 (1977): 392-409.

Grob, Alan. *The Philosophic Mind: A Study of Wordsworth's Poetry and Thought 1797-1805*. Columbus, Ohio: Ohio State Univ. Press, 1973.

Hamilton, Carson C. *Wordsworth's Decline in Poetic Power: Prophet into High Priest*. New York: Exposition Press, 1963.

Hardy, Thomas. *Jude the Obscure*. Vol. 3 of *Works in Prose and Verse with Prefaces and Notes*. 18 vols. Wessex Edition. New York: AMS Press, 1984.

Harson, Robert R. "Wordsworth's Narrator in 'The Childless Father.'" *American Notes and Queries* 13 (1975): 138-40.

Hartman, Geoffrey H. *The Unremarkable Wordsworth*. Foreword by Donald G. Marshall. Theory and History of Literature 34. Minneapolis: Univ. of Minnesota Press, 1987.

———. *Wordsworth's Poetry 1787-1814.* New Haven and London: Yale Univ. Press, 1964.

Havens, Raymond Dexter. *The Mind of a Poet.* Baltimore: Johns Hopkins Univ. Press, 1941.

Hay, W. H. "Berkeley's Argument from Nominalism." *A Treatise Concerning the Principles of Human Knowledge with Critical Essays.* Edited by Colin Murray Turbayne. Indianapolis: Bobbs-Merrill Co., Inc. 1965. 37-46.

Hayden, John O. *The Romantic Reviewers.* Chicago: Univ. of Chicago Press, 1968.

Hazlitt, William. *The Complete Works of William Hazlitt.* Edited by P. P. Howe. 21 vols. London and Toronto: J. M. Dent and Sons, Ltd., 1931.

Hempton, David. *Methodism and Politics in British Society 1750-1850.* Stanford: Stanford Univ. Press, 1984.

Herman, Judith B. "The Poet as Editor: Wordsworth's Edition of 1815." *The Wordsworth Circle* 9 (1978): 82-87.

Hewitt, Regina. "Faery Lands Fit and Forlorn: Keats and the 'Problem' of Wordsworth's 'Ego.'" *Essays in Literature* 14 (1987): 65-79.

Hirsch, E. D. *Wordsworth and Schelling: A Typological Study of Romanticism.* New Haven: Yale Univ. Press, 1960.

Hodgson, John A. *Wordsworth's Philosophical Poetry, 1797-1814.* Lincoln and London: Univ. of Nebraska Press, 1980.

Holland, Norman N. "Unity Identity Text Self." *Reader-Response Criticism: From Formalism to Post-Structuralism.* Edited by Jane P. Tompkins. Baltimore and London: The Johns Hopkins Univ. Press, 1980. 118-33.

Hume, David. "Dissertation on the Passions." Vol. 4 of *The Philosophical*

Works. 4 vols. Edited by T. H. Green and T. H. Grose. 1882. Darmstadt: Scientia Verlag Allen, 1964.

___. *Treatise of Human Nature.* Edited with an analytical index by L. A. Selby-Bigge. 1888. 2nd ed. with text revised and variant readings by P. H. Nidditch. Oxford: Clarendon-Oxford Univ. Press, 1978.

Iser, Wolfgang. *The Act of Reading: A Theory of Aesthetic Response.* Baltimore and London: Johns Hopkins Univ. Press, 1978.

___. *The Implied Reader: Patterns of Communication from Bunyan to Beckett.* Baltimore and London: Johns Hopkins Univ. Press, 1974.

___. *Prospecting: From Reader Response to Literary Anthropology.* Baltimore and London: Johns Hopkins Univ. Press, 1989.

Jackson, Geoffrey. "Nominal and Actual Audiences: Some Strategies of Communication in Wordsworth's Poetry." *The Wordsworth Circle* 12 (1981): 226-31.

Jackson, Wallace. *The Probable and the Marvelous: Blake, Wordsworth, and the Eighteenth-Century Critical Tradition.* Athens, Georgia: Univ. of Georgia Press, 1978.

Jacobus, Mary. *Tradition and Experiment in Wordsworth's* Lyrical Ballads (1798). London: Clarendon-Oxford Univ. Press, 1976.

Jauss, Hans Robert. *Toward an Aesthetic of Reception.* Trans. Timothy Bahti. Intro. by Paul de Man. Theory and History of Literature 2. Minneapolis: Univ. of Minnesota Press, 1982.

Jay, Paul. *Being in the Text: Self-Representation from Wordsworth to Roland Barthes.* Ithaca: Cornell Univ. Press, 1984.

Johnson, Lee M. *Wordsworth and the Sonnet.* Copenhagen: Rosenkilde and Baggar, 1973.

Johnson, Samuel. *A Dictionary of the English Language.* 4th ed. London: W. Strahan, 1773.

——. *The Works of Samuel Johnson.* 11 vols. 1825. New York: AMS Press, 1970.

——. *The Yale Edition of the Works of Samuel Johnson.* Edited by John H. Middendorf. 23 vols. New Haven and London: Yale Univ. Press, 1958-in progress.

Johnston, Kenneth R. *Wordsworth and* The Recluse. New Haven and London: Yale Univ. Press, 1984.

Jones, Howard Mumford. *Revolution and Romanticism.* Cambridge: Belknap-Harvard Univ. Press, 1974.

Jones, John. *The Egotistical Sublime: A History of Wordsworth's Imagination.* London: Chatto and Windus, 1954.

Kelley, Theresa M. *Wordsworth's Revisionary Aesthetics.* Cambridge and New York: Cambridge Univ. Press, 1988.

Klancher, Jon P. *The Making of English Reading Audiences, 1790-1832.* Madison and London: Univ. of Wisconsin Press, 1987.

Kroeber, Karl. "Beyond the Imaginable: Wordsworth and Turner." *The Age of William Wordsworth: Critical Essays on the Romantic Tradition.* Edited by Kenneth R. Johnston and Gene W. Ruoff. New Brunswick and London: Rutgers Univ. Press, 1987. 196-213.

——. *Romantic Landscape Vision: Constable and Wordsworth.* Madison: Univ. of Wisconsin Press, 1975.

Langbaum, Robert. *The Poetry of Experience.* New York: Random House, 1957.

Lindenberger, Herbert. *On Wordsworth's* Prelude. Princeton: Princeton Univ. Press, 1963.

Locke, John. *An Essay Concerning Human Understanding.* Edited with an Intro. by Peter H. Nidditch. Oxford: Clarendon-Oxford Univ. Press, 1975.

Luce, A. A. *Berkeley and Malebranche: A Study in the Origins of Berkeley's Thought.* 1934. Oxford: Clarendon-Oxford Univ. Press, 1967.

Lyles, Albert M. *Methodism Mocked: The Satiric Reaction to Methodism in the Eighteenth Century.* London: The Epworth Press, 1960.

Lyon, Judson Stanley. The Excursion: *A Study.* 1950. New York: Archon Books, 1970.

Lyons, John O. *The Invention of the Self: The Hinge of Consciousness in the Eighteenth Century.* Carbondale, Illinois: Southern Illinois Univ. Press, 1978.

McFarland, Thomas. "Wordsworth's Hedgerows: The Infrastructure of the Longer Romantic Lyric." *The Age of William Wordsworth: Critical Essays on the Romantic Tradition.* Edited by Kenneth R. Johnston and Gene W. Ruoff. New Brunswick and London: Rutgers Univ. Press, 1987. 239-58.

McGann, Jerome. *The Romantic Ideology.* Chicago and London: Univ. of Chicago Press, 1983.

McInerney, Peter F. "Natural Wisdom in Wordsworth's *The Excursion.*" *The Wordsworth Circle* 9 (1978): 188-99.

MacLean, Kenneth. *John Locke and English Literature of the Eighteenth Century.* 1936. New York: Russell and Russell, 1962.

Manning, Peter J. "Placing Poor Susan: Wordsworth and the New Historicism." *Studies in Romanticism* 25 (1986): 351-69.

Mayo, Robert. "The Contemporaneity of Wordsworth's *Lyrical Ballads.*" *PMLA* 69 (1954): 486-522.

Meisenhelder, Susan Edwards. *Wordsworth's Informed Reader: Structures of Experience in His Poetry*. Nashville, Tennessee: Vanderbilt Univ. Press, 1988.

Moore, G. E. "The Refutation of Idealism." *A Treatise Concerning Principles of Human Knowledge with Critical Essays*. Edited by Colin Murray Turbayne. Indianapolis: Bobbs-Merrill Co., Inc., 1965. 57-84.

Nuttall, A. D. *A Common Sky: Philosophy and the Literary Imagination*. London: Chatto and Windus for Sussex Univ. Press, 1974.

Owen, W. J. B. "Wordsworth and Jeffrey in Collaboration." *Review of English Studies* ns 15 (1964): 161-67.

——. "Wordsworth's Imaginations." *The Wordsworth Circle* 14 (1983): 213-24.

Oxford English Dictionary. Edited by James A. H. Murray et al. 13 vols. London: Clarendon-Oxford Univ. Press, 1933.

Palumbo, Linda J. "The Later Wordsworth and the Romantic Ego: Bede and the Recreant Soul." *The Wordsworth Circle* 17 (1986): 181-84.

Parrish, Stephen Maxfield. *The Art of the Lyrical Ballads*. Cambridge: Harvard Univ. Press, 1973.

——. "The Worst of Wordsworth." *The Wordsworth Circle* 7 (1976): 89-91.

Patterson, Annabelle. "Wordsworth's Georgic: Genre and Structure in *The Excursion*." *The Wordsworth Circle* 9 (1978): 145-54.

Perkins, David. *Wordsworth and the Poetry of Sincerity*. Cambridge: Belknap-Harvard Univ. Press, 1964.

Pfau, Thomas. "Rhetoric and the Existential: Romantic Studies and the Question of the Subject." *Studies in Romanticism* 26 (1987): 487-512.

Prickett, Stephen. *Coleridge and Wordsworth: The Poetry of Growth*. Cambridge: Cambridge Univ. Press, 1970.

——. *Wordsworth and Coleridge: The Lyrical Ballads*. London: Edward Arnold, 1975.

Quintana, Ricardo. *Two Augustans: John Locke and Jonathan Swift*. Madison: Univ. of Wisconsin Press, 1978.

Rader, Melvin. *Wordsworth: A Philosophical Approach*. London: Clarendon-Oxford Univ. Press, 1967.

Raleigh, Walter. *Wordsworth*. London: Edward Arnold, 1903.

Ramsey, Jonathan. "Seeing and Perceiving in Wordsworth's *An Evening Walk*." *Modern Language Quarterly* 36 (1975): 376-89.

Reed, Mark L. *Wordsworth: The Chronology of the Early Years 1770-1799*. Cambridge: Harvard Univ. Press, 1967.

Reid, Thomas. *The Works of Thomas Reid, D.D.* Edited by Sir William Hamilton. 2 vols. 8th ed. Edinburgh: J. Thin, 1895.

Reiman, Donald H. "Poetry of Familiarity: Wordsworth, Dorothy, and Mary Hutchinson." *The Evidence of the Imagination: Studies of Interaction between Life and Art in English Romantic Literature*. Edited by Donald Reiman et al. New York: New York Univ. Press, 1978. 142-77.

——. *Romantic Texts and Contexts*. Columbia, Missouri: Univ. of Missouri Press, 1987.

——, ed. *The Romantics Reviewed: Contemporary Reviews of British Romantic Writers*. 9 vols. New York and London: Garland Publishing Co., Inc. 1972.

Riffaterre, Michael. "Interpretation and Descriptive Poetry: A Reading of Wordsworth's 'Yew-Trees.'" *New Literary History* 4 (1973): 229-56.

Robinson, Henry Crabb. *The Correspondence of Henry Crabb Robinson with the Wordsworth Circle*. Edited by Edith J. Morley. 2 vols. London:

Clarendon-Oxford Univ. Press, 1927.

——. *Henry Crabb Robinson on Books and Their Writers.* Edited by Edith J. Morley. 3 vols. London: J. M. Dent and Sons, Ltd., 1938.

Ross, Jr., Donald. "Poems 'Bound Each to Each' in the 1815 Edition of Wordsworth." *The Wordsworth Circle* 12 (1981): 13-40.

Ruoff, Gene. "Critical Implications of Wordsworth's 1815 Categorization, with Some Animadversions on Binaristic Commentary." *The Wordsworth Circle* 9 (1978): 75-82.

Ryskamp, Charles. "Wordsworth's Lyrical Ballads in Their Time." *From Sensibility to Romanticism: Essays Presented to Frederick A. Pottle.* Edited by Frederick W. Hilles and Harold Bloom. Oxford and New York: Oxford Univ. Press, 1965. 358-68.

Rzepka, Charles J. *The Self as Mind: Vision and Identity in Wordsworth, Coleridge, and Keats.* Cambridge and London: Harvard Univ. Press, 1986.

Scoggins, James. *Imagination and Fancy: Complementary Modes in the Poetry of Wordsworth.* Lincoln: Univ. of Nebraska Press, 1966.

Shaftesbury, Anthony, Lord. *Characteristics of Men, Manners, Opinions, Time, Etc.* Edited with an Intro. and Notes by John M. Robertson. 2 vols. 1900. Gloucester, Massachusetts: Peter Smith, 1963.

——. *The Life, Unpublished Letters and Philosophical Regimen of Anthony, Earl of Shaftesbury.* Edited by Benjamin Rand. London: S. Sonnenschein and Co., Ltd.; New York: The Macmillan Co., 1900.

Shairp, John C. "Wordsworth: The Man and the Poet." *North British Review* 81 (August 1864): 1-29.

Sharp, Steven E. "Principle and Whimsey: Thomas Holcroft and *Descriptive Sketches*." *The Wordsworth Circle* 9 (1978): 71-74.

____. "The Unmerited Contempt of Reviewers: Wordsworth's Response to Contemporary Reviews of *Descriptive Sketches*." *The Wordsworth Circle* 8 (1977): 25-31.

Shepherd, T. B. *Methodism and the Literature of the Eighteenth Century*. London: The Epworth Press, 1940.

Simpson, David. *Wordsworth and the Figurings of the Real*. Atlantic Highlands, New Jersey: Humanities Press, 1982.

____. *Wordsworth's Historical Imagination: The Poetry of Displacement*. New York and London: Methuen, 1987.

Siskin, Clifford. "Revision Romanticized: A Study in Literary Change." *Romanticism Past and Present* 7 (1983): 1-16.

Smith, Adam. *The Theory of Moral Sentiments*. Edited by D. D. Raphael and A. L. Macfie. Vol. 1 of *The Glasgow Edition of the Words and Correspondence of Adam Smith*. 6 vols. London: Clarendon-Oxford, 1976.

Smith, David Q. "The Wanderer's Silence: A Strange Reticence in Book IX of *The Excursion*." *The Wordsworth Circle* 9 (1978): 162-72.

Sperry, Willard L. *Wordsworth's Anti-Climax*. Cambridge: Harvard Univ. Press, 1935.

Spiegelman, Willard. *Wordsworth's Heroes*. Berkeley, Los Angeles, and London: Univ. of California Press, 1985.

Stace, W. T. "The Refutation of Realism." *A Treatise Concerning the Principles of Human Knowledge with Critical Essays*. Edited by Colin Murray Turbayne. Indianapolis: Bobbs-Merrill Co., Inc., 1965. 85-99.

Stallknecht, Newton P. *Strange Seas of Thought: Studies in William Wordsworth's Philosophy of Man and Nature*. Bloomington and London: Indiana Univ. Press, 1958.

Steiner, George F. "Contributions to a Dictionary of Critical Terms. 'Egoism' and 'Egotism.'" *Essays in Criticism* 2 (1952): 444-52.

Swingle, L. J. *The Obstinate Questionings of English Romanticism.* Baton Rouge and London: Louisiana State Univ. Press, 1987.

Thomas, Keith G. *Wordsworth and Philosophy: Empiricism and Transcendentalism in the Poetry.* Ann Arbor, Michigan: UMI Research Press, 1989.

Tompkins, Jane P. "The Reader in History: The Changing Shape of Literary Response." *Reader-Response Criticism: From Formalism to Post-Structuralism.* Edited by Jane P. Tompkins. Baltimore and London: The Johns Hopkins Univ. Press, 1980. 201-32.

Tuveson, Ernest Lee. *The Imagination as a Means of Grace: Locke and the Aesthetics of Romanticism.* 1960. New York: Gordian Press, 1974.

Van Iten, Richard J. "Berkeley's Alleged Solipsism." *A Treatise Concerning the Principles of Human Knowledge with Critical Essays.* Edited by Colin Murray Turbayne. Indianapolis: Bobbs-Merrill Co., Inc., 1965. 47-56.

Watson, J. R. *Wordsworth's Vital Soul: The Sacred and Profane in Wordsworth's Poetry.* London and Basingstoke: The Macmillan Press, Ltd., 1982.

Wellek, Rene. *Immanuel Kant in England, 1793-1838.* Princeton: Princeton Univ. Press, 1931.

Wesley, John. *The Appeals to Men of Reason and Religion and Certain Related Open Letters.* Vol. 11 of *The Oxford Edition of the Works of John Wesley.* Edited by Gerald R. Cragg. London: Clarendon-Oxford Univ. Press, 1975.

———. *The Journals of the Reverend John Wesley, A. M.* Edited by Nehemiah Curnock. 8 vols. London: Robert Culley, 1909.

Willey, Basil. "On Wordsworth and the Locke Tradition." *The Seventeenth-Century Background*. 1934. London: Chatto and Windus, 1949. 1-17.

Wolfson, Susan J. *The Questioning Presence: Wordsworth, Keats, and the Interrogative Mode in Romantic Poetry*. Ithaca and London: Cornell Univ. Press, 1986.

____. "The Speaker as Questioner in *Lyrical Ballads*." *Journal of English and Germanic Philology* 77 (1978): 546-88.

Woodring, Carl. "The New Sublimity in 'Tintern Abbey.'" *The Evidence of the Imagination: Studies of Interaction between Life and Art in English Romantic Literature*. Edited by Donald Reiman et al. New York: New York Univ. Press, 1978. 86-100.

____. *Politics in English Romantic Poetry*. Cambridge: Harvard Univ. Press, 1970.

____. *Wordsworth*. Cambridge: Harvard Univ. Press, 1968.

Wordsworth, Christopher. *Memoirs of William Wordsworth*. Edited by Henry Reed. 2 vols. Boston: Ticknor, Reed, and Fields, 1851.

Wordsworth, Johnathan. *The Music of Humanity: A Critical Study of Words-worth's* Ruined Cottage *Incorporating Texts from a Manuscript of 1799-1800*. New York: Harper and Row, 1969.

Wordsworth, William. *The Poetical Works of William Wordsworth, Edited from the Manuscripts, with Textual Notes and Critical Notes*. Edited by Ernest de Selincourt and Helen Darbishire. 5 vols. Rev. ed. Oxford: Clarendon-Oxford Univ. Press, 1952-59.

____. *The Prose Works of William Wordsworth*. Edited by W. J. B. Owen and Jane Worthington Smyser. 3 vols. Oxford: Clarendon-Oxford Univ. Press, 1974.

Wordsworth, William and Dorothy. *The Letters of William and Dorothy Wordsworth*. Edited by Ernest de Selincourt. 6 vols. Oxford: Clarendon-Oxford Univ. Press, 1935-39. 2nd ed., 1967-82.

Yates, Arthur D. *The Doctrine of Assurance with Special Reference to John Wesley*. London: The Epworth Press, 1952.

Yolton, John. *John Locke and the Way of Ideas*. London: Oxford Univ. Press, 1956.

Young, Edward. *Conjectures on Original Composition*. Edited by Edith J. Morley. Manchester: The University Press, 1918.

Index

Notes included in references to the main text have not been entered separately.